Sarah Orı

By

Carroll F. Burcham

Lubbock, Texas

2013

ISBN: 9781493634361

Sarah Orne Jewett Revealed

Introduction

Sarah Orne Jewett was one of the most accomplished regional writers of her time. She had the gift of turning the prosaic lives of her Maine neighbors of the last half of the Nineteenth Century into pastoral poetry. Miss Jewett portrayed the hardworking men and women, the old sea captains, the plain fisher-folk, the hill farmers, and the isolated lumbermen of Maine in such a quaint and delightful way that the stories have become memorable to all who love local-color Americana. She pictured her New England world with exquisite freshness of feeling. Her New England shaped her life, her thought, and her literary art in such a way that she became the sympathetic recorder of the lives of the people of Maine. Her own story was set in that arena.

Miss Jewett's Family

She was born on September 3, 1849, to a well-respected couple, Dr. Theodore Herman Jewett (1815-1878) and his wife, Caroline Frances Perry Jewett (1820-1891). Her hometown was South Berwick, Maine. In this picturesque town she lived all her life. The place gave her the characters and setting for most of her stories and sketches. Here she gathered the materials for her writing from the time that she was born. The impressions of the old Jewett mansion, her family, and South Berwick and its country neighbors are the foundation of her life and her art.

Her deep sense of morality and her devotion to God and man came from her inherited Christian faith. Her surroundings deepened her awareness of her fellowmen and her love of nature. Those ancestors that gave her a proper foundation are reflected in her name. She was known as "Miss Sarah," but her full name is Theodora Sarah Orne Jewett. Theodora came from her father and grandfather, whose first names were Theodore. Her name, Sarah Orne, came from her grandmother whose maiden name was Sarah Orne. Jewett had been a prominent name in South Berwick from the time her grandfather had come to South Berwick in 1819.

Her two sisters impacted the way she related to others. She was the second of the three Jewett sisters; Mary was born June 18, 1847, Sarah was born in 1849, and Caroline or "Carrie" was born in 1855. Caroline was the only one who married. Her husband, Edwin Eastman was a South Berwick pharmacist and they had an only child, Theodore Jewett Eastman. Miss Jewett loved her sisters and honored them for their influence. Carrie lived just a short distance away and made frequent visits to see them. Mary lived 83 years, Sarah nearly 60, and Caroline 41. The three sisters counted South Berwick as their permanent home. Mary and Sarah continued to live in the family mansion until their deaths.

One can trace the life of Sarah Orne Jewett in her poems, short stories, novels, letters, and magazines, journal articles, and in her friends and acquaintances. Also her biography can be amplified by those who wrote to her and about her. These details will reveal who she was and what she did.

"Looking Back on Girlhood" *Youth's Companion*, January 7, 1892

In her early forties, Miss Jewett wrote this article in *"Youth's Companion"* about her early life. In it she reveals the influence that her family, her home, her town, and her country neighbors had on her as a person. She tells of her initial writing experiences. At an early age, she began writing about life as she viewed it, within the scope of her mental powers and the range of her imagination, not for money but for the pleasure of it. She wrote poems, short sketches and short stories sometimes as a game to occupy her time. At eighteen, she saw her first story; "Jenny Garrow's Lovers" appear in the *"Flag of Our Union"* and a poem printed in *"Our Young Folks."*

At twenty she published a story in a national magazine. Arthur Quinn in *"American Fiction: An Historical and Critical Survey"* records her early literary output. He tells of her story published in the *"Atlantic Monthly"* when she was twenty years old. It was entitled "Mr. Bruce" and it was written as she confessed, in "two evenings after ten." The story is about a girl who masquerades as a waitress in her father's home. The story is included in her book, *"Old Friends and New"* published in 1897. At age twenty-two, in 1870 she submitted another story to the *"Riverside Magazine,"* a children's magazine. They published her story, "The Shipwrecked Buttons." The magazine also accepted three more of her stories for that year and credited them to her real name in the index.

During her early years of writing, other stories and poems appeared in various juvenile and general magazines.

Sarah Orne Jewett's Works:

Deephaven, James R. Osgood, 1877
Play Days, Houghton, Osgood, 1878
Old Friends and New, Houghton, Osgood, 1879
Country By-Ways, Houghton-Mifflin, 1881
A Country Doctor , Houghton-Mifflin, 1884
The Mate of the Daylight, and Friends Ashore, Houghton-Mifflin, 1884
A Marsh Island, Houghton-Mifflin, 1884
A White Heron and Other Stories, Houghton-Mifflin, 1886
The Story of the Normans, Told Chiefly in Relation to Their Conquest of England, Putnam's Sons, 1887
The King of Folly Island and Other People, Houghton-Mifflin, 1888
Tales of New England, Houghton-Mifflin, 1890
Betty Leicester: A Story for Girls, Houghton-Mifflin, 1890
Strangers and Wayfarers, Houghton-Mifflin, 1890
A Native of Winby and Other Tales, Houghton-Mifflin, 1893
Betty Leicester's English Christmas: A New Chapter of an Old Story, privately printed for the Bryn Mawr School, 1894
The Life of Nancy, Houghton-Mifflin, 1895
The Country of the Pointed Firs, Houghton-Mifflin, 1896
The Queen's Twin and Other Stories, Houghton-Mifflin, 1899
The Tory Lover, Houghton-Mifflin, 1901

An Empty Purse: A Christmas Story, privately printed, 1905

She also wrote many sketches, short stories, collections of stories, children's stories, letters, and poems that appear in books, journals, and magazines. There are many books that contain her literary works.

She was the product of her place and her time. Her hometown, South Berwick, Maine, was an important part of her story. She was a realist about the history of South Berwick and its prospects for the future, yet she clung to the pleasant memories she had of the town in her youth. Its surroundings affected the course of her work as a writer and the nature of her character as a person. Yet in *"Looking Back on Girlhood,"* she could not stop herself from looking back when she wrote, "there is never-ending pleasure in making one's self familiar with such a region. One may travel at home in a most literal sense, and be always learning history, geography, botany, or biography --whatever one chooses. I have had a good deal of journeying in my life, and taken great delight in it, but I have never taken greater delight than in my rides and drives and tramps and voyages within the borders of my native town. There is always something fresh, something to be traced or discovered, and something particularly to be remembered. One grows rich in memories and associations."

Her grandfathers, both paternal and maternal, likewise gave her a fine inheritance of grace and manners. About the value of old truths learned from grandparents, she wrote "People do not know what they lose when they make away with the reserve, the separateness, the sanctity of the front yard of their grandmother." And to this separateness, sanctity and reserve, Miss Jewett responded with deep appreciation and total acceptance for she wrote in a letter to Sarah Wyman Whitman; "I look upon that generation as the one to which I belong,--I who was brought up with grandfathers and grand-uncles and aunts for my best playmates. They were not the wine that one can get so much the dozen now." Her friend, Sarah Wyman Whitman (1842-1904), was one of America's most important designers of book covers starting in 1884. She worked with Houghton, Mifflin & Company. She designed several book covers for Miss Jewett's books. She also designed for a stained glass factory in near Boston.

As an old-timer in the town, her grandfather, Theodore Furber Jewett, had bought the house in the 1820's in which she lived all her life, and he had brought his household goods to South Berwick from nearby Portsmouth, New Hampshire. As a sympathetic student of her grandfather's life, she recorded his story in *Looking Back...*"

"He was a sea-captain, and had run away to sea in his boyhood and led a most adventurous life, but was quite ready to forsake seafaring in his early manhood and at last joined a group of acquaintances who were engaged in the flourishing West India trade of that time. For many years he kept and extended his interest in shipping, building ships and buying large quantities of timber from the northward and eastward, and sending it down the river to the sea." Her grandfather was always interested in the business of the sea. He owned in whole or in part nearly every ship that was built in Berwick. Some of the vessels that he had an interest in were barques, brigs and schooners with such names as *"Perseverance," "Pactolus," Sea Duck," "John Henry"* and *"Dart."* His sea-going experiences influenced Miss Jewett who was always interested in the sea and the lives of the men and women who were connected with the sea. To show her great interest in the affairs of the sea, she wrote, "My young ears were quick to hear news of a ship's having come into port, and I delighted in the elderly captains, with their sea-tanned faces, who came to report upon their voyages, dining cheerfully and heartily with my grandfather, who listened eagerly to their exciting tales of great storms on the Atlantic, and winds that blew them North-about and good bargains in Havanna, or Barbados, or Havre."

Through her grandfather died when she was eleven years old, his influence was felt throughout her life mainly because he had such a strong character, such a penetrating knowledge of the world, and such a wide reputation in his community. To show his cosmopolitan character and his range of occupational experiences, Richard Cary of Colby College described Grandfather Jewett as "a citizen of the whole geography," and said that he "led a life of affairs and hazards which appealed to Miss Jewett's early romantic drift. Bound out as a boy, he ran away and shipped aboard a whaler. With only two companions, he was left for over eight months on an uninhabited island in the Pacific Ocean to guard stores and secure seals. He returned to New England, became a sea captain, ran a vessel to the West Indies at the height of the Embargo, was captured by the British and confined on the infamous Dartmoor Prison Ship. Back in South Berwick he turned to the less turbulent occupation of shipbuilding, he married four times, and he finally retired as a merchant. In his declining years he maintained the W. I. Store on Main Street in South Berwick, a multifarious general store replete with potbelly stove and cracker-barrel."

Because of the varied background of his life and the multiple responses he made to that life, Miss Jewett learned to appreciate old Captain Jewett and his philosophy of life. She was fond of him after he got old. She wrote in a letter to Annie Fields how old men in general were valuable for their contributions based on experience and personality: "Egotism is the best of a man after eighty. He is chiefly valuable then for what he has been, and for the wealth of his personality, and what is silly self-admiration at forty is a treasure of remembrance. The stand-point has changed."

Miss Jewett viewed the older generation, to which her grandfathers belonged, with respect and admiration. Her maternal grandfather was honored for his active and useful life when she dedicated her book, "*The Story of the Normans*" "To my dear grandfather, Doctor William Perry of Exeter." She called Dr. William Perry (1788-1887) Grandpa. He was originally of Norton, Massachusetts. He lived most of his life practicing medicine in nearby Exeter, New Hampshire. As was her other grandfather, Dr. Perry was a colorful figure. His youth was spent on a farm after which he went to Harvard Medical School for his professional training. As a part of a history-making event while a student at Harvard, he made a trip in Robert Fulton's first steamboat, "The Clermont" down the Hudson River. After graduating from Harvard in 1811 he was an apprentice with Dr. James Thatcher of Plymouth. He then opened his own medical practice in Exeter in 1814. During his long life, he practiced medicine throughout the county, invented and patented new surgical devices for the treatment of certain kinds of physical injuries, agitated for the State Asylum for the Insane, and lectured to medical students at Bowdoin Medical College. He always cast the first ballot of his townsmen in the national presidential elections, owned part of the Exeter Mill and Water and Power Company, and was involved financially in the manufacture of potato starch. He still raced horses when he was eighty years old. He died at the old age of ninety-six after living a healthful and active life.

Her grandfathers, though from widely separate backgrounds and wholly different occupations, had their personalities and lives fused into a single, vital force in the person and life of Sarah Orne Jewett, their grand-daughter.

Dr. Perry's son and Miss Jewett's uncle, Dr. William G. Perry (1823-1910), a graduate of Dartmouth College in 1842 was also a country doctor in Exeter serving with his father for several years. Exeter, New Hampshire, held its special memories for her because it was the hometown of several of her kinfolks. Because so much of her time was spent with relatives, Miss Jewett wrote of Exeter as a place, "Where I always find my childhood going on as if I had never grown up at all, with my grand-aunts and their old houses and their elm-trees and their unbroken china plates and big jars by the fireplaces. And I go by the house where I went to school, aged eight, in a summer that I spent with my grandmother."

Her other school experiences were in South Berwick where she went to Miss Olive Rayne's school for reading, writing and arithmetic. Her final school years were spent at Berwick Academy studying the traditional subjects of French, rhetoric, logic, history and the classics. The school was across Portland Street from her home, as was her grandfather's West Indies store. She graduated in 1865. Berwick Academy was known throughout the region for its high standards, and it was one of the oldest preparatory schools in the state. Its charter was granted while the State of Massachusetts still held jurisdiction over that part of the country. The signers of the Berwick charter included John Hancock also a signer of the *"Declaration of Independence."*

Two of her friends who graduated from Berwick Academy were William Hayes Ward and his sister, Susan Hayes Ward both of whom helped Miss Jewett establish her place in the world of letters. William Ward was the editor of *"The Independent,"* a semi-religious weekly, and he published stories and essays by her and about her. Miss Jewett welcomed the Wards to her home in South Berwick and at the Boston home of her friend Annie Fields (Mrs. James T. Fields). Several of Miss Jewett's letters were written to William and Susan Ward. Most of her letters to others were collected in the volume *"Letters of Sarah Jewett"* edited by Annie Fields in 1911.

Miss Jewett supported Berwick Academy throughout her life. She thought that the Academy with its emphasis on Christian morality was to be commended. She condemned schools who omitted the moral component of education. She said of them, "Memory is developed at the expense of what in general we are pleased to call thought and character."

She even liked the setting of the school with the hill back of it. She often took walks down the street beside it. She attended the Centennial celebration of the Academy on July 1, 1891. Three years later she got her friend, Sarah

Whitman to design the stained glass windows and the interior decoration of the Fogg Memorial Library at the Academy. For years, Miss Jewett, her sister Mary and her nephew Theodore Eastman served as members of the library's administrative committee.

The house where she was born and lived all of her life was impressive on the outside and on the inside. The house had great halls, square rooms and a staircase of fine design and detail. A window of flowered glass lighted the landing. The stairway took two men one hundred days to complete.

The exquisite French wallpaper in the front room had a history which gives the house the flavor of the high seas. The wall paper was meant for the Governor of one of the French West Indies, but it was taken from a vessel captured by an American pirate. The paper was brought to Salem and bought by Captain Jewett.

The finely furnished library with its great books was the heart of the home. It was her favorite place in their home. She said that "the old house was well provided with leather-bound books of a deeply serious nature, but in my youthful appetite for knowledge, I could even in the driest find something vital and in the most entertaining I was completely lost." The library contained letters from famous persons, children's books, books on antiques, medical books, and great literary works. There were Seventeenth Century printings of "*The Essays of Montaigne* (1659), Thomas Browne's "*Religio Medici*," (1668), and "*Pseudodoxia Epidemica*" (1646), the collected works of Samuel Daniel (1602), Eighteenth Century printings of the nine volume edition of Alexander Pope (1756), Alexander Pope's five volume translation of "*The Odyssey*" (1752), and six volume translation of the "*Iliad*" (1750). Also there were John Dryden's six volume "dramatic Works" (1725), and his three volume "*Virgil*" (1709, and James Boswell's three volume "*Life of Samuel Johnson*" (1792) and "*Works*" in twelve volumes (1792), and many nineteenth century books.

She had a full appreciation of the library and the wealth of literature that she found there. In her article "*Looking Back on Girlhood*" "My bookcase is the home of my dearest books, and a kind of hotel for those for which I have varying and lesser affection. Sometimes I leave one there for months, but there are few who have lived in the same places ever since I was a child."

As an integral part of the life of the Jewett family, the library served as a gathering place with famous guests from America and Europe, as a place of consultations between Dr. Jewett and his patients, as a place of family gatherings and discussions, and as a place where one could have long solitary visits with the books themselves. When only Mary and Miss Jewett lived in the home, the library continued to play an important role in their lives. The library is now housed in the Houghton Library at Harvard University.

Miss Jewett had much to do with the upkeep of their home. She kept the house in order. She noted that one time when she discovered three gilded feathers of the breakfast-room mirror were broken, she carved replacements out of pine. She glued them back on and then gilded them. After she had finished, she felt personally satisfied with the job.

In a letter to Annie Fields, she told of her work one morning when she "did some hammering and housekeeping" and that she "box-pleated sixteen breadths of silk ruffle this afternoon." She did not sit back and let the servants do all the work. She did much of it herself because she wanted to. She even concerned herself with such matters as having the carriage painted.

In the Jewett home, she experienced many pleasures. She wrote in her letters about them. She watched small boys playing marbles on the sidewalk in front of her house. She looked at high snowdrifts in winter as she kept snug by the big fire of walnut logs. During those long winter months she enjoyed waiting for the spring thaws with their deep mud and the reappearance of the brown landscape, and the change from dull brown to bright green.

Her hometown was rooted in the past, and Miss Jewett found it difficult to accept the changing order of things that were occurring in her day. She disliked and distrusted the changes of the old landmarks and traditions. The town was decaying as she watched. South Berwick's fading aristocracy and its declining economy were the reality that had to be reckoned with. Yet, the town proudly and defiantly remembered its pleasant historical heritage when the living was elegant and the traditions gracious. The Jewett family served as a prime example of aristocracy that had once flourished but now was dying out.

South Berwick possessed mansions of historical romance, namely the Simpson House, one of the oldest in the state; the Goodwin House, former home of General Ichabod Goodwin who had been the commander of the Berwick Company in the Revolutionary War; the Jonathan Hamilton House in which Admiral John Paul Jones had been a frequent guest; and the Jewett House which was built by the same builder as the aristocratic Wentworth Gardner House of Portsmouth, New Hampshire. The elegant houses were full of the finest furnishing that could be acquired in the new world and finest that could be bought in foreign markets. The women in these houses dressed in French silks and their tables were set with antique silver. The prosperity of the town, though giving way to an industrial economy, still kept the present descendants furnished with adequate incomes to continue life in almost the same luxurious fashion.

Miss Jewett considered the Hamilton mansion the one house that was unrivaled for its beauty and its grand air. She gives a description of it in her short story, "River Driftwood." She wrote, "It is square and gray, with four great chimneys, and many dormer windows in its high-peaked roof; it stands on a point below which the river is at its widest. The rows of poplars and its terraced gardens have fallen and been spoiled by time, but a company of great elms stand guard over it, and the sunset reddens its windows, and the days of the past seem to come back, when one is near it, its whole aspect is so remote from the spirit of the present. Inside are great halls and square rooms with carved wood-work, arched windows and mahogany window-seats, and fireplaces that are wide enough almost for a seat in the chimney corner. In the country about, I have heard many a tradition of the way this house was kept; of the fine ladies and gentlemen, and the great dinner parties, and the guest who used to come up the river from Portsmouth, and go home late in the moonlight evening at the turn of the tide." In her fictitious and historical biography of Berwick, "The Tory Lover," Miss Jewett recounts some of the traditions that she had learned from her neighbors about the Hamilton mansion and the historical houses of Berwick.

In earlier days South Berwick had been as she said, "As proper a place to live in as Boston." Many important activities had taken place in the town. In South Berwick John Paul Jones had gathered his crew for his Ranger to go fight the English on their own soil during the Revolutionary War. Men had made fortunes trading the tall pines, the upland timber for West Indian rum and molasses, great ocean-going ships had been built for the great sea enterprises of the world, and salmon fisheries up and down the Piscataqua River had done a grand business. Its location made it especially desirable as an inland port. South Berwick is located in southwestern Maine. The town stands in close proximity to the sea, being only twenty miles from the Atlantic Ocean. Ships came to the town's very doorstep up the Piscataqua River which joins the Salmon Falls River just below South Berwick.

Using the history of South Berwick as her subject, Miss Jewett wrote a paper for the centennial celebration of the town for the Berwick "*Scholar*" and for the "*New England Magazine.*" Because she was interested in the history of the town and the area, she became an active member of the South Berwick Historical Society whose meetings were often held in her own home. As a result of her love for the town in its setting, she praised the town in the "*Youth's Companion*" and showed her love for the town's natural beauty. She wrote "with its high hills and pine forests, and all its ponds and brooks and distant mountain views, there are few such delightful country towns in New England as the one where I was born."

Burton Trafton, Jr. quotes her as writing in 1894, "I am proud to have been made of Berwick dust; and a little of it is apt to fly in my eyes and make them blur whenever I tell the old stories of bravery, of fine ambition, of good manners, and the love of friend for friend and the kindness of neighbor to neighbor in this beloved town." Trafton in his article for the *"Boston Post"* also told how involved she became in the life of the town. He wrote, "She was never surprised to see one of the selectmen coming up the lilac-bordered path to ask for help in naming a street or locating a water pipe. She had visited the sick with her father and had poured over his journals to such a degree that she was quite a doctor in her own right, and the villagers knew it and called on her when the need came."

In *"Looking Back on Girlhood"* she described the river which flowed by South Berwick by writing that the river is "at the head of tide-water, and these, with the great inflow from the sea, make a magnificent stream bordered on the seaward course now by high-wooded banks of dark pines and hemlocks, and again by lovely green fields that slope gently to long lines of willows at the water's edge."

She was acquainted with the weasels, minks and squirrels along the river banks. She travelled down the river past High Point, Devil's Reach, and the old Hodgdon Farm, the mouth of Dover River and past Dover Point to the mouth of the Great Bay. To her the singing of the Piscataqua included the noise of the falls above South Berwick and she wrote "you hear the noise of them by night in the village like the sound of the sea." About its purpose she said, "This fine water power so near the coast, beside a great salmon fishery famous among the Indians, brought the first English settlers to the town in 1627...I know some families who still live upon the lands which their ancestors bought from the Indians, and their single deed bears the queer barbaric signatures."

The river, the town, and the countryside affected her in profound ways. She said, "I believe that we should know our native towns much better than most of us do, and never let ourselves be strangers at home, particularly, when one's native place is really as interesting as my own." She was an out-of-doors woman at heart and in experience. She knew every nook and cranny of her hometown and the countryside from her solitary walks, her carriage rides, and by her horse trips.

When she felt tired "because of the things she had to do" not only did she love long walks alone but she loved to take long rides alone on her horse. Sometimes she would go out with their servant John to York Long Sands to escape from the pressing moments of daily life. In the fall of 1877 she bought a saddle horse that she named Sheila. The horse was a thoroughbred of a beautiful chestnut color. Much to her delight Sheila followed her about for the sugar and apples that she liked to give to her. Miss Jewett rode her horse along country roads and across vast tracts of pastureland or down by the river or along the sea-shore. On occasion she would ride as far as fifty miles away from home on some solitary outing. She said in the spring of 1878 that "My horse goes splendidly and I have had some splendid long rides after I finish writing in the afternoon." One of the stories she considered to be some of her best writing was "*October Ride*: (1880) in which she described a girl's rough-riding. She wrote, "This has at least the virtue of being true, on my horse, the 'farm' and the old parsonage—which is more than I can say for my sketches usually." These walks and rides through the country-side were exhilarating to her.

Sometimes she walked at night in the moonlight or in the fog; sometimes she got up at the break of day and took walks before anyone else was up. In 1889 she wrote Annie Fields on one such walk: "I went up the street, and out into the garden, where I had a beautiful time, and was neighborly with the hop-toads and with a joyful robin who was sitting on a corner of the barn, and I became very intimate with a big poppy which had every arrangement to bloom as soon as the sun came up."

About a similar occasion, Miss Jewett wrote a poem entitled, "Flowers in the Dark" which is collected in her book of poems, "*Verses.*"

Flowers in the Dark
"Late in the evening, when the room had grown
Too hot and tiresome with its flaring light
And noise of voices, I stole out alone
Into the darkness of the summer night.
Down the long garden-walk I slowly went;
A little wind was stirring in the trees;
I only saw the whitest of the flowers,
And I was sorry that the earlier hours
Of that fair evening had been so ill spent,
Because, I said, I am content with these
Dear friends of mine who only speak to me
With their delicious fragrance, and who tell
To me their gracious welcome silently.
The leaves that touch my hand with dew are wet;
I find the tall white lilies I love well.
I linger as I pass the mignonette,

And what surprise could dearer be than this:
To find my sweet rose waiting with a kiss!"

The plants were of special interest to her. She wrote of the dearness of the "trig little company of anemones in a pasture." In a letter to Annie Fields, she described the first time she had known anemones, "Yesterday I went traveling in my own land, and found the most exquisite place that ever was. We followed a woods road into an old farm where I used to go with father years and years ago, the first time I knew anemones, was there, I remember." It is high on a great rocky hillside and deep in the woods, and what I had completely forgotten was the most exquisite of glens."

She described wild Hepaticas as being "like some people, very dismal blue, with cold hands and faces." In wandering through the woods she liked to pick herself a luncheon of currants, or find a mess of watercress in some stream and eat it with bread and butter. To Annie Field she stated, "I thought of you today for I was over in the fields and found a brookful of delicious crisp watercress, but I shall let them grow until you come, for I don't think anybody cares much for them." She would go into the pasture and eat the yellow apples that grew there or she would pick bouquets of white wee daisies. She reported to Annie Fields on one such occasion, "I found a white-weed daisy fully blown, but only an inch high, so that it looked as if somebody had snapped it off and dropped it on the ground."

She visited old pine trees that were her friends for they held a special place of affection in her heart. Once she said to Annie Fields, "I wonder if your pine boughs smell as sweet as mine tonight." On a visit to Wells, she saw a four-foot thick pine tree and exclaimed, "In all my life I never was in such glorious woods." When the pine trees of Maine were cut for lumber, she bewailed their passing as a tragedy. At one time, she mourned the passing of a tree that she had visited many times. She stated, "Alas, when I went to see my beloved pitch-pine tree that I loved best of all the wild trees that lived at Berwick, I found only the broad stump of it beside the spring, and the top branches scattered far and wide." Speaking of a fallen oak in a poem entitled "*The Fallen Oak*, she reflects again her love for trees and her anguish at the fall of each one.

The Fallen Oak

"Where the oak fell, a great road leads away,
Across the country to the door of day,
To find no ending where the sky begins:—
What the oak knew our larger outlook wins."

Miss Jewett loved to dig clams and to fish. She said, after one highly successful fishing trip "I know where the cunners hold county conferences out in the harbor; where two other little boys and I caught 130 one day." At Carter's Notch she caught seven trout and described an encounter with a squirrel. "Once I was standing on a log that had fallen across the stream, and I looked round to see a solemn little squirrel that had started to cross his bridge!"

Wild and domesticated birds fascinated her. She wrote to Annie Fields of a special robin that had its nest in a tree next to her house, "Oh, you should see the old robin by my bedroom window a-fetching up her young family! I long to have you here to watch the proceedings. She is a slack house-keeper, this robin, of the blown-away ruffles that she wove into her nest have suffered so much from neglect, combined with wind and weather, that they ravel out unsightly strings. But oh, the wide mouths of the three young ones,--how they do reach up and gape altogether when she comes near the nest with a worm! How can she attend to the mural decorations of her home? I am getting to be very intimate with the growing family. I waited by the window an hour at tea-time, spying on them." She wrote a poem about her canary who patiently endured its prison.

A Caged Bird

High at the window in her cage
  The old canary flits and sings,
Nor sees across the curtain pass
  The shadow of a swallow's wings.

A poor deceit and copy, this,
  Of larger lives that mark their span,
Unreckoning of wider worlds
  Or gifts that Heaven keeps for man.

She gathers piteous bits and shreds,
  This solitary, mateless thing,
To patient build again the nest
  So rudely scattered spring by spring;

And sings her brief, unlisted songs,
  Her dreams of bird life wild and free,
Yet never beats her prison bars
  At sound of song from bush or tree.

But in my busiest hours I pause,
    Held by a sense of urgent speech,
Bewildered by that spark-like soul,
    Able my very soul to reach.

She will be heard; she chirps me loud,
    When I forget those gravest cares,
Her small provision to supply,
    Clear water or her seedsman's wares.

She begs me now for that chief joy
    The round great world is made to grow,—
Her wisp of greenness. Hear her chide,
    Because my answering thought is slow!

What can my life seem like to her?
    A dull, unpunctual service mine;
Stupid before her eager call,
    Her flitting steps, her insight fine.

To open wide thy prison door,
    Poor friend, would give thee to thy foes;
And yet a plaintive note I hear,
    As if to tell how slowly goes

The time of thy long prisoning.
    Bird! does some promise keep thee sane?
Will there be better days for thee?
    Will thy soul too know life again?

Ah, none of us have more than this:
    If one true friend green leaves can reach
From out some fairer, wider place,
    And understand our wistful speech!

She wrote of watching a crow in flight, "I was in some underbrush, going along the slope, and saw a crow come toward me flying low, and when I stood still he did not see me and came so close that I could hear his wings creak their feathers—and nearly in the same spot I thought I heard the last of the 'creakits.'" The sparrows and the cardinals along with all the other birds of Maine and Massachusetts captivated her interest and attention. In order to give her views on discontent, she wrote a poem, *"Discontent"* which uses a robin to give advice to a discontented buttercup. The story is simply told and the lesson is obvious.

Her garden was a delight to her. She wrote to Annie Fields, "Oh! The garden is so splendid! I never dreamed of so many hollyhocks in a double row and all my own!" She transplanted sunflowers, hired boys to dig plantains from the grass "at fifteen cents the hundred;" put hellebore on her gooseberry bushes; gathered twigs of her double flowering cherry trees for room decorating and dug asparagus for the table.

Miss Jewett's Love of Animals

She enjoyed all the dogs that she had owned. She had a special relationship with her large Irish setter, Roger. She said that he had "great dignity of character" and was allowed to go with her everywhere. Roger was a spoiled dog who had easy access to the house and the gardens, the town and nearby fields. After Roger's fight with another of her dogs, Browny, Miss Jewett showed concern over her broken furniture, Roger's lame paw and Browny's damaged ears. She wrote to Annie Fields that the dogs were, all of a sudden, a discount. In winter, she and Roger, with his copper-colored coat, enjoyed his stay in Boston at the home of Annie Fields where they were welcome guests. Roger's friendly ways lighted the eyes of many a tired-hearted person on their romps along Charles River and in the market place. Gertrude Van R. Wickham in her article entitled, "*Sarah Orne Jewett's Dog*" in "*St. Nicholas*' in May 1889 wrote that Miss Jewett would sometimes forget her errand when she stopped to talk to others about Roger. Not only did she take Roger along with her, but Annie Fields often took him "to walk along the beach and chase sandpipers."

About another dog that she owned, she wrote to Mrs. Fields to say that "Beverley doggie" had come by express and was some trouble to look after, even though he was liked by Stubbs, their servant. With yet another dog, Jock, Miss Jewett, as she was enjoying a period of peace and quiet out on a solitary hill, happened to look up and see a great trail of fog and mist advancing from the sea. She raced Jock back to the house just in time to escape a soaking in the mist that followed them. When the little amiable dog named Crabby died, Miss Jewett mourned him and said, "I hate to think we shall never see him again."

As a part of her love for animals, she was also fond of cats as is seen in her stories as well as in her letters. Helen Winslow in an article in "*St. Nicholas*" entitled "*Some Literary Cats*" described Miss Jewett's love for cats. She quoted Miss Jewett as saying, "I look back over a long line of cats; from a certain poor 'Spotty,' who died in a fit under the library window when I was less than five years old, to a lawless fluffy coon-cat now in my possession. I shall tell you of two in particular: one the mortal enemy and the other the friend of my dog, 'Joe.' I may mention, that Joe and I grew up together, and were fond companions until he died of far too early old age, and left me to take my country walks alone."

Polly, the mortal enemy of Joe, and the best mouser of all was described as a business cat with a brain that was shrewd in catching mice and birds and as an impatient cat with fierce eyes and a twitching tail. She related an amusing incident about one of the confrontations between Joe and Polly. She writes, "I was sitting at my desk, one day, when Joe suddenly appeared, grinning in the funny way he had, and wagging his tail until he enticed me out to the kitchen. There I found Polly on the cook's table, gobbling away on some chickens which were waiting to be put in the oven. I caught and cuffed her…" The other cat which was the friend of Joe was an ordinary cat about which no amusing anecdote is told. Yellow "Danny" as she called him was much beloved by all the family especially poor Joe, "who must sometimes have had the worst dreams about the day of old Polly and her sharp unsparing claws… Danny was the most amicable and friendly pussy that ever walked on four paws.'

Miss Jewett's Life in South Berwick and Its Surroundings

Her love of the land of quiet nature with its high hills and grey days, its windmills and scattered country homes was described by a critic in 1909 in the "*Outlook*." "A villager to the end of her life in her sense of the significance of local things, of the interest of local characters, of the happy intimacy which comes from unfolding out of the soil in which one's roots were planted, Miss Jewett was also a woman of the modern world."

She was familiar with the nearby Negutaquit woods in which a band of thieves had lived many years. She heard stories about them. Her trips into the mountains were delightful, especially to Agamenticus, the tallest mountain in Southern Maine which was only six miles from her house. She could see the White Mountains of New Hampshire too. From the Jewett home, she could see Butler's Hill with its high Oak woods, the top of Garrison Hill at Dover to the west, and the dark, pine-forested region of the Rocky Hills to the south.

She admitted that the town always seemed a little sad to her. In *"Looking Back..."* she wrote "The old houses look at each other as if they said, 'Good heavens! The things that we remember!' But after the leaves come out they look quite prepared for the best and quite touchingly cheerful."

The town was ideally situated for sea and timber trade, but in her youth the town's days of sea trade and lumber trade were numbered. People moved to other places and abandoned the ways of their parents. She could see that things as they had been would be no more. "It was easy," she said, "to be much disturbed by the sad discovery that certain phases of provincial life were fast waning in New England." The Embargo Act of 1807-1809 virtually killed the Maine shipping industry and left decaying, shipless harbors all along the Maine coast including South Berwick and the neighboring towns. The Civil War (1861-1865), marked the city, for it emptied the town of its young men and reduced the vitality of the town. She remembered, "My grandfather died in my eleventh year and presently the Civil War began. From that time the simple village life was at an end. Its provincial character was fading out; shipping was at a disadvantage, then there were no more bronze sea-captains coming to dine and talk about their voyages, no more bags of filberts or oranges for the children, or great red jars of olives."

The Civil War drained the town of two hundred young men who had the taste of other places and did not return or who were killed in the war. Three other wars had also taken other young men in earlier times. Older people talked about these three wars in her girlhood, namely, the Siege of Louisburg, the Revolution, and the War of 1812 or the "last war," as everyone called it. Later, when the Spanish-American War occurred, she gave an interesting insight into her thinking about war.

The area's economy and the population of South Berwick declined with the great movement westward by young families going to the California Gold Rush of 1849. The migrating families left more people in the cemeteries than in the houses of South Berwick. One whole island gave up all its inhabitants to the Gold Rush.

She felt the impact of America's advance into the Industrial Age with its effect on the mind set of her generation. They had lost their aristocratic and agrarian ways to the invasion of fast moving machinery and an urban outlook. At fifteen she became aware of the effect of the French Canadians and Irish immigrants as they moved in and pushed aside the old ways. Writing in "*Outlook*" she wrote that at that time "the first city boarders began to make their appearance near Berwick, and the way they misconstrued the country people and made game of their peculiarities fired me with indignation. I determined to teach the world that country people were not the awkward ignorant set those people seemed to think. I wanted the world to know their grand simple lives, and so far as I had a mission, when I first began to write, I think that was it."

The rural way of life gave way to the industrial, and the air over South Berwick became polluted with smoke from the textile mills barely outside the town. Unusual for the town, slums developed, and the traditional village life ceased when the foreigners crowded in upon the natives. The outsiders shoved aside some of the townspeople, but there were those whose roots went deep. They could not be changed or shoved aside. In a letter she wrote, "Berwick itself is growing and flourishing in a way that breaks my heart, but out from the village among the hills and near the sea there are still the quietest farms, where I see little change from one year to another, and the people would delight your heart."

Some of the memories that she grew rich in were centered in the country fairs, hospital fairs, and church fairs that she attended in town and city. Fairs for various purposes attracted her attention, for she attended the local county and church fairs as well as fairs in neighboring counties. About a church fair in South Berwick, she wrote to Anna Laurens Dawes, "And you probably know what that means to a small town." Once for the hospital fair in Portland, Maine, she wrote three papers, "*Birds and Nests*," "*Doctors and Patients*," and "*Protoplasm and House-Cleaning.*" These sketches appeared in the Portland paper "*The Tonic.*" This love of fairs caused her in 1900 to help conduct a charity fair for the Trinity Church in Boston, where she helped Mrs. Mary Francis Parker Parkman and Sarah Whitman furnish items for the fair by sending a $15 check to Henry Green, and elder in the Maine Shaker

Community, for the Shaker-made products to exhibit at the fair.

Her memories grew rich in the stories that she eagerly listened to in her childhood, stories of the seafaring and timber-trading past. The past, however, lingered on the scene in the minor furnishings of the houses that had come by sea from Bristol and Havre. But the stories that she listened to were of past adventures. She records in *"Looking Back..."* that she listened to a story of a courageous Berwick lad, repeated here in her own words: "There was a Berwick lad who went out on one of the privateers that sailed from Portsmouth in the Revolution. The vessel was taken by a British frigate, and the crew put in irons. One day one of the English midshipmen stood near these prisoners as they took their airing on deck, and spoke contemptuously about 'the rebels.' Young Lord heard what was said, and turned himself about to say boldly, 'If it were not for your rank, sir, I would make you take that back!' 'No matter about my rank,' said the gallant middy, 'if you can whip me, you are welcome to.' So they had a 'capital good fight,' standing over a tea-chest, as proud tradition tells, and the Berwick sailor was the better fighter of the two, and won. The Englishman shook hands, and asked his name and promised not to forget him—which was certainly most handsome behavior. When they reached an English port all the prisoners but one were sent away under guard to join the other American prisoners of war; but the admiral sent for a young man named Nathan Lord, and told him that His Grace, the Duke of Clarence, son of his Majesty the King, begged for his pardon, and left a five-pound note at his disposal. This was not the first or last Berwick lad who proved himself of good courage in a fight, but there never was another to whip a future King of England, and moreover to be like the better for it by that fine gentleman." A kinsman of Nathan Lord, Dr. Lord of South Berwick, visited Miss Jewett in her home and entertained her with interesting talk about his experiences in England for he had known Cardinal Wiseman, Archbishop Whately, and Carlyle-during his three-year stay there. She drew out many of the details of his experiences which proved delightful to her.

As important as they were, the physical surroundings of South Berwick were not as important to her as were the honest people who lived there. Characteristic of her nature, she admired the pastoral people of her region more than anything else. She loved the people because she lived among them. She sympathized with them, and they became her models for the characters in her stories. So, in a sense, her stories record the lives of the New England people who lived there and as the writer of her obituary in the "*Nation*" said, "If for nothing else, Miss Jewett's stories will live as the memorials of a locality and a people. She understood what lay beneath the surface. She said to Anna Laurens Dawes, "I thank God that you and I have some slight capacitate at any rate for liking people for themselves—what they are—and not what they have!" She shared the joys and sorrows of her fellow countrymen and women even those "whom irreverence and thoughtlessness had flouted" and even the ones with those with personal peculiarities.

She came to know the local people in their homes and businesses and even the travelling peddlers with their carpet-bags full of medicines, essences and perfumes. She learned the local folk ways when she shopped at her grandfather's general store for fresh eggs and butter and listened to their conversations and their stories.

As a child growing up, she especially liked visiting her mother's friend, old Miss Elizabeth Cushing. In Miss Cushing's home she sat high on the ottoman and ate pound cake and watched the wrinkled faced old woman with her "pair of beautiful childlike blue eyes," who, as she described her, "always hid herself from the gayeties of the house." Miss Cushing died at the age of 92, and Miss Jewett mourned her death. She had admired the proud, dutiful, and aristocratic old lady in her reduced circumstances.

Other friends were Miss Grant, the village dressmaker, Miss Polly Marsh, a nurse, and old Miss Barrell, a friend of Miss Jewett's mother. Miss Jewett liked to listen to the stories of Miss Grant, especially when she was in "the full tide of successful narration." Miss Polly Marsh was a faithful servant of the sick and well thought of by the local people. When she visited Miss Barrell on her death bed, she told of how the old woman held her "with her poor old bird's claw of a hand and kissed and kissed" her, while the old lady's eyes were so full of pleasure at seeing her friend who cared enough to come visit her. "Dear quaint little creature nobody knows how appealing it was." The recognition gave her a sense of fellowship with the woman that she had not had in the same measure before. Somehow these older women had a greater bearing on her life than any young person her own age. These mature women touched a past life that became increasingly important to her as she herself grew older.

Miss Jewett felt that it was one of her religious privileges to make social calls on the poor who lived in the shoetown part of South Berwick, to the newcomers to their village, and to the old people. In a letter to Anna Dawes, she described the condition of one woman that she went to see. She wrote, "One sister informed us as we left that she'd about given up hope of seeing anybody—she'd been here five years and had only one or two calls

In addition to her personal contact with the ordinary citizens, she became friends with the prominent and wealthy citizens too. One well-to-do family, the Doe family, lived only a mile from her home, and the Jewett sisters were frequent guests of the Does. Charles Doe was highly respected by the community as he had served as an associate Justice of the New Hampshire Supreme Court. In a letter on one occasion, Miss Jewett showed that the Does were good friends by mentioning a good time at their home, "We dined at the Doe's last Wednesday and had such a jolly time." With her unpretentious feelings toward humanity, she felt as much at home with the rich as she did with poor.

In addition to her many friends, she had several prominent relatives living in South Berwick. In the article in "*Outlook*" we find that she felt at ease with them in their colonial homes "in which breathed the refinement of an earlier New England society; she conveyed the charm of the high breeding of that older society; its love of books, its simplicity and dignity." One of her relatives and one of the prominent men of the town was her father's first cousin, Elisha Hanson Jewett. He had served as a senator from the town in the state legislature, and he had interests in banking and in railroading. Another one was her uncle, William Durham Jewett who operated a drugstore in South Berwick. His store, along with other village shops, among them

"Stacy's" and Willards" was frequented by the Jewett sisters. In these shops she observed the country and village people and she said "I used to linger about the busy country stores, and listen to the graphic country talk. I heard the greetings of old friends, and their minute details of neighborhood affairs, their delightful jokes and Munchhausen-like reports of tracts of timber-pines ever so many feet through at the butt." She recalled in *"Looking Back..."* that when she was a small girl that "when the great teams came in sight at the head of the village street, I ran to meet them, if possible to mount and ride into town in triumph; but it was not many years before I began to feel sorry at the sight of every huge looped stem or oak or pine that came trailing along the slow stepping, frosted oxen. Such trees are irreplaceable. I only know of one small group now in all this part of the country of those great timber pines."

Later in her life, she told Annie Fields, "I wish you knew some of the village people,--not the new ones, but those whom in their early days Berwick was the round world itself." The round world of Berwick had a profound effect on her and she reflected, "The quiet village life, the dull routine of farming or mill life, early became interesting to me. I was taught to find everything that an imaginative child could ask, in the simple scenes close at hand." So powerful was the effect on her mind that it produced a pleasure of such magnitude that she felt duty-bound to share with others. "I long to impress upon every boy and girl this truth: that it is not one's surroundings that can help or hinder—it is having a growing purpose in one's life to make the most of whatever is in one's reach."

Writing in "*The Country of the Pointed Firs*" about the hidden fire of enthusiasm in the breasts of her fellow New Englanders, Miss Jewett further reflected that "In quiet neighborhoods such inward force does not waste itself upon those petty excitements of every day that belong to cities, but when, at long intervals, the altars of patriotism, to friendship, to the ties of kindred, are reared in our familiar fields, then the fires glow, the flames come up as if from the inexhaustible burning heart of the earth; the primal fires break through the granite dust in which our souls are set." Gladys Hasty Carroll in "*New England Sees it Through*" wrote that Miss Jewett "had the artistic wisdom never to touch material which she did not thoroughly know." Miss Carroll praised Miss Jewett's art of characterization, "Her gentle narratives of the elderly, of herb gatherers and shepherdesses, of retired seamen, cheery invalids, and tranquil lighthouse-keepers are carved with the delicate precision of cameos; never an ill-chosen word; never a blurred stroke, always an extraordinary skill and a loving care and an abiding tenderness."

During those years she helped her mother in the kitchen, preparing meals, canning jellies, cleaning up. One of her mother's recipes for pepper tomato she gave to Alice Dunlap Gilman. In her letter to Miss Gilman, she wrote, "Take the tomatoes and put them in hot water a little while so they will peel easily and then put them in a kettle without any water and the proportion is three pounds of sugar to four pounds of fruit. Boil them until they get dark and thick (almost all day, I guess) and put in cayenne pepper as strong as you like it."

Miss Jewett with her mother and father often visited their neighbors. On a visit to old "Mr. G.," she and her mother were greeted with a cry of great delight. He was bedridden in his isolated farmhouse and he welcomed their visit. She tells of his prized white rosebush which caused her to call this region the White Rose Road, a location she used in several of her short stories.

Her love of books was given her from both her parents. She would sit in her mother's room and read. One time she wanted to buy a seventy volume set of Voltaire but her mother thought it too extravagant.

She thought her mother looked like an Old Testament figure. She described her mother's reaction when Mary returned from a trip. Miss Jewett said "Mother's look as she came running out to meet Mary was something that I never shall forget. It was like some old painter's picture of a Bible scene! With her arms out, and her aging face and figure." Her mother died on October 21, 1891.

She described her new feeling of nearness in a letter shortly after her mother's death, "I never felt so near to my mother or kept such a sense of her love for me and mine for her as I have since she died. There are no bars of shyness or difference or inexpressiveness or carelessness; it seems as if I had never known my mother before." Her mother and father taught her to have a ready wit with her wisdom and to be sweet in her disposition. She recalled the old days together and noted that they had about them "all their wit and wisdom and sweetness."

In "*Looking Back...*" she wrote, "My father had inherited from his father an amazing knowledge of human nature, and from his mother's French ancestry, that peculiarly French Trait, called "*gaiete' de Coeur*." Through all the heavy responsibilities and anxieties of his busy professional life, this kept him young at heart and cheerful. His visits to his patients were often made perfectly delightful and refreshing to them by his kind heart, and the charm of his personality."

When Miss Jewett was sickly and missed school, she went with him to call on his patients, spending many hours with him. These visits were to his patients who lived in the mansions at Lower Landing and in the cottages at "Old Fields" and "Emery's Bridge" as well as to several other places. She described her trips with him, "In those days I was given to long, childish illnesses, and it must be honestly confessed, to instant drooping if ever I were shut up in school I had apparently not the slightest desire for learning, but my father was always ready to let me be his companion in long drives about the country."

She was fortunate that she had a wonderful teacher and friend in her father and the outdoor climate was good for her health and her character. In a short story "Lady Ferry" in *"Old Friends and New"* she wrote, "One often hears of the influence of climate on character: there is a strong influence of place: and the inanimate things which surround us indoors and out make us follow out in our lives their own silent characteristics." At one time she was so impressed with her father's life and the medical profession that she expressed a desire to be a doctor herself. Instead she settled for the writing profession because of her periodic poor health and her greater inclination to write. Even in her writing, her father gave her sound literary advice by telling her "don't try to write about people and things; tell them just as they are. How often my young ears heard these words without comprehending them! But while I was too young and thoughtless to share in an enthusiasm for Sterne or Fielding, and Smollett or Don Quixote, my mother and grandmother were leading me into the pleasant ways of '*Pride and Prejudice*,' and '*The Scenes of Clerical Life*,' and the delightful stories of Mrs. Oliphant."

Miss Jewett grew up in a port-town and was acquainted with the sea lore and the men who made the sea their lives. She had always known the sea. She loved the sea and many of her friends had been sailors. She was a friend to captains and sailors alike. In one of the fish houses at Wells she enjoyed a visit of an old sea captain. F. O. Matthiessen in his biography of Miss Jewett lets her describe her one such visit to the old captain in 1885. She said "I lagged along from one fish-house door to the next, and thought I wasn't going to see D___B____, the knitter, but early in the afternoon he rolled along as if he trod a quarter deck all the way, and mentioned after a time that he saw me driving down—he saw a team and got his glass and found out it was I." She was saddened by the fact of his age and how he looked as though he were about to go join his Poor Dear in death. Miss Jewett was pleased that he had asked her to bring him some good detective books to read—an indication that he was not through with life yet.

Miss Jewett's Christian Beliefs and Religious Associations

Wed to her love for nature was her love for Nature's God. Her devotion to the Christian's God was one of the significant parts of her character and her life. Her devotion developed early in her experiences because her parents took her to worship services where she learned about Jesus Christ and his work of redemption. They participated in various church activities, and invited ministers into their home for religious discussions and fellowship. She was born into a family whose Christian ties were with the Congregational Church of South Berwick. Later she changed her affiliation after she became an independent person. In her early twenties, on November 27, 1870, she changed her allegiance to the St. John's Episcopal Church of Portsmouth where she was baptized in the name of the Father, the Son, and the Holy Spirit and was confirmed. There she accepted the Creeds of the Episcopalian Church whose statement is, "We will always have questions, but in the two foundational statements of faith – the Apostles' Creed used at baptism, and the Nicene Creed used at communion – we join Christians throughout the ages in affirming our faith in the one God who created us, redeemed us, and sanctifies us.

The Apostles' Creed

I believe in God, the Father almighty,
creator of heaven and earth;
I believe in Jesus Christ, his only Son, our Lord.
He was conceived by the power of the Holy Spirit
and born of the Virgin Mary.
He suffered under Pontius Pilate,
was crucified, died, and was buried.
He descended to the dead.
On the third day he rose again.
He ascended into heaven,
and is seated at the right hand of the Father.

He will come again to judge the living and the dead.
I believe in the Holy Spirit,
the holy catholic Church,
the communion of saints,
the forgiveness of sins
the resurrection of the body,
and the life everlasting. Amen.
(Book of Common Prayer)

The Nicene Creed

We believe in one God,
the Father, the Almighty,
maker of heaven and earth,
of all that is, seen and unseen.

We believe in one Lord, Jesus Christ,
the only Son of God,
eternally begotten of the Father,
God from God, Light from Light,
true God from true God,
begotten, not made,
of one Being with the Father.
Through him all things were made.
For us and for our salvation
he came down from heaven:
by the power of the Holy Spirit
he became incarnate from the Virgin Mary,
and was made man.
For our sake he was crucified under Pontius Pilate;
he suffered death and was buried.
On the third day he rose again

in accordance with the Scriptures;
he ascended into heaven
and is seated at the right hand of the Father.
He will come again in glory to judge the living and the
dead,
and his kingdom will have no end.

We believe in the Holy Spirit, the Lord, the giver of life,
who proceeds from the Father and the Son.
With the Father and the Son he is worshiped and glorified.
He has spoken through the Prophets.
We believe in one holy catholic and apostolic Church.
We acknowledge one baptism for the forgiveness of sins.
We look for the resurrection of the dead,
and the life of the world to come. Amen.

Since there was no Episcopal Church in South
Berwick she continued to attend the Congregational Church
with her parents. In addition to worship attendance either
at Portsmouth or South Berwick, she read religious
magazines in her leisure moments and she participated in
various church works. When her sister Carrie was
confirmed in the St. John's Episcopal Church, Miss Jewett
said in a letter to Anna Laurens Dawes, "it brought back
my own confirmation most vividly; and it came over me
how much happiness and how many good things have
'come true' and are realities which used to be only dreams
and wishes."

She was not naïve nor gullible about her religious
faith for many of the old fashioned sermons in the
Episcopal Church, she confessed, "Carried me back more
than forward," and she would wait patiently for the long

ones to end. During these periods of unprofitable talk, she learned to take advantage of the situation. According to her, if the summer weather were hot, the congregation sleepy, and the sermon dull, she would compose her sketches of New England people and places in her mind. She wrote to Annie Fields about one such time, "This morning at church I was dreadfully bored with a sermon, and I made up a first rate story which will have to be written very soon after Christmas." Other times she stayed away from services as she said in a letter to Annie Fields, "For one reason or another I have not been preached at for some months! This afternoon, after the communion service, I had a great pleasure in seeing the very old church silver which is not often used, and some time I wish to show it to you. One exquisite old flagon is marked 1674, and the cups are such beautiful shapes."

Not all sermons were boring to her, however. Shortly after her confirmation into the Episcopal Church, she described in a letter to Lucretia Perry, how much she enjoyed hearing the Episcopal Bishop at several of the area towns. She expressed her pleasure by saying "I have enjoyed myself today very much, for the Bishop preached at Dover this morning and Mary and I drove over to hear him and were repaid by a very fine sermon--and this afternoon he preached in Salmon Falls at the little old Episcopal church—and everybody went to hear him and was delighted with him, and I was very proud of my Bishop." In addition to her fairly regular attendance at worship she went to county conferences where all the old – fashioned country ministers, their devout wives and other church delegates would assemble for special religious affairs.

At the age of 18, she wrote in her diary that a person must be virtuous to be happy. She believed that her diary was left as a moral guide for some young lady who might read it later. She humorously wrote about the effect the diary might have on someone who read it. "A hundred years is a tremendous while. I think it would be funny if, a hundred years from now, some girl like me should find this diary somewhere and wonder about me. I guess I will write my journal with a view to your getting some improving information, young woman. Let me tell you first that I am a 'sinfle' bad girl, and it is very much for your interest that you live in the time you do instead of the age in which you might have come across me, and I will add for your instruction the maxim 'Be virtuous and you will be happy.' Now if anybody gets this book before the hundred years, don't burn it, so the young woman can have the benefit of what is intended for her."

Miss Jewett visited in the homes of ministers and corresponded with other ministers that were acquainted with her through her books. She was a friend to the children of ministers. In her teens and twenties one of the ministers and his family she visited were the Gordons, whose daughter, Grace, married Treadwell Walden, rector of St. Paul's in Boston. Their fellowship continued to bear fruit because Miss Jewett visited Grace Walden and her husband in their cottage at Wonalancet on several occasions.

An example of her correspondence with a minister that she knew as a personal friend is shown in her letters to Annie E. Mower and her husband, Irving B. Mower, who was the Baptist minister in South Berwick. On the other hand, Miss Jewett received letters of thanks from ministers for the moral tales that she wrote. Especially enthusiastic about her work was Andrew Preston Peabody, the long-time Unitarian minister of Portsmouth, New Hampshire and twice acting president of Harvard. He wrote to her of his appreciation of "Betty Leicester."

Great moments came when she listened to the renowned Phillips Brooks preach in Boston. One of his sermons had as its subject the comparison of the highlights of life with the mundane affairs of life. The one sentence that struck a chord in her mind was, "Nobody could stay on the mount, but everyone knew it and went his way with courage by reason of such moments." Several years later when Mr. Brooks died, Miss Jewett was one of hundreds who attended his funeral. She wrote to Mrs. George D. Howe that the funeral was one of the most impressive events in her life. She described it fully, "I have never seen anything like the effect upon the city the day of the funeral—the hush, the more than Sunday-like stop, the mighty mourning crowd about the church, and in the church a scene that thrills me now, as I think of it. The light kept coming and going—it was a spring-like day with the sky full of shining white clouds, and on all the plain black hangings Sara Whitman had made them put great laurel wreaths, with a magnificent one of red carnations and green on the front of the pulpit, that was like a victor's trophy." She said it was like "a great sunset that suddenly turned itself into dawn" after she sat through the funeral sermon, after she had viewed the white lilies and the purple pall, and after she had listened to the hymn 'For All Thy Saints Who from Their Labor's Rest.'"

Her sympathy with ones who had lost loved one led her to attend funerals of all kinds: walking funerals, boat

funerals, and graveside funerals. She attended those of her
neighbors and friends in South Berwick, where many times
she would go to a farmhouse to view the body, listen to a
simple burial service, and walk to the cemetery for burial.
One of the great tragedies of life to her was the death and
burial of men at sea. Her poem is collected in "*Verses.*"

"The Gloucester Mother"

When Autumn winds are high
They wake and trouble me,
With thoughts of people lost
A-coming on the coast,
And all the ships at sea.
How dark, how dark and cold,
And fearful in the waves,
Are tired folk who lie not still
And quiet in their graves: --
In moving waters deep,
That will not let men sleep
As they may sleep on any hill;
May sleep ashore till time is old,
And all the earth is frosty cold. --
Under the flowers a thousand springs
They sleep and dream of many things.
God bless them all who die at sea!
If they must sleep in restless waves,
God make them dream they are ashore,
With grass above their graves.

After looking at the face of a neighbor's child that
had died she commented in a letter to Annie Fields "…that
old, wise, little dead face, which made me feel one's self
the ignorant child, and that poor baby an ancient wise

creature that knew all that there was for a baby to know of this world and the next."

Once when she saw a child's grave, she was stirred to write a poem about questions that the scene raised in her mind.

A Child's Grave

More than a hundred years ago
   They raised for her this little stone;
'Miss Polly Townsend, aged nine,'
   It says, is sleeping here alone.

'Twas hard to leave your merry mates
   For ranks of angels robed and crowned,
To sleep until the judgment day
   In Copp's Hill burying-ground.

You must have dreaded heaven then——
   A solemn doom of endless rest,
Where white-winged seraphs tuned their harps—
   You surely liked this life the best!

The gray slate headstones frightened you,
   When from Christ Church your father brought
You here on Sunday afternoon,
   And told you that this world was nought;
     And you spelled out the carven names
   Of people who beneath the sod,
Hidden away from mortal eyes,
   Were at the mercy of their God.

You had been taught that He was great—
   You only hoped He might be good—
An awful thought that you must join
   This silent neighborhood!

Did you grow up to womanhood
    In Heaven, and did you soon lose sight,
Because you are so happy there,
    Of this world's troubles infinite?

No one remembers now the day
    They buried you on Copp's Hill-side;
No one remembers you, or grieves
    And misses you, because you died.

I see the grave and serious men
    And pious women, meek and mild,
Walk two by two in company,
    The mourners for this little child.

The harbor glistened in the sun;
    The bell in Christ Church steeple tolled;
And all her playmates cried for her—
    Miss Polly Townsend, nine years old.

Her interest in the unseen spiritual world was constantly with her. It was hard for her to determine the line between imagination and the consciousness of the spiritual world. She mused in a letter to Annie Fields, "yet where imagination stops and consciousness of the unseen begins, who can settle that even to one's self." In a poem called "*The Widow's House*" she pictures the sad lot of women in a Moravian Home for widows. She described the mateless women as "tired hearted" and who were alone who have nothing to do but patiently wait for the release of their souls from their mortal bodies.

The Widow's House

What of this house with massive walls
   And small-paned windows, gay with blooms?
A quaint and ancient aspect falls
   Like pallid sunshine through the rooms.

Not this new country's rush and haste
   Could breed, one thinks, so still a life;
Here is the old Moravian home,
   A placid foe of worldly strife.

For this roof covers, night and day,
   The widowed women poor and old,
The mated without mates, who say
   Their light is out, their story told.

To these the many mansions seem
   Dear household fires that cannot die;
They wait through separation dark
   An endless union by and by.

Each window has its watcher wan
   To fit the autumn afternoon,
The dropping poplar leaves, the dream
   Of spring that faded all too soon.

Upon the highest window-ledge
   A glowing scarlet flower shines down.
Oh, wistful sisterhood, whose home
   Has sanctified this quiet town!

Oh, hapless household, gather in
   The tired-hearted and the lone!
What broken homes, what sundered love,
   What disappointment you have known!

They count their little wealth of hope
   And spend their waiting days in peace,
What comfort their poor loneliness
   Must find in every soul's release!

And when the wailing trombones go
   Along the street before the dead
In that Moravian custom quaint,
   They smile because a soul has fled.

Miss Jewett was tolerant of other religions. She viewed Swedenborgism as a foundation that lifted up one's other thoughts, and in reading Edwin Arnold's "India Revisited" she praised the power of morality in Buddha's teaching. Believing that an eclectic view would have its value, she wrote to Annie Fields of Buddhism, "If we had better interpreters of Buddha's teaching we might reach heights and depths of power and goodness that are now impossible; but we have fallen from the old wisdom and none of us today are so advanced." But regardless of her generosity toward other religions, she was basically a Christian.

Miss Jewett Personal Attributes

Concerning Miss Jewett's personal appearance, Willa Cather in *"Daughters of the Revolution Magazine,"* praised her dignity and refinement and her many charming personal attributes, "the distinguished outward stamp—it was that one felt immediately upon meeting Miss Jewett: a lady, in the old high sense. It was in her face and figure, in her carriage, her smile, her voice, and her way of greeting.

There was an ease, a graciousness, a light touch in conversation, a delicate unobtrusive wit."

Miss Jewett had a quaint beauty about her face with its dark eyes and dark hair; her figure took on a slender dignity; and her overall countenance indicated the moral durability of the New England Yankee. Her appearance is recounted in an article in "*Outlook*," 1909, whose writer said, "Those who recall Sarah Orne Jewett on the threshold of her career can never forget the sweet serenity of her face, the beauty of her brow, the gentle truthfulness of her eye, the atmosphere of candor in which she lived, the harmony of keen observation, quiet sympathy, and poise of judgment which moved with her."

Miss Jewett retained throughout her life her straight stance, her direct eye, and her friendly warmth. In April 1899, "*Life*" magazine included a verse and a drawing about Miss Jewett.

"If I could look as she looks,
 I wouldn't be bothered with books.
 If I could write as she writes,
 My looks wouldn't vex me o'nights.
 But to write as she writes,
 And look as she looks,
 And charm as she charms—
 Who is there can do it.
 Save only Miss Jewett."

As a woman who loved to keep her personal appearance above reproach, she took pains in buying her clothes and her accessories. She appeared in the pages of a newspaper account which described her "black hat with many nodding plumes." In a letter to Annie Fields, she described the way she dressed up on the occasion of her sister's return from a trip when her sister brought presents galore. Miss Jewett was proud of the seal-skin cape on her shoulders and the other gifts: an Edinburgh pin, new undergarments, stockings and a white petticoat. She wished Mrs. Fields could see "Pinny with such splendor!" Another day found her getting ready to make two "elegant calls" for which she said, "I dressed me all up."

Miss Jewett's Lifelong Struggle with Poor Health

Miss Jewett was a delicate child and she continued to suffer periodic attacks of influenza in winter months throughout her life. One time she called her "grippe" a "Bad hindrance," but on another occasion she wrote to Aunt Lucretia Perry how quickly she had recovered from a bad cold, "for when I last went to Boston I was scarcely able to sit up the day before and had not been 'outside the door' for a week with a bad cold 'on my lungs' and that same afternoon was out shopping minus any extra wrappings and stayed out until dark in the midst of December drizzle and half snow-storm and have continued in good health to the present time!"

She was a lifelong sufferer of rheumatism and respiratory ailments. She tried different remedies. One was drinking mineral water imported from various places. Her cousin, Charles Gilman, owner of a mineral spring and organizer of The Paradise Spring Company, sent her mineral water to drink. Alice Longfellow introduced her to Mouse Island where she drank from the mineral spring in the midst of its twenty acres of woods. She sought relief from her sufferings by bathing in the mineral waters at resorts in this country and in European countries. She stayed at the Spring House in Richfield Springs, New York; she travelled south with Annie Fields to Hot Springs, Virginia, where she stayed in the Homestead Hotel and to St. Augustine, Florida. On her trips abroad she likewise tried the mineral waters at various places, especially did she like the one in Aix-les-Bains, France.

Since she had been a "drooping child" in her youth, susceptible to respiratory diseases all of her life, and being the daughter of a doctor, Miss Jewett quickly sympathized with others who were ill and in pain. When U. S. Grant, former president of the United States died after having suffered so much at the end of his life, she sympathized with his suffering. She wrote, "Good heavens, what a thing it is for a man of Grant's deliberate, straightforward, comprehending mind, to sit day after day with that pain clutching at his throat, looking death straight in the face! And with all his clear sight he was no visionary or seer of spiritual things...and now he knows all, the step is taken, and the mysterious moment of death proves to be a moment of waking. How one longs to take it for one's self."

On the death of Miss Grant, the local dressmaker, who had served as a model for several characters in Miss Jewett's stories, she wrote, "I can't take it in that I shall see that lively, friendly, quaint, busy creature no more." In her letters she continued to be sympathetic to others who had suffered disease and who were bereaved because she knew from firsthand experience what it was all about.

Miss Jewett's quiet beauty, the charming dignity about her person, and her quick sympathy with those in distress of mind and body are the result of her aristocratic outlook on life. Another example of her personal philosophy is shown by the fact that she wrote little about the racial problems of her day. She did lean toward the separation of the races and national stocks. In a letter to Annie Fields she wrote, "When I read the '*Saturday Review*' and '*Spectator*' I find myself calling one politician a Saxon and the next a Norman! Indeed I can pick them out here in Berwick." Ferman Bishop in his article entitled, Sarah Orne Jewett's Ideas of Race" in the "*New England Quarterly*" (June 1957.) wrote "To the end of her career, then, Sarah Orne Jewett—despite her admiration for Whittier and Harriet Beecher Stowe—maintained an aristocratic emphasis upon the racial inequalities of mankind. It is true that she advocated very little social action based upon her system of belief."

Miss Jewett's Love of Books

Miss Jewett, whose knowledge came from books as well as from life's experiences, was a prolific reader. Her interest ranged from the reading of children's books, handbooks on anatomy, to reading the great giants of world literature. She had books all over her house, in the library, in her room, and in a book closet in the garret where she kept her copies of the "*Atlantic Monthly*" as well as her other magazines. In her letters and essays, she made many references to her reading habits. Every comment helps to reveal her personality and character. In Dorothy Wordsworth's "*Tour of Scotland*" Miss Jewett revealed her love of nature in a letter to Annie Fields, "There is no more charming book in the world. It is just our book and the way we enjoy things isn't it when we are footing it out of doors?"

In a letter to Horace Scudder, she shows her constant yearning for the joys and simplicities of childhood. She wrote, "I'm not a bit grown up if I am twenty and I like my children's books just as well as ever I did, and I read them just the same." On her 48th birthday she confessed to Sara Norton in a letter, "This is my birthday and I am always nine years old." Annie Fields noted that Miss Jewett's yearning for the simple things of childhood were always with her. Mrs. Fields said after Miss Jewett's death, "she never put her dolls away." Miss Jewett not only read juvenile literature but she also produced many stories and poems for the juvenile magazines and in her published books.

Miss Jewett was always impressed with the humanity she found in the books of others. To show her love for human affection, after reading Christopher North's "*Genius and Character of Burns*," she begged Annie Fields, "Do let us read bits of Burn's together sometime, just for the bigness of his affection and praise." In order to share the common humanity in other works, she read to Annie Fields those works that were mutually meaningful to the two women. Both women loved these periods of intimate contact of heart with heart.

Miss Jewett admired Adeline Dutton Train Whitney because of the moral quality that was present in her books of fiction for teenage girls. Miss Jewett especially enjoyed reading "*Lights and Insights*" and "*A Summer in Leslie Goldthwaite's Life,*" saying "I think Mrs. Whitney has done an immense deal of good." Miss Jewett expressed this love of books by saying to Annie Fields, "I long to read some page to you, for the humanity—the knowledge of life and sympathy with everyday trouble is more and more wonderful." In letters to Annie Fields she showed her admiration for books with human worth and dignity and sympathy. Miss Jewett deeply enjoyed reading Thackeray's *"Pendennis"* because it was full of humanity and that it was more simple and sincere than *"Vanity Fair"* and greater than Tolstoy's *"Anna Karenina."* She exclaimed about Thackeray that he was a great Christian. "He does not affect, he humbly learns and reverently tries to teach out his own experience." She said that *"Pendennis"* belongs to America more than it belongs to England.

She thought *"Vanity Fair"* was a good example of realism. And she praised its stand for morality. And she thought that it was Tolstoy, Zola, Daudet, Howells, Mark Twain, Turgenieff and Miss Thackeray all rolled into one. She praised its wisdom, its scorn for meanness and wickedness.

Besides her enthusiasm for books and authors, she got others to share in her enthusiasm. According to Carl J. Weber in his book, *"Hardy in America,"* she was the first American to introduce Thomas Hardy to the literary community of her state. Weber wrote, "Until we find the footprints of an earlier pioneer, she must be given credit for being the first to introduce Hardy to the State of Maine."

In addition to her love of books which are full of the knowledge of life in general, she liked to read books that reminded her of her own country people of southwestern Maine. Jane Austen's works reminded her of the pre-civil war days in New England. Early in her life, she had criticized Miss Austen, but later she was completely sympathetic to Miss Austen. Early in her life, 1871, she wrote, "I don't think I remember Miss Austen very well, in spite of my fondness for her. It all comes back to me as I read, but I had forgotten stories almost entirely. . . I think one reason was that they were nearly all the same kind of books (novels) and there is no effort about reading them. All the reasoning is done for you and all the thinking, as one might say. It seems to me like hearing somebody talk on and on and on, while you have no part in the conversation, and merely listen."

But upon reading Jane Austen's *"Persuasion"* twenty-five years later, she changed her mind and reflected upon the nostalgia that the book brought to her heart. She wrote to Annie Fields, "Yesterday afternoon I amused myself with Miss Austen's '*Persuasion*.' Dear me, how like her people are to the people we knew years ago! It is just as much New England before the war—that is, in provincial towns—as it ever was old England. I am going to read another, '*Persuasion*' tasted so good!"

Through books Miss Jewett could live in the past when life seemed more pleasant and the provincial people more amiable. Burton Trafton, Jr. wrote, "Though Miss Jewett lived much in the past she was no recluse. She often helped choose books for the local library, and it is not a rare thing to take a book from those shelves even today and find her handwriting on the flyleaf."

Sometimes she would get so emotionally involved in a story that she would weep, or at other times she would make deep resolutions to follow certain courses of action. When she read Matthew Arnold's essay on George Sand she said that she finished it with tears in her eyes. After reading a story by Tolstoy she declared to Annie Fields, "That story of Tolstoy's was such an excitement that I did not sleep until almost morning! . . . but now I know what he means, and I know that I can dare to keep at the work I sometimes despaired about because you see people are always caught by fringes of it, and liked the stories if they like them at all for some secondary quality, I know there is something true, and yet I myself have often looked only at the accidental and temporary part of them."

In letters to Annie Fields she further stated her ideas about books. In order to read a volume of George Sand's letters in 1888, Miss Jewett declared, "I am willing to study French very hard all winter in order to read her comfortably in the spring." Two years later she said, "I really know Madame Sand," since she had read her letters. In the preface to "*Deephaven*" she quotes a letter of Madame Sand's to support her views on the value of provincial differences and provincial ways of life and thought those views were her own as she said, "We Americans had better build more fences than take any away from our lives."

Letters of all kinds were meaningful to her, as is shown in the fact that her library had volumes of letters of Jane Welsh Carlyle, Madame de Sevigne, Voltaire, William Thackeray, Edward Lear, Thomas Lovell Beddoes, Fitzgerald, Dickens, Lady L. Duff-Cordon, William Cowper, and Lady Louisa Stuart. She also owned Edward T. Mason's three volume edition of British Letters. After reading Dickens's letters and especially enjoying his letter to his sons in Australia, she remarked to Annie Fields, "What a lovely spirit there is in them."

In her own letters, Miss Jewett often referred to books she had been reading. In her letters she made direct reference to Edwin Arnold, Balzac, Rousseau, Matthew Arnold, John Donne, Wordsworth, Milton, "*Spectator*,"

"*Saturday Review*," and many others. The following notes help to further one's impression of her thoughts on literary topics. About William Wordsworth she said, "I can't get enough of him." The same was true of Dorothy Wordsworth whom she greatly admired. After reading "*Madam Bovary*" she commented, "It is quite wonderful how great a book Flaubert makes of it . . . A master writer gives everything weight, and makes you feel the distinction and importance of it, and count it upon the right or wrong side of a life's account."

According to Louis Auchincloss in "*Pioneers and Caretakers*," Miss Jewett was so impressed with Flaubert "who sees so far into the shadows of life," that she kept pinned to a little drawer at the back of her writing desk as a constant reminder these two statements by him: "Ecrire la vie ordinaire comme on ecrit l' historie," (write ordinary life as one writes history) and "*Ce n'est pas de faire rire— mais d'agir a la facon de la nature, c'est a dire de faire rever.*" (It is not to provoke laughter, nor tears, nor rage, but act as nature does, that is to provoke dreaming.)

She made a perceptive judgment on Balzac's "*Alchemist*" when she wrote to Annie Fields, "I think that Balzac got tired of it toward the end—there where he makes Margaret regain her lost fortune over and over, as lobster grows a new claw." Even though her mind was vexed with "*Clarissa Harlow*" she stated that "I learn a good deal and profit much from the old novel, it accounts for so much in literary traditions." She found "*Royal Commentaries of the Incas*" by the Hakluyt Society very interesting, and speaking of "*Tom Brown at Rugby*," she said, "It is one of the books I like best." After she had been reading Jane Welsh Carlyle's "*Reminiscences*" she said that

"Carlyle is like a great stone face on a mountain top." About Thomas Carlyle, whom she called a "cross Scotchman," she said that he carried a yardstick to measure literary ideas "as if he were a commissioner from the Book of Judgment." There are numerous references to other authors and works that she read with joy and delight. In fact, on one occasion because she had been reading hard in Thierry, she said that she had been overeating with her head, and on another she said that her eyes were blurred from so much reading.

In a letter to Lucretia Perry, she discussed her daily reading allowance. She stated, "I allow myself a certain number of pages every day of course exceeding if I like, however, I find English history goes off very fast at fifty pages a day, at any rate, and sometimes a hundred." She read religious works as well as historical and literary books. She was interested in *Mother's Magazine*" which helped her in her work of surveying Sunday school books for use in her church in Portsmouth.

When Miss Jewett read her own books, she marked passages and made notes in the margins of things she wanted to remember of things that she thought while reading a certain passage. She described her habit to Sara Norton, "I have a bad habit of writing in my books as if no one else were ever going to read them."

Miss Jewett's Writing Habits

As a romanticist Miss Jewett wrote sporadically and impulsively. Early on she wrote without plan, but in later years she said that it was best to be systematic. Sometimes when she would write furiously for a few weeks and then would go for weeks between writing periods. As a usual rule she would write for five or six weeks at a time before she would stop for a rest. During her writing furor she would write, at times, 6,000 to 7,000 words per day. Since she was relieved of most household chores by servants who worked under the direction of her older sister, Mary, her daily writing schedule consisted of her mornings being devoted to letter writing and her afternoons and evenings to her sketches. Sometimes her work was begun before breakfast and sometimes it lapsed into the hours after dark. After enjoying an unusually early morning stroll in her garden, she wrote to Annie Fields, "Really, so much happened in that hour that I could make a book of it—I had a great temptation to go to writing." After her steady output of words for thirty years, she remarked in a letter to Horace Scudder dated July 12, 1901, "It seems as if I must have been writing every minute since I arrived in this world."

At the age of twenty-four, Miss Jewett began to mature in her writing ability and she felt that writing was her profession. She described her earnestness in her new-found profession as getting quite ambitious. She came to feel that writing was her life's work. She thought that it was better than just amusing herself.

In a letter to Annie Fields she indicated that her French ancestry came to the fore on occasion and made "her nibble all around her stories like a mouse." And she increased her proficiency in the quality of work and in the quantity of output. Later she was quoted by Carl Weber in "*Hardy in America*" as saying that "The tracks of my story-telling pen amaze me: and the stories themselves seem like the sands of the sea." Those stories to her, though as long "as yardsticks at the beginning, were at the end the size of old-fashioned peppermints which retained some shape and flavor to them."

Her writing became her profession, but it never became a bread and butter affair with her. She was independently wealthy and could afford to remain idle if she chose. In fact, later in her life, she declared to Annie Fields that "the business part of writing has grown very noxious to me, and I wonder if in heaven our best thought—poet's thoughts, especially—will not be flowers, somehow, or some sort of beautiful live things that stand about and grow and don't have to be chaffered over and bought and sold." On the business side of her writing, she constantly communicated with her publishers about her stories and books, and she bargained with them about her literary merchandise. In writing an autobiographical sketch for the "*Youth's Companion*" in 1892, she bargained with the associate editor, William Rideing, about the length and the price of the article. She wanted at least $100 for 1500 words instead of the 4,000 words that he had suggested. Another aspect of the business side of writing that did not appeal to her was the constant reading of proofs. She said that the reading of proofs caused her severe eye strain and that she did not enjoy it at all!

At times she wanted to stop writing because of her yearning for other experiences such as painting pictures, gardening, and travelling, but she never could get away from the writing urge that kept pushing her back to her desk and to her pen and paper. In 1883 she explained her mixed feelings to Annie Fields, "I am tired of writing things. I want now to paint things, and drive things, and kiss things, and yet I have been thinking all day what a lovely sketch it would be to tell the story of the day we went to Morwentow with bits of '*Lorna Doone*' and '*The Vicar*' intertwined with the narrative." In a series of letters, she told Annie Fields that the stories and sketches kept coming into her mind without conscious effort. Miss Jewett likened the coming of the stories into her mind to divine inspiration. About "*A Player's Queen*" she said that even though it had lagged, it is beginning to write itself." About another work she said, "For two weeks I have been noticing a certain string of things and having hints of character, etc., and day before yesterday the plan of the story comes into my mind, and in half an hour I have put all the little words and ways into their place and can read it off to myself like print. Who does it? For I grow more and more sure that I don't." This statement in a belief of external forces driving her to write is similar to a statement of her friend Harriet Beecher Stowe who likewise claimed supernatural guidance in the writing of "*Uncle Tom's Cabin.*"

The inspiration to write came to Miss Jewett in strange places. She would make up a sketch as she rode from one place to another as she did the "Marsh Rosemary," of which she said, "I made it up as I drove to the station in Wells this morning." Her inspiration was basically the result of her trained eye and ear that caught the sights and sounds of her surroundings and translated them into lasting and meaningful interpretations for future generations to see and to hear and to understand.

Thinking and planning her stories over and over set her mental wheels turning and caused her to produce stories that came in a sudden flash. To Annie Fields she explained one such happening. "It was funny; I had the solitary man whom I talked about at first, and then came 'the man who never smiles' and I coquetted over these two estimable characters for some days, when suddenly without note or warning they turned a double somersault and one swallowed the other, and I found they were really one person." Other times she would be bewitched with a story as she told Annie Fields, "I have nothing to say to you about it yet."

Even though it is sometimes difficult to do in regard to most authors, Willa Cather in her preface to "*The Country of the Pointed Firs*" successfully defined Miss Jewett's mental processes in getting her thoughts down on paper. Miss Cather wrote, "Miss Jewett was very conscious of the fact that when a writer makes anything that belongs to literature, limiting the term here to imaginative literature, which she of course meant, his material goes through a process very different from that by which he makes merely a good story or a good novel. No one can exactly define this process; but certainly persistence, survival, recurrence in the writer's mind, is highly characteristic of it. The shapes and scenes that have 'teased' the mind for years, when they do at last get themselves rightly put down, make a very much higher order of writing, and much more costly, than the vivid and vigorous transfer of impressions."

Some of her writing time was occupied in writing memorials, thank-you notes and reviews and rewriting stories she had already submitted to editors who returned them for some revision. She wrote a memorial in behalf of Mrs. James Osgood, the wife of the publisher of Houghton Mifflin Company. The memorial to Mrs. Osgood appeared in the "*Transcript.*" Miss Jewett wrote thank-you notes to those people that had sent her gifts of one kind or another.

Many of the thank-you notes went to authors who had sent copies of their lately published books to her. She thanked Frederick Tupper for his book, "*Echoes from Dream-Land*, (1891), Robert Johnson for his book, "*The Winter Hour and Other Poems*, (1892), and F. Hopkinson Smith for his books, "*Well-worn Roads*," and "*White Umbrella*," (1889).

Additionally she wrote many reviews of books for journals, and some she declined to write, such as a review of Helen Hunt Jackson's book, "*A Calendar of Sonnets*" when asked to do so by Edwin Morse, editor "*The Book Buyer*." She refused to write the review on other grounds than friendship because she and Helen Hunt Jackson were close friends. Helen Hunt Jackson coveted Miss Jewett's critical opinion about her work for in January, 1883 she sent the following note to Mrs. Fields, "I think this storm will keep you and Miss Jewett at home this afternoon—and I want to come and read to you my two papers on the Franciscan Missions—It will take nearly two hours.—I blush at my impudence—but this is why I want to do it—I am uneasy about the papers."

Letter writing occupied much of her time even though she sometimes wrote from a land where it was not easy to write letters. In 1872 she remarked to her cousin, Lucretia Perry, about the letters she could think up in her bed at night. She wrote, "Oh, dear! If one could only remember those letters one composes in bed o'night! I know mine would be so entertaining that my friends would insist upon their 'being preserved in a volume.'" In 1876 to Anna Laurens Dawes, she expressed her fondness for letter writing because she felt that "sometimes one may 'get acquainted' more easily through letters than by being together." She wrote, "I like to write letters and I like to get them and it is only when I owe more than fifteen that my heart grows faint within me." The letters that she composed in the daytime were sufficient to want her friend, Annie Fields, to collect her letters into a volume in 1911. A later friend, Richard Cary, professor of English at Colby College in Maine collected other letters of Miss Jewett and published them in 1963.

The one tragedy of her life occurred when after her accident in 1903; she complained to Sara Whitman that she could hardly write. She complained that "one ought not to expect to write forever, but I seem never to be thinking about anything now—it's very dull." Even though she had lost the energy and the stamina to continue her sketches, she continued to write letters of encouragement and cheer to her friends.

Miss Jewett's Acquaintances: Literary and Otherwise

Horace Scudder

In conjunction with her literary career, Miss Jewett was blessed with the association of the literary establishment of the latter half of the nineteenth century. Among those men of letters with whom she was intimately associated was Horace E. Scudder, who was James Russell Lowell's biographer. Scudder edited the *"Riverside Magazine for Young People"* when Miss Jewett sent her first story to it. He succeeded Thomas Bailey Aldrich as editor of *"The Atlantic Monthly."* The friendship between the two began when she sent the story, "The Shipwrecked

Buttons" to him at the Riverside offices and it was accepted and printed. On that occasion she wrote a letter to Mr. Scudder and asked him to criticize her writing Since she was just beginning her career, she wanted any advice that he had to offer, for she said, "I know I must need it very much and I realize the disadvantage of never hearing anything about my stories except from friends." In the letter she confessed that at the early age of nineteen "I couldn't write a perfect story, and secondly, I didn't try very hard on that. I wrote it in two evenings after ten, when I was supposed to be in bed and sound asleep, and I copied it in part of another day." Since the days of her early correspondence with him, Miss Jewett counted him as a friend and on several occasions, called at his home at No. 3 Berkeley Street in Boston.

Early in her career, Mr. Scudder advised her to drop the assumed names that she had attached to her earlier stories. Some of the pseudonyms she used were: A. C. Eliot, Alice Eliot, Sarah Jewett, Sarah O. Sweet, and S.O.J. The reason that she used these names was because she was embarrassed to use her real name. In *Looking Back on Girlhood* she confessed, "I was very shy about speaking of my work at home, and even sent it to the magazine under an assumed name and then was so timid about asking the post-mistress for those mysterious and exciting editorial letters which she announced upon the post-office list as if I were a stranger to the town."

His advice was wise advice because her stories were nothing to be ashamed of and they merited carrying her real name. Mr. Scudder recognized her art while she was still in her early twenties for he praised *Deephaven Cronies* as being worthy to carry her own name in dignity. Later, in an article entitled, "Miss Jewett" in the "*Atlantic Monthly*," January, 1894, he praised her as "one of our most happily endowed writers" and that "from time to time, and very often at that, the reader is surprised by the success with which a girl scarcely out of her teens caught the likenesses of these shore folk, and gave to her sketches a breadth as well as a refinement which seemed to come from careful training, yet really, we must believe, were the unerring product of a genuine gift of literary art illumined and warmed by an affectionate sympathy." He summed up his reasons for believing in her literary genius by saying, "in the books which have followed "*Deephaven*" there have been at all times expressions of a more conscious purpose of construction, and it has been apparent that Miss Jewett, aware of the somewhat fragmentary and sketchy character of her writing, has aimed at a more deliberate structure; but the naturalness, the direct look at life, the clear sense of the value of the moment, have always been her protection against an artificial method; and with an increase of experience has come also an excess of strength, though this strength has been shown rather in a firmer conception of the contrasting pathos and humor of life than in any outburst of passion or kindling emotion."

William Dean Howells

Another American author who discovered Miss Jewett to be an excellent writer and who became her personal friend was William Dean Howells. His discovery of her talent was made while he was yet serving as an assistant editor under James T. Fields of the "*Atlantic Monthly*." Later when he was editor of the "*Atlantic*

Monthly," Howells expressed his pride about the fact that he had, at her young age, recognized in her the genius to capture New England life at the turn of the century. He records the time when she began to publish "her incomparable sketches of New England character." He said "if any long-memoried reader chooses to hail me as an inspired genius because of my instant and constant appreciation of Miss Jewett's writings, I shall be the last to snub him down." In fact, he was so impressed with her work that he likened her to the incomparable English author, Jane Austen in his book, "*Literature and Life*" (1902) where he said of Miss Jewett, "If Miss Jewett were of a little longer breath than she has yet shown herself in fiction, I might say the Jane Austen of Portsmouth was already with us, and had merely not yet begun to deal with its precious material."

Despite what William Dean Howells said about this age frowning on the romantic and condemning it as an art form, Miss Jewett in a letter to Annie Fields said "but dear me, how much of it there is left in everyday life after all." In her works and her personal philosophy, she favored the romantic above the realistic of her day and to her mind realism wasn't seen from any viewpoint for "its shadows fall in every direction and it fails at being art." In her works she tried to bring the imagination to bear upon the realistic and, as a result, her works are called "poetic realism." For this reason, according to Olive Beatrice Floyd, Miss Jewett advised a young writer, Andress Small Fry of New York, "to write of great things in a great way and with at least imaginative realism." Edward Garnett described Miss Jewett's work as "homely realism," because "her people are felt to be living as intensely individual life" and because the "spiritual aroma (was) so subtle, that to come to it is like coming to one of the quiet beaches or woody hill-sides of Maine she so tenderly describes for us."

Floyd said that in advising others in their writing endeavors, Miss Jewett emphasized that a writer should not use the crutch of personal introduction to the editor of a publishing enterprise to win acceptance of a work. She said that it was her experience that an introduction "hinders an editor's interest in an unknown writer's manuscript" and that "it is apt to make him think that it is afraid to come on its own merits."

As a literary critic, Miss Jewett said that the use of language is the key. She wrote in a letter to Annie Fields, that the literary artist uses words effectively to paint pictures and to present ideas, by the use of "the reticence or the bravery of speech, the power of suggestion that is in it, or the absolute clearness and finality of revelation; whether it sets you thinking or whether it makes you see a landscape with a live human figure living its life in the foreground."

A tribute to Miss Jewett in the "Outlook" in 1909 also likened her to Jane Austen. The critic stated, "The resemblance between her work and that of Jane Austen's has often been noted. Press too far, that resemblance dissolves into thin air; but superficially the two women had many things in common. Both were free from the blight of an over-developed literary consciousness; both met life and studied it, not so much on its highways as in its byways; both looked not only for the eccentricities and inconsistencies of character, but for its fundamental goodness, its saving sweetness, its normal expression of normal ambitions; both found what they looked for."

Later generations have thanked Mr. Howells for urging Miss Jewett to collect her stories from the "*Atlantic Monthly*" into her first volume of short stories. The result of his advice to publish a book of stories was "*Deephaven*" (1877). In his review of it, Howells praised Miss Jewett's portrayal of the characters that she introduced in her book. He believed that the local life was fully explored, that life which included "three or four aristocratic families, severally dwindled to three or four old maiden ladies; the number of ancient sea-captains cast ashore by the decaying traffic; the queer sailor and fisher folk; the widow and old-wife gossips of the place, and some of the people of the neighboring country. These are all touched with a hand that holds itself far from every trick of exaggeration, and that subtly delights in the very tint and form of reality; we could not express too strongly the sense of conscientious fidelity which the art of the book gives, while over the whole is cast a light of the sweetest and gentlest humor, and of a sympathy as tender as it is intelligent." In his article, Howells praised her "simple treatment of the near-at-hand, quaint and picturesque" in conjunction with his praise of her description of New England landscape. He also admired the characteristic speech of her New England folk. Because of his admiration or her ability to use specific and concrete details and to display the personality of her characters, Howells expressed a hope that more writers could attain the same powers of observation and characterization that Miss Jewett had attained. He wrote that her "true feeling for the ideal within the real" made him glad that her sketches had been written in such a simple yet refined way.

William Dean Howells, editor of the *"Atlantic Monthly,"* in his book, *"Literature and Life"* (1902) said that when new stories by Miss Jewett appeared in a journal or in a new book, he read the stories with much anticipation and delight. Sometimes he read the stories aloud to his wife. Sharing his enthusiasm for Miss Jewett's work, Mrs. Howells was also sympathetic to the way of life described in her stories. Mrs. Howells in a letter dated February, 1891, thanked Miss Jewett for *"The White Rose Road"* that appeared in her book, *"Strangers and Wayfarers."* Mildred Howells wrote that upon reading the story, her husband wept because of "the everlasting ache" in his heart "for all that is poor, and fair and pitiful." Howells in his letter about the book wrote, "You have a precious gift, and you must know it and be the worse for your knowledge. We all have a tender pleasure in your work, which there is no other name for but love. I think no one has shown finer art in a way, than you, and that something which is so much better than art, besides. Your voice is like a thrush's in the din of all the literary noises that stun us so."

Mildred Howells edition of *"Life in Letters of William Dean Howells"*, recorded that after Howells read Miss Jewett's *"Second Spring"* aloud to his wife and they had rejoiced in it, he wrote another letter that expressed his love for every touch and tint that she had used in the story. He wrote, "What a divine creature you are in it, and how you do make other people's joinery seem crude and clumsy! No, you are too friendly and kind for that, but it seems so, out of a mere sense of shame and unworthiness."

A personal friend of the Howells, Miss Jewett dined frequently in their home on Berkeley Street in Boston and they in turn visited her in South Berwick and at Mrs. James

T. Fields' home in Boston. Mr. Howells made frequent
trolley trips to South Berwick from his summer home in
nearby Kittery Point, Maine. On one of his summer visits
he took Henry James for a special visit to see Miss Jewett
where the two men confessed that they ate too much cake
with their tea. James said that Miss Jewett had made them
feel at home because of her ready wit, her gracious
hospitality, and their lively conversation on literary topics.

James Russell Lowell

According to M. A. DeWolfe Howe in his *"New
Letters of James Russell Lowell"* (1932), Miss Jewett was
highly prized by James Russell Lowell "both for her
writings and for herself," and she thought that he was a
help to her thoughts and purposes in everyday life. Lowell,
who was an outstanding poet, a professor of French and
Spanish at Harvard and the first editor of the *"Atlantic
Monthly,"* entertained Miss Jewett several times in his
home at Elmwood. He thought it delightful to mimic her
Maine accent and colloquialisms. In keeping with their
literary friendship he introduced her to John Donne's
poetry, and he praised her literary efforts, as well as her
Christian character. Each visit with the Lowell's at his
home was filled with pleasure as she expressed in a letter to
Thomas Bailey Aldrich, "I cannot tell you with any pen
how much I care about 'Elmwood,'" and she felt that she
belonged to his household and kindred." At another time
she attended a birthday dinner in honor of Lowell's
seventieth birthday at the Tavern Club in Boston. On
February 23, 1889, Lowell wrote to Mrs. Fields of his
delight in meeting her and Miss Jewett on the occasion, "a

rain of flowers came down on me yesterday as on a virgin-martyr, and the hard seventieth step of my climb was velveted with them. They were very sweet but such gracious words from you two (to me, too) were even sweeter. That two such charming women—since there are two of you I can say what I like without impertinence—should think of me so kindly makes all <u>man</u>kind a matter of indifference."

Later, Lowell in a letter to Mrs. Fields on August 27, 1889, asked her to give his kindest regards "to Miss Jewett if she be with you as I hope she is for both your sakes." In a letter two years later he asked Mrs. Fields (Annie) to "Give my love to Miss Jewett and tell her that I shall put some dream-eggs under her pretty little bird and hope some of them will hatch one of these days." Lowell died the same year, and the last thing he wrote before he died was a tribute to Miss Jewett to her London publisher. Miss Jewett said of his note about her, "I suppose that the last bit of writing for print that he may have done was that letter for me. I have been looking over two or three of his letters or notes to me, which I happen to have here, with such affection and pleasure. . . How I treasure that last time I saw him, and the fringe tree in bloom, and Mabel gone to Petersham, and he and I talking on and on, and I thinking he was really going to be better, in spite of the look about his face."

James Russell Lowell compared her idylls to those of the ancient pastoral poet from Greece, Theocritus. Lowell wrote, "I am very glad to hear that Miss Jewett's delightful stories are to be reprinted in England. Nothing more pleasingly characteristic of rural life in New England has been written, and they have long been valued by the judicious here. They are probably idylls in prose and the life they commemorate is as simple in its main elements, if not so picturesque in its setting, as that which has survived for us in Theocritus. Miss Jewett has wisely chosen to work within narrow limitations, but these are such only as are implied in an artistic nature and a cheerful compliance with it. She has thus learned a discreet use of her material and to fill the space allotted without over-crowding it either with scenery or figures. Her work is narrow in compass, like that of the gem-cutter, but there is always room for artistic completeness and breadth of treatment which are what she aims at and attains. She is lenient in landscape, a great merit, I think, in these days. Above all she is discreet in dialect, using it for flavor but not, as is wont of many, so oppressively as to suggest garlic. She has a gift of quiet pathos and its correlative, equally subdued humor. I remember once, at a dinner of the Royal Academy, wishing there might be a toast in honor of the Little Masters such as Tenniel Du Mauier, and their fellows. The tine woodcuts traced by those who gave rise to the name attract an affectionate partiality which the spacious composition of more famous contemporaries fail to sign. They are artists in the best sense, which could make small means suffice for great ends. It is with them I should class Miss Jewett, since she both possesses and practices this precious art." This is a quote from F. O. Matthiessen's work on "*Sarah Orne Jewett.*"

Miss Jewett and Lowell were mutual admirers of each other because both believed in the aristocratic tradition of elevating the educated to positions of rule and responsibility instead of insisting on government by the ignorant. Miss Jewett praised this belief of Lowell's in a letter to Mrs. Fields, "I think . . . as Mr. Lowell did, that the mistake of our time is in being governed by the ignorant mass of opinion, instead of by thinkers and men who know something. How great that was of Gladstone, 'He has no foresight because he has no insight.'"

After Lowell's death, Miss Jewett read with interest George S. Woodberry's essay on Lowell in *"The Century,"* November 1, 1891, and sent a personal thank-you letter to him for his estimate that had deserved and won her admiration. She also sent a thank you note to Thomas Bailey Aldrich for his poem in memory of Lowell.

S. S. McClure

S. S. McClure, who strongly believed that he could make a success of a literary syndicate, began in 1884, to contact already established writers to join his service. He personally visited Miss Jewett in South Berwick and converted her to his new idea of furnishing serials and short stories for simultaneous publication in important newspapers across the country. Miss Jewett advised McClure to merge with a syndicate established by Allen Thorndike Rice, to quit overworking what she called "poor economy" to keep from enlarging his business too fast which she said was for his sake and his wife's.

Henry Wadsworth Longfellow

Miss Jewett met Henry Wadsworth Longfellow shortly before his death in 1882. She did not have time to have a long and deep friendship with him. In 1881 she was in attendance at the birthday party celebrating his 74th birthday. Longfellow noted in his journal for February 26, 1881, "a birthday dinner in advance; at Mr. Houghton's. Holmes, Howells, Aldrich, Miss Bates, and Miss Jewett, author of '*Deephaven.*'" More than a year later in a letter to Mrs. Fields, Miss Jewett noted Longfellow's death and reminisced about her visits with him and the contribution he had made to American letters. She reflected, "Are not you glad that we saw him on that pleasant day when he was ready to talk about books and people, and showed so few signs of the weakness which troubled us in those other visits? . . . I can't help saying that I am glad he has gone away before you had to leave him and know it was the last time you should see him. . . Change grows every year a harder part of our losses. . . A man, who has written as Longfellow wrote, stays in this world always to be known and loved- - to be a helper and a friend to his fellowmen. His works stand like a great cathedral in which the world may worship and be taught to pray, and long after its tired architect goes home to rest."

In 1887, Miss Jewett served as secretary of the committee that conducted an Author's Reading in the Boston Museum to raise money for the Longfellow Memorial. At the reading Miss Jewett's friend, Charles Eliot Norton, presided. Five dollars admission fee was charged, yet the house was filled with admirers of Longfellow who came to hear the many literary men and women present their readings. Mark Twain began the program with his speech entitled, "*English as She is Taught.*" He was followed by Dr. Oliver Wendell Holmes who read "*The Chambered Nautilus.*" Others who read their own works were Mrs. Julia Ward Howe who read "*Her Orders,*" and "*Battle Hymn of the Republic,*" Dr.

Edward Everett Hale read *"The Great Harvest Year,"* Mr. George William Curtis read extracts from *"Potiphar Papers,"* T. W. Higginson read *"Vacation for Saints,"* William Dean Howells read extracts from *"Their Wedding Journey,"* and James Russell Lowell closed the program by reading Longfellow's *"Building of the Ship."* According to Mrs. Thomas Bailey Aldrich (Lilian) the event was "one of the most notable entertainments ever given in Boston" as recorded in her book, *"Crowding Memories."*

A few years later, in 1905 Miss Jewett again helped honor the memory of Longfellow by being present at the Longfellow Centennial Celebration and by participating in the program. Julia Ward Howe and Miss Jewett were the only women present on the platform during the program. Mrs. Howe recorded in her diary a delightful account of the occasion dated February 27, 1905. She recorded, "In the evening went with the Jewett sisters to the celebration of Longfellow's Centennial. I had copied my verses written for the first Author's Reading in re Longfellow rather hoping that I might be invited to read them. This did not happen. I had had no reason to suppose that it would, not having been thereunto invited. Had a seat on the platform among the poet's friends, myself one of the oldest of them. It seemed as if I could hardly hold my tongue, which, however, I did. . . I sat on the platform where Sarah Jewett and I were the only women in the charmed circle." This event was Miss Jewett's last time to honor Longfellow in a public way.

Harriet Beecher Stowe

At the age of fourteen in 1863, Sarah Orne Jewett for the first time read Harriet Beecher Stowe's "*The Pearl of Orr's Island*," a novel about the coast of Maine. Because it was about the locality where Miss Jewett grew up, she read it with great interest and admiration. Reflecting on the book's influence on her thought, Miss Jewett in a letter dated July 5, 1889, to Mrs. Fields, said, "I have been reading the beginning of "*The Pearl of Orr's Island*" and finding it just as clear and perfectly original and strong as it seemed to me in my thirteenth or fourteenth year, when I read it first. I shall never forget the exquisite flavor and reality that it gave me. . . It is classical - - historical - - anything you like to say, if you can give it high praise enough." In fact, she admired the book so much that she decided to depict the same Maine scenes and characters in the tales and sketches that she wrote in the years to come. In a letter to Frederick Hopkins she said, "I tried to follow Mrs. Stowe in those delightful early chapters of "*The Pearl of Orr's Island*" in writing about people of rustic life just as they were." She did not have the same respect for the last part of "*The Pearl*" that she had for the first part. She noted, "Alas that she couldn't finish it in the same noble key of simplicity and harmony; but a poor writer is at the mercy of much unconscious opposition. You must throw everything and everybody aside at times, but a woman made like Mrs. Stowe cannot bring herself to that cold selfishness of the moment for one's work's sake and the recompense for her loss is a divine touch and there is an incomplete piece of work." Miss Jewett, though, thought the work as a whole was a great work. As a consequence of her deep delight in the book, Miss Jewett reread Mrs. Stowe's many times during her life. In a letter to her cousin, Charley Gilman, she wrote on October 17, 1877, "I have been reading *"The Pearl"* over again to refresh my memory." *"The Pearl"* was one of her great reading experiences. It gave her the opportunity to lessen the suspicion that country people had for city people. The introduction to a later edition of *"Deephaven,"* began with a reference to *"The Pearl."* Mrs. Stowe's book gave her new eyes to see the old shore paths, the weather beaten homes, and the settled folk. The book inspired her in the genre of reverently and gently picturing the lives and the places of her homeland. She was not a writer of despair, but a writer of ordinary lives lived out in a settled place.

Forrest Wilson in his book, *"Crusader in Crinoline: The Life of Harriet Beecher Stowe"* (1941) tells about Miss Jewett's first visit with Mrs. Stowe in Hartford, Connecticut in the summer of 1878. Afterwards, the two women kept in touch with each other by personal visits and correspondence. Later, Miss Jewett in company with Mrs. Fields visited Mrs. Stowe in her Hartford home in the fall of 1884. The women took gifts of their latest books with them. Miss Jewett's new novel, *"A Country Doctor,"* was her gift and the new edition of Mrs. Fields' volume of poetry, *"Under the Olive,"* was her gift. The women and their gifts were graciously received. Mrs. Stowe in her last letter to Mrs. Fields dated September 24, 1884, praised the book for its "strong and earnest thought. . . How many delightful memories your short, little visit brought back to me! I must thank you, too, for bringing Miss Jewett. I have just finished reading her book, having been delayed in indulgence to Mr. Stowe's eagerness to read it. It is not only interesting and bright but full of strong and earnest thought. The conversation between two doctors is full of gems from the deepest mines of thought. Will you give her my love and thanks for the book, which will always be a treasure to me . . . with best love to you and Miss Jewett; I am ever, the same old friend, H. B. Stowe."

Several meetings between Miss Jewett and Mrs. Stowe took place in the home of Governor and Mrs. William Claflin at Newton, Massachusetts. Miss Jewett enjoyed the letters she received from Mrs. Stowe, and she graciously accepted literary advice from the older woman. Miss Jewett wrote to Mrs. Fields of a letter she had received from Mrs. Stowe, "and dear Mrs. Stowe, with her new suggestions for my happiness, standing ready like a switchman at the division by the rails. How sweet her letters are, though, hers to you most lovely, for it says all we felt, and knew she thought that evening." The friendship came to an end at the burial of Mrs. Stowe on July 3, 1896, in Andover Chapel cemetery as she was laid to rest between her husband and son. Miss Jewett and Annie Fields attended the service. Mrs. Fields laid purple fleurs-de-lis on the coffin and where Miss Jewett mourned that none present could "really know and feel the greatness of the moment." Professor Smith read Mrs. Stowe's hymn *"Still, Still with Thee,"* the crowd sang *"Nearer My God, to Thee"* and the minister spoke the regular Episcopal burial service.

A humorous side note to Miss Jewett's acquaintance with Mrs. Stowe and her books is seen in the nickname that Mrs. Fields and Celia Thaxter called Miss Jewett. They nicknamed her, "Pinny Lawson" after Mrs. Stowe's character, Sam Lawson's daughter. Mrs. Fields said that they called Miss Jewett, "Pinny," because her head was no bigger than a pin and that she stood as straight and thin.

Charles Dudley Warner

Her good friend, Charles Dudley Warner, had many associations with her in the whole of her career. He complimented her artistry by writing, "Her portrayal of character, habits, traits, speech, was all perfectly true, although drawn from that very rural and village New England life which other writers, clever and merciless, had convinced the world to be wholly sordid and melancholy."

The exchange of letters between Miss Jewett and Warner was merely an indication of the friendship that existed between the two. For years she had been a regular and frequent visitor at the Warner's home in Hartford, Connecticut, with the Warner's reciprocating with visits to South Berwick. On one occasion Mr. Warner wrote to Annie Fields, "If SOJ is not with you I might run up to South Berwick and see her." Again in a letter to Miss Jewett, Warner said, "I want to see you ever so much and talk to you about your novel, and explain to you a little what I tried to do with Evelyn in my own." In another letter to her, he thanked her for some pointed fir that she had sent him, "The Pointed Firs in your note perfumed the house as soon as the letter was opened, and were quite as grateful to me as your kind approval. . ." The friendship ended with his death, October 20, 1900.

Julia Ward Howe

Another literary acquaintance was Julia Ward Howe, the author of the *"Battle Hymn of the Republic"* which was in the *"Atlantic Monthly"* for 1862. Julia Ward Howe visited Miss Jewett's home in South Berwick. It was an honor having her in her South Berwick home. She was accompanied by her two daughters, Laura E. Richards and Maud Howe Elliott, the co-authors of a biography of their mother entitled: *"Julia Ward Howe (1819-1910)."* In their book, they discussed Mrs. Howe's association with Miss Jewett in a chapter entitled, "Stepping Westward." From this chapter it is learned that Miss Jewett on April 2, 1901, treated Mrs. Howe to the performance of *"Ben Hur"* just as Miss Jewett had earlier treated her to the opera. The following year, Mrs. Howe, who was called "Diva" by her friends, attended a lecture in South Berwick where she visited Miss Jewett, Mary Jewett and Annie Fields. In Mrs. Howe's diary dated November 1, 1903, she described a delightful experience that she had with the two ladies. She wrote, "A delightful drive. Mary Jewett, Annie Fields and I to visit Mrs. Tyson in the Hamilton House described by Sarah in her 'Tory Lover.' Most interesting. Mrs. Tyson very cordial and delightful. . . She came over later to dinner and we had such a pleasant time." The next day they left South Berwick after having a wonderful dish of pigeons for dinner.

Laura Richards and Maud Howe Elliott, the daughters of Mrs. Howe, expressed their delight in the good time when they wrote, "It was delightful to see our mother and Miss Jewett together. They were the best of playmates, having a lovely intimacy of understanding.

Their talk rippled with light and laughter. Such stories as they told! Such songs as they sang." The girls also recalled an amusing incident that took place at the Jewett home. The daughters felt their mother had eaten enough fruitcake, but Miss Jewett insisted that Mrs. Howe eat all she wanted and take as much home with her as she desired. Miss Jewett told her, "You shall have all you want, Mrs. Howe, and a good big piece to take home besides! Put it somewhere where the girls can't find it! She nodded. 'There is a corner in my closet, which even Maud dare not explore! The fruit cake was duly packed, transported, and eaten - - we are bound to say without ill effect."

Mrs. Howe, who had been an intimate friend of Margaret Fuller and her biographer, helped Miss Jewett touch the great transcendental movement in America. Mrs. Howe, who had received an honorary L.L.D. from Smith College, stood on common ground with Miss Jewett who also received an honorary degree from Bowdoin College. Mrs. Howe was president of the New England Woman Suffrage Association, and an associate editor of "*Woman's Journal*." She gave strength to Miss Jewett in her own endeavors to be independent. Miss Jewett, however, did not participate as fully in the reform movements as Mrs. Howe did. Mrs. Howe had helped her husband edit "*Commonwealth*," an abolitionist paper, and frequently lectured in Unitarian churches. In addition to her being a biographer, an editor, a poet and a reformer, Mrs. Howe, as the aunt of F. Marion Crawford, a well-known novelist of the period, also shared a deep interest in literature with Miss Jewett.

Mrs. Howe and Miss Jewett had much in common which made for easy friendship. Both were interested in women's rights, the writing of biography and in the composing of poetry.

The Charles Eliot Norton

Miss Jewett visited at various times in the "Shady Hill" home of Mr. and Mrs. Charles Eliot Norton of Boston and in their summer home in Ashfield. Miss Jewett enjoyed a close association with their daughter, Sara, who accompanied her once to Hartford, Connecticut in January 1897 to visit Mrs. Charles D. Warner whose home was a haven for artists and writers. At other times Sara visited in Miss Jewett's home in South Berwick. Later, Sara edited the *"Letters of Charles Eliot Norton"* (Boston, 1913) in two volumes in conjunction with Mark Antony DeWolfe Howe. Miss Jewett was fortunate to be closely associated with the Norton family because of their position in the world of arts and letters. Mr. Norton was the co-editor with his brother-in-law, James Russell Lowell, of the *"North American Review."* Mr. Norton edited the works and letters of Carlyle, Ruskin, Rossetti, Lowell, and Emerson, and he taught the history of art at Harvard.

Madame Marie Therese Blanc

Miss Jewett was a friend of Madame Blanc (1840-1907), a French author of over thirty novels, a literary critic whose articles appeared in journals on both sides of the Atlantic, and a translator of American authors' works into French. Through correspondence and personal visits, their friendship became an enduring personal and professional one for both women. Madame Blanc, writing under the pseudonym of Th. Bentzon after her grandfather's name, began writing reviews of Miss Jewett's works for French literary journals in 1885. Shortly afterwards, she translated several of Miss Jewett's works into French. When Mme. Blanc sent a copy of a French translation of one of Miss Jewett's books to Miss Jewett, Miss Jewett said she received it with much "pride of heart." Returning the compliment, Miss Jewett translated Madame Blanc's works into English. One example of her work as a translator is the article entitled, *"Family Life in America"* which appeared in *"Forum XXI* (March, 1896), pages 1-20. Miss Jewett also helped promote Mme. Blanc's literary works on the American literary market.

Commenting about the feeling she experienced when she received a letter from Madame Blanc, Miss Jewett said in a letter to Annie Fields, "I have a curious sense of delight in the fragrance that blows out of Madame Blanc's letter every time I take it out of its envelope, it is so refined, so personal, and of the past." Through the Blanc letters Miss Jewett came to have a deeper impression and a fuller knowledge of Paris and France, as well as becoming more intimately acquainted with the person of Madame Blanc.

Early in 1892 after years of correspondence with each other, the two women, already friends, met for the first time when Miss Jewett and Annie Fields visited Madame Blanc in Paris. Miss Jewett described the encounter in a letter she wrote to Mrs. George D. Howe. She wrote, "I can tell you that I went on her stairs with my heart much a-freard, - - it is an awful experiment to see so old a friend for the first time, - - but I found her even more dear and kind and delightful than she has been in her letters for these eight long years. There has been no end to her friendliness."

In an article on Mme. Blanc for "*Century*," Mrs. Fields verified Miss Jewett's account of their meeting, "Eight years later we visited Paris, and found ourselves on the staircase of an old mansion in the ancient part of the city. 'Perhaps we shall do better to turn back,' Miss Jewett said, 'it is really taking a great risk to see so old a friend for the first time. This dear and intimate friendship of ours may be in danger.' But her companion, being of a more daring mind in such matters rang the bell, and the trial moment was soon most happily over." While in Paris they were introduced to Madame Blanc's many literary friends. She also took them to her country place, *La Ferte sous Jouarre*, where they took long walks in the meadows and in the woods and enjoyed the French summer together. The Frenchwoman also took them to Barbizon at the edge of the Fontainebleau forest. While there they visited a French comtesse in her storybook house, *Place Vendome*.

Madame Blanc then took a trip to Boston to visit Miss Jewett and Mrs. Fields in the Fields' home. It was not until Madame Blanc's second visit to America did she have an extended visit in Miss Jewett's South Berwick home. She began her visit on May 25, 1897. In June Miss Jewett wrote to a fellow author and friend, Harriet Prescott Spofford, about the visit. "Just now we are here keeping the old house together and looking at the green fields with the eager delight of children. I have given her some sweet fern and some bayberry and some young checkerberry leaves, and so now she knows New England."

The Frenchwoman was impressed with the wide streets and scattered houses of the village of South

Berwick. She liked the well-to-do look of the general populace. And she had to endure a terrible New England rainstorm that washed out bridges and railroad embankments. She and Miss Jewett visited the 3,000-acre Shaker Colony in Alfred, Maine. Madame Blanc wrote detailed descriptions of her stay for several French newspapers and magazines. Annie Fields in her article in "*Century*," said that Mme. Blanc "has devoted herself assiduously to understanding and to making known the aspirations of our country."

Carl J. Weber wrote an entertaining and informative essay on Mme. Blanc's visit in an article entitled, "New England through French Eyes Fifty Years Ago," in the "*New England Quarterly*" in September 1947.

During their friendship they exchanged small mementos and gifts. Mme. Blanc gave Miss Jewett a silver dish decorated with green oak leaves and white flowers which she loved. She also gave Miss Jewett a twenty-year-old picture of herself that have been engraved by Amaury Duval which had taken the medal at the Salon. In a letter Miss Jewett said that it was sweet to look at because it reminded her of the woman across the Atlantic that meant much to her, and it gave her a sense of closeness to the woman. Madame Blanc died February 5, 1907 - - only two years before Miss Jewett's own death in 1909.

Violet Page (1856-1935)

Violet Page was a mutual friend both of Mme. Blanc and Miss Jewett. Violet Page wrote thirty books of fiction, drama, and essays under the pseudonym, Vernon Lee. Violet Page was a frequent visitor and correspondent with Miss Jewett. On her library shelves Miss Jewett had copies of four books written by Violet Page. They were *"Ariadne Mantua"* (1903), *"Hortus Vitae"* (1904, which was dedicated to Madame Blanc, *"Sister Benvenuta and the Christ Child,"* and *"The Sentimental Traveler"* (1905). Miss Page sent Miss Jewett a little flowered Italian bowl which Miss Jewett prized highly and kept on her bedroom shelf. According to Miss Jewett's letters, the two had lunch together in Italy and had shared the friendship of Madame Blanc and Mrs. Fields.

Willa Cather (1873-1947)

Miss Jewett and Willa Cather enjoyed a short friendship, for it was born during the last years of Miss Jewett's life. According to Miss Cather's *"Not under Forty"* the first time that they met was in 1906 when Miss Cather, was a staff member of *"McClure's Magazine."* She was working on her first assignment. The second meeting took place in the home of Mrs. James T. Fields in 1908 when Cather was managing editor of *"McClure's Magazine."* Cather had already become an author in her right by publishing a collection of poems, *"April Twilights"* and a collection of stories, *"The Troll Garden."* The relationship between them lasted only sixteen months because of Miss Jewett's death in 1909.

In 1906 Miss Cather was introduced to Miss Jewett and Mrs. Fields by Mrs. Louis D. Brandeis - - the sister of Pauline Goldmark, a friend of Elizabeth Shepley Sergeant who wrote *"Willa Cather, A Memoir."* Miss Sergeant's book was published by the University of Nebraska Press in 1953. It recounts their relationship. Miss Jewett gave

Cather valuable literary advice. And Jewett praised the work and character of Miss Cather. On the other hand, Miss Cather admired the work and character of Miss Jewett.

Miss Cather devoted one of her six chapters of *"Not Under Forty"* to the life and thought of Miss Jewett. In her book, she praised the humor of Miss Jewett because it came "from her delicate and tactful handling of this native language of the waterside and countryside, never overdone, never pushed a shade too far." In further describing the art of Miss Jewett, she said that she admired the way Miss Jewett related to her stories and her character, and she called the relationship that Miss Jewett had with her stories "spirited, gay, tactful, and noble in its essence and a little arch in its expression." Writing of her use of language, she spoke of the source of her power of dialogue in the following manner: "From her early years she must have treasured up those pithy bits of local speech, of native idiom, which enrich and enliven her pages. The language her people speak to each other is a native tongue. No writer can invent it. It is made in the hard school of experience, in communities where language has been undisturbed long enough to take on color and character from the nature and experiences of the people." Because she had such a good opinion of Miss Jewett's works she predicted a long life for her works but a limited audience for them. She stated that a taste for Miss Jewett's works "must always remain a special taste, - - but it will remain."

Miss Cather said that Miss Jewett was one who enjoyed the seasons of nature as well the seasons of humankind. The picture is of one who loved her garden in spring and summer and with equal deference loved small dinner parties and luncheons with friends and acquaintances. She described Miss Jewett as a young woman who "devoted her mornings to horseback riding in fine weather, and was skillful with a sailboat," and that "every day, in every season she enjoyed the beautiful country in which she had the good fortune to be born. Her love of the Maine country and seacoast was the supreme happiness of her life."

Miss Cather portrayed her as a world traveler who had visited the Alps, the Pyrenees and the Apennines, and as a friend to great men of letters along with the lowly country people of her own community. Cather included in her book a comment by Henry James, who was himself one of Miss Jewett's dear friends and who said of her that she "had a sort of elegance of humility, or fine flame of modesty." Cather wrote "She had friends among the most interesting and gifted people of her time, scores of friends among the village and country people of her own state -- people who knew her as Doctor Jewett's daughter and regarded 'Sarah's writing' as a ladylike accomplishment. These country friends, she used to say, were the wisest of all, because they could never be fooled about fundamentals."

Miss Cather hailed Miss Jewett as one of the first Americans to see the importance of Joseph Conrad. Recalling one of the ironies of Miss Jewett's life, she wrote that Miss Jewett was "reading a new volume of Conrad, late in the night, when the slight cerebral hemorrhage occurred from which she died some months later."

After visiting in South Berwick, Miss Cather pictured the bedroom and study of Miss Jewett for Elizabeth Sergeant. Miss Sergeant in her book, *"Willa*

Cather, A Memoir," (1953) records, "Willa began, as the light from the stove faded, to tell me about the small green bedroom - - the smallest and plainest of the four upstairs chambers where Miss Jewett wrote her stories. The room had a fireplace with Delft tiles, half-paneled walls, and a rather homely Victorian desk with sloping top and drawers at the sides. She made me see it so clearly that I had a shock of recognition when Miss Laura Hills, remembering Sarah Orne Jewett for me, in her rose-leaf mood of the nineties in Newburyport, quoted her: 'I was born here and I know the room I want to die in, leaving the lilac bushes green and growing, and all the chairs in their places.'"

Being completely sympathetic to Miss Jewett, Miss Cather was elaborate in her praise of Miss Jewett's "*The Country of the Pointed Firs*" honoring it along with Hawthorne's "*The Scarlet Letter*" and Mark Twain's "*Huckleberry Finn*" as one of the "three American books which have the possibility of a long, long life." Miss Cather said of the book, "I can think of no others that confront time and change so serenely," and that the sketches of the novel 'are living things caught in the open with light and freedom and airspaces about them. They melt into the land and the life of the land until they are not stories at all, but life itself." In Miss Jewett's work Miss Cather found her own model of the pioneer woman in Miss Jewett's character, Mrs. Almira Todd of "*The Country of the Pointed Firs,*" and when Miss Cather came to dedicate "*O Pioneers!* whose characters had been discussed with Miss Jewett she said that it was dedicated to the memory of Sarah Orne Jewett, "in whose beautiful and delicate work there is the perfection that endures."

In Eleanor M. Smith's *"The Literary Relationship of Sarah Orne Jewett and Willa Sibert Cather,"* in the *"New England Quarterly,"* (December, 1956) refers to an interview that Miss Cather had with Latrobe Carroll. It is the story of her own inspiration in writing *"O Pioneers!"* She said, "And from the first chapter, I decided not to 'write at all - - simply give myself up to the pleasure of recapturing in memory people and places I had believed forgotten. This was what my friend Sarah Orne Jewett had advised me to do. She said to me that if my life had lain in a part of the world that was without literature, and I couldn't tell about it truthfully in form I most admired, I'd have to make a kind of writing that would tell it, no matter what I lost in the process."

Because Miss Jewett's stories were honestly and reverently told, Miss Cather delighted in reading and rereading them. She said her experience of reading the sketches of Maine life was like "watching the movement of a yacht." One of the reasons she reread the sketches was, according to her own statement, for their "inherent, individual beauty" and not because they were clever stories with arresting situations.

Miss Jewett' influence on Willa Cather is of great importance in the annals of American Literature since Miss Cather now stands in a high place in American literature. She expressed her gratitude to Miss Jewett for the influence that she had on her life in the introduction to her own novel, *"Alexander's Bridge"* (1922), where she publicly proclaimed that Miss Jewett had been a real inspiration to her and had helped her in her own writing career. Miss Cather wrote of the advice that Miss Jewett had specifically given to her in these words, "one of the few really helpful words I ever heard from an older writer, I had from Sarah Orne Jewett when she said to me: 'of course, one day you will write about your country. In the meantime, get all you can. One must know the world so well before one can know the parish." The advice was the result of her knowledge of success in writing fiction. Miss Jewett's advice was frank and refreshing to Miss Cather who, in turn, followed it with great success for herself. In addition, Miss Jewett advised her to "work in silence and with all one's heart," and spoke of her own method of composition as an old house and an old woman coming together in her mind with a click to indicate that a story was coming on.

Not only was the literary advice to Miss Cather, general in nature, but it was also specific at times. In a letter in November, 1908, Miss Jewett critiques a story of Miss Cather's that had appeared in "*McClure's Magazine.*" In the letter Miss Jewett wrote, "The lover is as well done as he could be when a woman writes in the man's character- - it must always, I believe, be something of a masquerade. I think it is safest to write about him as you did about the others, and not try to be he!"

Both women shared the same feeling toward Annie Fields and gave the same allegiance to the literary salon in Mrs. Fields' Boston home. Both were entertained by Mrs. Fields on several occasions whose charm was enhanced by her setting. Miss Cather in "*Not Under Forty*" in describing Mrs. Fields' home said, "The unique charm of Mrs. Fields' house was not that it was a place where one could hear the past, but that it was a place where the past lived on - - where it was protected and cherished, had sanctuary from the noisy push of the present." This mutual love for their heritage brought the three women together as friends and literary companions. Miss Jewett, in Willa Cather's mind, was a chronicler of New England past, as in fact Miss Cather was a chronicler of the Nebraska past. According to Miss Cather, Miss Jewett wrote "of everyday people who grew out of the soil, not about exceptional individuals at war with their environment."

As a memorial to the woman she respected and loved, Miss Cather kept the letters that she had received from Sarah Orne Jewett and looked through them for literary observations, as well as for matters relating to their friendship. In one letter Miss Cather found an observation of Miss Jewett's that stayed in her mind for Miss Jewett had written, "The thing that teases the mind over and over for years, and at last gets itself put down rightly on paper - - whether little or great, it belongs to literature." In agreeing with her, Miss Cather said that "the artist spends a lifetime in pursuing the things that haunt him, in having his mind 'teased.'" As others had done before her Miss Cather compared Miss Jewett to the great writer of Greek idylls, Theocritus, saying that her writings lingered in one's mind leaving the reader "an intangible residuum of pleasure," and "an experience in memory."

In December 13, 1908, Miss Cather received a letter from Sarah Orne Jewett. Miss Jewett wrote: "My dear Willa, — I have been thinking about you and hoping that things are going well. I cannot help saying what I think about your writing and its being hindered by such incessant, important, responsible work as you have in your hands now. I do think that it is impossible for you to work so hard and yet have your gifts mature as they should — when one's first working power has spent itself, nothing ever brings it back just the same, and I do wish in my heart that the force of this very year could have gone into three or four stories. . . I want you to be surer of your backgrounds, — you have your Nebraska life, — a child's Virginia, and now an intimate knowledge of what we are pleased to call the 'Bohemia' of newspaper and magazine-office life. These are uncommon equipment, but you don't see them yet quite enough from the outside [...] You need to dream your dreams and go on to new and more shining ideals, to be aware of 'the dream' and to follow it; your vivid, exciting companionship in the office must not be your audience, you must find your own quiet center of life, and write from that to the world that holds offices, and all society, all Bohemia; the city, the country — in short, you must write to the human heart, the great consciousness that all humanity goes to make up."

To Miss Cather, Miss Jewett's work would be read by later generations with pleasure and profit, where they would learn "the characteristic flavor, the spirit, the cadence, of an American writer of the first order, - - and of a New England which will then be a thing of the past."

John Greenleaf Whittier

Miss Jewett's friendship with John Greenleaf Whittier, the Quaker Poet, began early in her literary career. They first met at Annie Fields' home in Boston, and the friendship was lengthened and deepened by the exchange of letters, by the mutual admiration of each other's works, by the writing of poems for each other, and by their continued visits together. After Miss Jewett had sent a copy of her recently published book, "*Deephaven*" (1877) to him, Whittier responded with prompt praise, "I must thank thee for thy admirable book, '*Deephaven*:' I have given several copies to friends, all of whom appreciate it highly, and I have been reading it over for the third time. I know of nothing better in our literature of the kind, though it recalls Miss Mitford's "*Our Village*" and "*The Chronicles of Carlingford.*" I heartily congratulate thee on thy complete success and am Very Truly thy Friend, John Greenleaf Whittier." The letters are in Samuel T. Pickard, "*Life and Letters of John Greenleaf Whittier*" (1894). In a letter two years later and after receiving Miss Jewett's "*Old Friends and New*" Whittier again expressed thanks for the refreshing material that Miss Jewett included in her books. He exclaimed, "I am glad to get the charming book from thy own hand. I have read '*Deephaven*' over half a dozen times, and always with gratitude to thee for such a book - - so simple, pure, and so true to nature. And '*Old Friends and New*' I shall certainly read as often. When tired and worried I resort to thy books and find rest and refreshing. I recommend them to everybody and everybody likes them. There is no dissenting opinion; and already thousands whom these have never seen love the author as well as her books." Miss Jewett continued to send copies to him of her other books as they were published, and Whittier admired each one. His admiration for them was based primarily on the quieting effect that her books had on his mind and emotions.

Miss Jewett wrote to Annie Fields about a visit that she had made to see Whittier. She said that the meeting was highly satisfying, "I was so glad that I went, 'Thy dear friend' was so glad to see me, and we sat right down and went at it and with pauses at tea-time, the conversation was kept up until after ten. He was even more affectionate and dear than usual, and seemed uncommonly well, though he had had neuralgia all day and made out to be a little drooping with the assistance of the weather and coming company. But oh, how rich we are with 'thy friend' for a friend!" At their meeting the conversation ranged from politics to the L.L.D. degree that Whittier had just received, to mutual friends and literature. She said, "We went over Julian Hawthorne and Lowell, and the President and Mrs. Cleveland."

After a visit with Miss Jewett at Annie Fields' literary salon in Boston in February, 1882, when he was 75 years old, Whittier wrote Miss Jewett in a letter from Danvers, Massachusetts, how much he enjoyed his visit with her. He wrote, "I wonder how I can reconcile myself to the old customary life here, after my pleasant stay in Boston, and our delightful companionship there. I cannot make thee understand how grateful and refreshing it all was and how much I thank thee for it."

In the summer of 1882, Miss Jewett invited Whittier to South Berwick for a visit prior to her going on a trip to Europe. In a letter of May, 1882, he declined the invitation for reasons of ill health and cold weather. He wrote, "How kind it was in thee to write me amidst the worries and cares of preparation for thy flitting across the water; and to add to all thy troubles the necessity of entertaining dull company by inviting me to South Berwick. I know it would be wickedly selfish for me to accept such an invitation; but I certainly should do so if I could . . . so I must let thee go with my written benediction and with grateful thanks for thy books, and still more for thyself." John Greenleaf Whittier composed a sonnet for the occasion of Miss Jewett's first voyage abroad entitled:

"Godspeed."

Outbound, your bark awaits you. Were I one
Whose prayer availeth much, my wish should be
Your favoring trade-wind and consenting sea.
By sail or steed was never love outrun,
And, here or there, love follows her in whom
All graces and sweet charities unite,
The old Greek beauty set in holier light;
And her for whom New England's byways bloom,
Who walks among us welcome as the Spring,
Calling up blossoms where her light feet stray.
God keep you both, make beautiful your way,
Comfort, console, and bless; and safely bring,
Ere yet I make upon a vaster sea
The unreturning voyage, my friends to me.

After Miss Jewett returned from Europe, she sent
Whittier a 56 line poem entitled "The Eagle Trees" which
was published in "*Harpers*" in 1882.

Great pines that watch the river go
    Down to the sea all night, all day,
Firm-rooted near its ebb and flow,
    Bowing their heads to winds at play,
Strong-limbed and proud, they silent stand,
    And watch the mountains far away,
And watch the miles of farming land,
    And hear the church bells tolling slow.

They see the men in distant fields
    Follow the furrows of the plough;

They count the loads the harvest yields,
  And fight the storms with every bough,
Beating the wild winds back again.
  The April sunshine cheers them now;
They eager drink the warm spring rain,
  Nor dread the spear the lightning wields.

High in the branches clings the nest
  The great birds build from year to year;
And though they fly from east to west,
  Some instinct keeps this eyrie dear
To their fierce hearts; and now their eyes
  Glare down at me with rage and fear;
They stare at me with wild surprise,
  Where high in air they strong-winged rest.

Companionship of birds and trees!
  The years have proved your friendship strong,
You share each other's memories,
  The river's secret and its song,
And legends of the country-side;
  The eagles take their journey long,
The great trees wait in noble pride
  For messages from hills and seas.

I hear a story that you tell
  In idleness of summer days:
A singer that the world knows well
  To you again in boyhood strays;
Within the stillness of your shade
  He rests where flickering sunlight plays,
And sees the nest the eagles made,
  And wonders at the distant bell.

His keen eyes watch the forest growth,
    The rabbits' fear, the thrushes' flight;
He loiters gladly, nothing loath
    To be alone at fall of night,
The woodland things around him taught
    Their secrets in the evening light,
Whispering some wisdom to his thought
    Known to the pines and eagles both.

Was it the birds who early told
    The dreaming boy that he would win
A poet's crown instead of gold?
    That he would fight a nation's sin? --
On eagle wings of song would gain
    A place that few might enter in,
And keep his life without a stain
    Through many years, yet not grow old?

And he shall be what few men are,
    Said all the pine-trees, whispering low;
His thought shall find an unseen star;
    He shall our treasured legends know:
His words will give the way-worn rest
    Like this cool shade our branches throw;
He, lifted like our loftiest crest,
    Shall watch his country near and far.

Miss Jewett's appreciation of Whittier's work and life matched his admiration for her person and books. Three notes show adequately this mutual admiration. In the summer of 1883 while Whittier was staying in the New Hampshire hills he wrote to Mrs. Pitman, "we are reading Sarah Orne Jewett's charming "*Country Doctor*" under the pines.

As an example of her appreciation of his work, in 1884 she wrote a complimentary letter to him about his poem, "*The Homestead.*" She praised the poem by writing, "I do not know when anything had touched me so nearly and dearly. Nobody has mourned more than I over the forsaken farmhouses which I see everywhere as I drive about the country out of which I grew, and where every bush and tree seem like my cousins. I hope this will make people stop and think, and I know it will bring tears to many eyes. That line about the squirrel in the forsaken house nobody else would have thought of but you. I send all the thanks one little letter can carry."

Filled with thanksgiving for Whittier's devotion to the ideals of God and country, Miss Jewett dedicated her book, "*The King of Folly Island and Other People,*" (1888) to Whittier. In response to the departure that Miss Jewett made in the book from her usual locale for her stories, Whittier said, "I do wonder that '*The Luck of the Bogans*' is attractive to the Irish folks, and to everybody else. It is a very successful departure from New England life and scenery, and shows that Sarah is as much at home in Ireland and on the Carolina Sea Islands as in Maine or Massachusetts." As a result of his admiration of Miss Jewett's character and work, Whittier boasted to Mrs. Fields, "I am very proud that I was one of the first to discover her." The friendship between the two is further acknowledged in letters to mutual friends and in public tribute. In 1891, Whittier in a letter to Annie Fields recalled his meeting with her and Miss Jewett at the Whittier Club of Haverkill on the occasion of his 84th birthday. He considered their brief meeting to be a high light of his birthday celebration. He wrote, "The best thing on my birthday was to meet thee and our dear Sarah on the stairs, and the worst was that you went away so soon." In 1892 when the *"Boston Journal"* dedicated an entire page of tributes to Whittier, there appeared a tribute to him by Miss Jewett. The friendship cannot be reckoned as a love affair for Whittier had once asked Miss Jewett, "Sarah, was thee ever in love?" She replied, "No! Whatever made you think of that?"

Whittier dedicated his book *"Among the Hills,"* to Annie Fields. She wrote in her book *"Authors and Friends"* of their sympathetic relationship: "Of Sarah Orne Jewett he was fond as of a daughter and from their earliest acquaintance his letters are filled with appreciation of her stories." Whittier's death in 1892 after several years of mutual insight into the essence of human relationships and spiritual affinities brought their ties to an end.

Mary E. Wilkins Freeman

Since the beginning of their published works, Miss Jewett and Mary E. Wilkins Freeman were selected by literary critics as the best of the nineteenth century local color writers of New England. The two women were acquainted with each other's works in their day, and they respected each other's art. They communicated that respect in an exchange of letters. According to F. O. Matthiessen in his book of *"Sarah Orne Jewett,"* Miss Jewett spoke highly of Mrs. Freeman's stories. Mrs. Freeman wrote "You are lovely to write me so about my stories, but I never wrote any story equal to your *'White Heron.'* I don't think I ever read a short story, unless I except Tolstoy's '*Two Deaths*,' that so appealed to me. I would not have given up that bird any more than you would if he had come back."

The two women wrote so similarly, that the two were spoken of in a single breath. In 1897, a critic in "*Leslie's Weekly*" in an article entitled, "*People Talked About*," placed the two women side by side. The writer stated that Miss Jewett's work "has been rather stimulated than otherwise by the competition of more recent comers, notably Mary Wilkins, who has contrived to wrest a literary livelihood from that inhospitable soil." Mark Sullivan in 1914 in "*Colliers Weekly*" also declared the fact of the mutual renown of the two women authors, "If I were to name the group of short story writers who are, to my taste, the greatest that America has had, I should certainly include among them Mary E. Wilkins and Sarah Orne Jewett."

Thomas Bailey Aldrich, editor of the "*Atlantic Monthly*" from 1881-1890, placed Miss Jewett, Mrs. Freeman, and Mrs. Harriet Beecher Stowe together in the category of great American Authors. Aldrich told Miss Jewett that "every generation has its own story-teller - - and very few of them ever survive their generation. The two or three who do are authors who have painted some special phase of life in some indelible local color. I think Mrs. Stowe had some of this in several of her Oldtown sketches, Miss Wilkins in her "*Humble Romance*" and you in at least a dozen pictures of New England country life." A later literary critic, Ludwig Lewisohn, compared the women and their work by saying that "their entire sincerity and formal simplicity make for mildly classical quality, for a sobriety and completeness of delineation within the tiniest of frames. They are at least never pretentious and rarely tricky; neither of them sought to treat large and intricate problems with the intellectual equipment of an average villager nor did they make romanticized scenery do for both character and action, they also avoided melodrama." This tribute is fitting to two women who adequately portrayed the people of New England whom they both appreciated and loved.

Thomas Bailey Aldrich

Thomas Bailey Aldrich from Portsmouth, New Hampshire, was a close personal friend of Miss Jewett. This closeness is shown in the nicknames that they had for each other. He called her "Sadie," and she called him, "Duke of Ponkapog" and his wife, "dear Ponkapog." Further evidences of their friendship is seen in Miss Jewett's correspondence with the Aldrich's when she visited them frequently in their summer home in Ponkapog, Massachusetts, and at the "Crags" at Tenants Harbor, Maine. The friends loved to be out-of-doors together as Miss Jewett noted in her letter to Lilian Aldrich, "Dear Ponkapog! How I should like to have a drive with you."

Aldrich was the editor of the *"Atlantic Monthly"* and a poet of some note. His "great gift and genius of verse" was praised by Miss Jewett, and in turn her gift of storytelling was praised by Aldrich. He wanted Miss Jewett's stories to appear in the *"Atlantic Monthly"* because they were widely read and liked. Annie Fields in the introduction to *"Letters of S. O. Jewett"* records the attitude that Aldrich had toward her and her stories. She said that he told her on receiving one of her stories, "Whenever you give me one of your perfect little stories the whole number seems to bloom!" He thought that her stories were so good that they would outlast the sketches of Hawthorne! He told her "I believe, for example, that Hawthorne's pallid allegories will have faded away long before those two little Dulham ladies will give up their daring railway journey to the neighboring town, in search of innocent personal decorations." Aldrich, himself a writer of nine volumes of fiction, the best of which is "*Marjorie Daw*," eight volumes of poetry, three volumes of non-fiction, and editor of one of the most notable literary magazines of his day, was according to Vernon Parrington, in "*The Beginnings of Critical Realism in America 1860-1920*" admired by Miss Jewett for she "never tired in praising the sprightliness of his humor."

Henry James

Miss Jewett was celebrated as a writer of note and as a person of enduring charm by Henry James, himself a celebrated American author of a dozen novels, a like number of novellas, numerous short stories and plays, several travel books, a well-kept notebook and hundreds of letters. James said of Miss Jewett in his book "*Mr. and Mrs. James T. Fields*," in his characteristic ambiguous and rambling language, "To speak in a mere parenthesis of Miss Jewett, mistress of an art of fiction all her own, even though of a minor compass, and surpassed only by Hawthorne as producer of the most finished and penetrating of the numerous 'short stories' that have the domestic life of New England for their general and their doubtless somewhat lean subject, is to do myself, I feel, the violence of suppressing a chapter of appreciation that I should long since somewhere have found space for. Her admirable gift, that artistic sensibility in her which rivaled the rare personal, that sense for the finest kind of truthful rendering, the sober and tender note, the temperately touched, whether in the ironic or the pathetic, would have deserved some more pointed commemoration than I judge her beautiful little quantum of achievement, her free and high, yet all so generously subdued character, a sort of elegance of humility or fine flame of modesty, with her remarkable distinguished outward stamp, to have called forth before the premature and overdarkened close of her young course of production."

This Jamesian statement was originally written for the "*Atlantic Monthly*," July, 1915, some six years after Miss Jewett's death. The tribute is a fitting judgment to climax a rich friendship that had thrived between the two of them for several years.

According to M. A. DeWolfe Howe in his book "*Memories of a Hostess*," Miss Jewett on her third European tour in 1898 with Mrs. Fields spent an enjoyable day of September 13, 1898, with Henry James at his home at Rye, England. Mrs. Fields described his intensive hospitality. He entertained the two women at his home by giving them a luncheon, a stroll in his garden, and an engaging conversation in his parlor. During the conversation in the parlor, he expressed his appreciation to Miss Jewett for her works by stating that he reread her works with increasing admiration. He said that her language was "so Absolutely true - - not a word overdone - - such elegance and exactness." Afterwards Mr. James took the women on a carriage ride to see Winchelsea and then saw them off at the railroad station at Hastings. To

James, Miss Jewett and Mrs. Fields, the day had been well spent.

In Leon Edel's "*The Selected Letters of Henry James,*" (1955) is a letter to Miss Jewett dated October 5, 1901, and posted in Rye, England. James, after receiving a copy of Miss Jewett's "*The Tory Lover,*" published in the same year thanked Miss Jewett for the book and at the same time criticized the book for being out of her usual style. He gave her wise literary advice concerning her future literary productions. He declared, "Let me not criminally or at all events gracelessly, delay to thank you for your charming and generous present of "*The Tory Lover.*" He has been but three or four days in the house, yet I have given him an earnest, pensive, a liberal- - yes a benevolent attention, and the upshot is that I should like to write you a longer letter. . . For it would take me some time to disembroil the tangle of saying to you at once how I appreciate the charming touch, tact and taste of this ingenious exercise, and how little I am in sympathy with the experiments of its general (to my sense) misguided stamp. . . You seem to me to have steered very clear of them - - to have seen your work very bravely and handled it firmly; but even you court disaster by composing the whole thing so much by sequences of speeches. . . Go back to the dear country of the Pointed Firs, Come back to the palpable present <u>intimate</u> that throbs responsive, and that wants, misses, needs you, God knows, and that suffers woefully in your absence. . ." James objected to her novel primarily because it was a historical romance which dealt with the pre-revolutionary days of South Berwick, Maine, and not with the contemporary lives of the people that Miss Jewett knew firsthand.

. In June 1905, Henry James and W. D. Howells visited Miss Jewett in her home in South Berwick. Later, James dined with Miss Jewett and Mark DeWolfe Howe at Mrs. Fields in Boston. In 1909 Miss Jewett, who read James' books with enthusiasm and appreciation, praised his *"The Jolly Corner"* in a letter to Mrs. Fields. She noted that "There are lovely things in it and a wonderful analysis of fear in the dark; so that it may please you better by day than by night, as it did me." Her favorite of James' stories was the *"Way It Came."* Miss Jewett, though an admirer of James, did say in a letter to Anna Laurens Dawes, "I don't like Mr. James' characters - that is I shouldn't like real people who acted and thought after his fashion, but I think he writes cleverly about them and makes them more or less interesting." In 1911 Henry James promised Mrs. Fields that he would write an introduction for a volume of Miss Jewett's letters that she had collected and edited for publication. For some unknown reason James was unable to keep his promise, but his estimate of her work six years after her death helped place Miss Jewett in the forefront of capable writers who should be studied and read with interest and pleasure. Other personal associations between the two authors occurred until her death, and James' praise of her work and person continued for several years after her death

Celia Thaxter

Another of Miss Jewett's personal friends and one who is mentioned often in her letters to Annie Fields was Celia Thaxter. Celia Thaxter was a popular and an accomplished poet and juvenile writer, who lived in Kittery

Point, Maine, only seventeen miles from South Berwick. The relatively close neighbors visited each other over a dozen years, and when personal visits were inconvenient or impossible they wrote to each other. The letters were filled with items of personal interest and literary advice. Collected in *"Letters of Celia Thaxter"* (1897) is a letter to Bradford Torrey dated December 27, 1889. Mrs. Thaxter recounted a most pleasant personal experience with Miss Jewett as they went on a drive through the woods together, "I heard the hermit thrushes in South Berwick woods. Sarah Jewett drove me down into the woods just after sunset, and we sat in the carriage and listened. I never heard them before. What an experience it was I leave you to guess." The two women were on such friendly terms that they affectionately called each other by nicknames. Celia Thaxter called her "Owlet" and Miss Jewett called her "Sandpiper." Miss Jewett shared Celia Thaxter's knowledge of nature. One of the favorite summer homes that Miss Jewett and Mrs. Fields visited during the summers was the Appledore Island home of Mrs. Thaxter where she had grown up in the Isles of Shoals where her brothers, Cedric and Oscar, operated the Appledore House, a resort hotel which accommodated 500 guests at three dollars a day in 1877. Among the guests that stayed at Appledore and who associated with Miss Jewett, Mrs. Fields, and Mrs. Thaxter were such famous men and women as Hawthorne, Emerson, Holmes, Whittier, Lowell, Aldrich, Harriet Beecher Stowe, and others. After Mrs. Thaxter's death in 1894, Miss Jewett wrote to Sara Whitman about Mrs. Thaxter and her Appledore home on August 29, 1894, "We were more neighbors and compatriots than most people. I knew the island, the Portsmouth side of her life, better than did others."

Miss Jewett knew the Isles of Shoals so well that her poem, "On Star Island" accurately describes one of the islands. The poem is collected in "Verses."

ON STAR ISLAND

High on the lichened ledges, like
   A lonely sea-fowl on its perch,
Blown by the cold sea winds, it stands,
   Old Gosport's quaint, forsaken church.

No sign is left of all the town
   Except a few forgotten graves;
But to and fro the white sails go
   Slowly across the glittering waves.

And summer idlers stray about
   With curious questions of the lost
And vanished village, and its men,
   Whose boats by these same waves were tossed.

I wonder if the old church dreams
   About its parish, and the days
The fisher people came to hear
   The preaching and the songs of praise!

Rough-handed, browned by sun and wind,
   Heedless of fashion or of creed,
They listened to the parson's words --
   Their pilot heavenward indeed.

Their eyes on week-days sought the church,
   Their surest landmark, and the guide
That led them in from far at sea,
   Until they anchored safe beside

The harbor-wall that braved the storm
   With its resistless strength of stone.
Those busy fishers all are gone -
   The church is standing here alone.

But still I hear their voices strange,
   And still I see the people go
Over the ledges to their homes:
   The bent old women's footsteps slow;

The faithful parson stop to give
   Some timely word to one astray;
The little children hurrying on
   Together, chattering of their play.

I know the blue sea covered some,
   And others in the rocky ground
Found narrow lodgings for their bones -
   God grant their rest is sweet and sound!

I saw the worn rope idle hang
   Beside me in the belfry brown.
I gave the bell a solemn toll -
   I rang the knell for Gosport town.

Mrs. Thaxter and Miss Jewett deepened their friendship with the exchange of mementos, letters, and favors. One time, Mrs. Thaxter gave Miss Jewett a copy of her book, "*The Isles of Shoals*," and a manuscript poem, "*Vesper*." Mrs. Thaxter dedicated two of her many books to Miss Jewett. The two books were "*Poems*," (1883) and "*An Island Garden.*" (1894). Miss Jewett after Mrs. Thaxter's death prepared a volume of Mrs. Thaxter's stories for children and wrote a preface for the work that was published. In addition, Miss Jewett treated Mrs. Thaxter's son, John Thaxter, with special interest by offering him literary advice though he published only a few of the many stories that he wrote. Several letters have been preserved that were written by Miss Jewett to John Thaxter.

Rudyard Kipling

Miss Jewett sent a copy of "*Country of the Pointed Firs*" to Rudyard Kipling, an English author of novels, poems, and short stories. Miss Jewett's intuition of what would interest him was accurate for Mr. Kipling graciously accepted the gift and wrote a note of thanks and praise of the book. In his letter of praise recorded by Annie Fields in the introduction to "*Letters of S. O. Jewett*", he said "I am writing to you to convey some small installment of our satisfaction in that perfect little tale. It's immense - - it is the very life, so many of the people of lesser sympathy have missed the lovely New England landscape, and the genuine New England nature." In his letter, Kipling went on to commend her art, for the grasp that she had of her materials and for the vigor with which she presented them. Kipling had read "*The Life of Nancy*" and he emphasized to her in a letter how well she had captured New England life and scenes, and described the people with true insight into their character. He especially liked the story, "The Quest of Mrs. Timms" and said of the whole work that "it had been worth spending three winters in New England to be able to draw the full flavor out of her stories."

F. Hopkinson Smith

Miss Jewett corresponded with F. Hopkinson Smith, the man who successfully engineered the foundation of the Statue of Liberty, the Block Island Breakwater, the seawall at Tompkinsville, Staten Island and the Race Rock Lighthouse and who turned to professional writing after he was fifty years old. The best of his eight novels, *"Colonel Carter of Cartersville,"* was reviewed by Miss Jewett in one of the literary journals. In her review she delighted in his hearty relish of life, in his sunny charm, and in his use of picturesque anecdotes. The two authors shared the same enthusiasm for the ideal, for the romantic, for the provincial character of the people – she in New England folk, he in New York State from the big city people and the rural dwellers. He, like Miss Jewett, was a regional storyteller.

John Burroughs

In a letter to Miss Jewett, John Burroughs, a well-known and widely respected author, expressed appreciation for her sketches of Maine and its people. His letter is recorded in F. O. Matthiessen's book. Burroughs said, "I remember your face at the Holmes breakfast, where I saw so many faces that I have forgotten. . . I remember also your first sketches in the *"Atlantic"* and the clear human impression which they made upon me - - an impression which your later works deepen and fill out. . . Now I know you are from Maine I can taste the flavor of the birch in your books. May the birches be kind to you."

Oliver Wendell Holmes

At Oliver Wendell Holmes seventieth birthday party, Miss Jewett was in the company of great authors at the Brunswick Hotel in Boston. It was "breakfast at noon," and had been postponed from August 29 to December 3. Among the distinguished guests were Helen Hunt Jackson, who "sat at Holmes' table, the third person to his right, between Whittier and Charles Dudley Warner," and H. O. Houghton, who was toastmaster for the event. Also present were Elizabeth Stuart Phelps, Mrs. Harriet Beecher Stowe, Julia Ward Howe, Rose Terry Cook, Mrs. James T. Fields, and others, "all the Brahmins, one hundred strong."

Others

Ellen Chase gave Miss Jewett photographs of Whitby, where Miss Jewett had visited with DuMaurier. Ellen Chase also gave her a little lemon tree that she kept on her window seat by her secretary where she wrote in her South Berwick home. Miss Jewett enjoyed the gift for it was always full of lemons.

Miss Jewett was friends with Daniel Chester French, the sculptor; Agnes Bartlett Brown who lived in Quincy Mansion in Boston and whose painting of a country hillside Miss Jewett wanted to buy; with Charles Townsend Copeland who had introduced her to Mark A. DeWolfe Howe; with Harriet Foot Seegar, a Boston schoolteacher and one who had visited her in South Berwick, and with

Harriet Prescott Spofford from Calais, Maine, who had reviewed one of Miss Jewett's stories for the *"Book Buyer."* Miss Spofford was also a poet, essayist and a short story writer to whom Miss Jewett wrote in 1902, "What any 'sister authoress' would really love to do would be to hold the pen that was equal to writing you." Miss Jewett was the friend of the wife of the *"Century"* editor, Mrs. Katharine McMahon Johnson, whose literary salon at Brown House in New York City was frequently visited by Miss Jewett.

Several people visited Miss Jewett or were visited by her at their homes. Miss Jewett visited Sarah Chauncey Woolsey annually at her Newport home called Liberty Hall. And Helen Bigelow Merriman, an artist, who wrote books on painting and painters, visited Miss Jewett in South Berwick. Visitors at her home included the illustrator, Jessie McDermott Walcott, who illustrated Miss Jewett's *"Katy's Birthday,"* in *"Wide Awake"* (June, 1883), the engraver, J. Appleton Brown, who presented her with an engraving of a river scene inscribed to her on June 29, 1886, a Baptist preacher, Reverend Irving B. Mower of South Berwick who had given her a piece of quartz that she kept on her desk, her aunt, Sarah Chandler Perry who gave her a Whittier spoon picturing his birthplace, and of Mrs. Riggs, whose book, *"Penelope in Ireland,"* Miss Jewett called "our beloved" book.

Miss Jewett was the friend of her Aunt Lucretia Perry who wrote her approval of *"The Shore House"* saying, "I do not think I ever told you how much I enjoyed your lifelike '*Shore House.*' It was as full of good things as a Christmas pudding, or plums, and I liked nearly as well your very graphic account of your visit to the old women in

Kittery in Mary's letter. You have a charm of naturalness in telling your stories, which seems so easy, yet it is so impossible to catch if one is not to the manner born. I hope you will always stick to your own style."

Miss Jewett was a friend of the wife of a railroad executive, Mrs. Edith Forbes Perkins, who sent flowers to Miss Jewett in 1903. Another friend was Charles Bell the Governor of Vermont whose first wife was cousin of Miss Jewett's mother and whose daughters provided companionship for both Mary and Sarah Jewett. Mr. and Mrs. John Burleigh of South Berwick visited her in her home. He was a member of Congress, 1873-1877 who also ran the woolen mill and lived in a Powderhouse Hill estate. Mellen Chamberlain served as a judge of the Boston Municipal Court and took Miss Jewett to visit the Boston Athenaeum.

She was a friend of Ella Walworth and attended her fashionable Boston wedding to George Little in 1875.

She was a friend of Rose Lamb, a watercolorist who helped Miss Jewett edit Celia Thaxter's letters. Another friend was Elizabeth Cabot Agassiz the founder and first president of Radcliff College. She was a member of the coterie of Mrs. Fields. Another friend was Katherine P. Wormeley who translated the entire Balzac works after she was 80 years old.

And there were many, many more friends and acquaintances that are mentioned here and there in her works that enriched her life and gave it dimension, but these listed here suffice to show what a broad range of associates and friends that she had in her lifetime.

Miss Jewett's Associates at "*The Atlantic Monthly*"

The personnel at the "*Atlantic Monthly*" offices became quite involved with Miss Jewett since they had published the bulk of her work that had appeared in magazine form. In the tribute to her life in August, 1909 reference was made to her life-long loyalty to "the House." The article reads, "If Miss Jewett placed a value upon associating this with life-long friends, - - and the loyalty in her voice when she spoke of 'the house' bore witness that she did, - - the Atlantic itself understood no less clearly what it was to count her as a constant contributor; for her work embodied in a peculiar degree the elements which every serious editor of an American magazine must find related to the complete fulfillment of his purpose."

Consequently Miss Jewett was closely associated with many of the editors of the "*Atlantic.*" Among them were James T. Fields who served as editor from (1861-1871), William Dean Howells (1871-1881), Thomas Bailey Aldrich (1881-1890), Horace Elisha Scudder (1890-1898), Walter Hines Page (1898-1899), and Bliss Perry (1899-1909). These and many other friends helped shape her life and thought.

Miss Jewett's Life with Annie Fields (Mrs. James T. Fields)

Miss Jewett wrote in "*The Country of the Pointed Firs*" a description of a woman who suits Annie Fields. She wrote "She had the gift which so many women lack, of being able to make themselves and their houses belong entirely to a guest's pleasure, - - that charming surrender for the moment of themselves and whatever belongs to them, so that they make a part of one's own life that can never be forgotten."

Miss Jewett admired Annie Fields because of the one-to-one relationship she had with her. Mrs. Fields was fifteen years older that Miss Jewett and she survived her by six years.

She said in a letter to Anna Laurens Dawes, "I like my friends one or two at a time so much better than in a crowd." Even though the two women had been acquainted for years, the enduring friendship between them began in earnest when the men, on whom they depended, died. Annie Fields' husband, James T. Fields, a native of Portsmouth, New Hampshire and the most notable publisher and editor in Boston died on April 24, 1881 leaving his wife a childless widow. On the other hand Miss Jewett's father, Dr. Theodore Jewett had died just nineteen months earlier on September 20, 1878, leaving Miss Jewett without male protection and comfort. As a result of these two deaths, Miss Jewett and Annie Fields were freed of their closest family ties and were in need of relief, through companionship, from grief and loneliness. They found in each other ideal companionship until Miss Jewett's death thirty years later.

Henry James was a friend to both women and in his article, "Mr. and Mrs. James T. Fields," in the *Atlantic Monthly* 106-31 (July, 1915) described the friendship between the two women in three of his rather lengthy, but typical sentences. He wrote, "She had come to Mrs. Fields as an adoptive daughter, both a sharer and a sustainer, and nothing could more have warmed the ancient faith of their confessingly a bit disoriented countryman than the association of the elder and younger lady in such an emphasized susceptibility. Their search together was of the firmest and easiest, and I verily remember being struck with the stretch of wing that the spirit of Charles Street could bring off on finding them all fragrant of a recent immersion in the country life of France, where admiring friends had opened to them iridescent vistas that made it by comparison a charity they should show the least dazzle from my so much ruder display. I preserve at any rate the memory of the dazzle corresponding, or in other words of gratitude for their ready apprehension of the greatness of big 'composed' Sussex, which we explored together almost to extravagance - - the lesson to my own sense all remaining that of how far the pure, the peculiarly pure, old Boston spirit, old even in these women of whom one was miraculously and the other familiarly young, could travel without a scarp of loss of its ancient immunity to set against its gain of vivacity."

Again Henry James mentioned how the two women lived in happy company with each other wherever they were, whether they were in Boston, South Boston, or in Mrs. Fields seaside home, Manchester-by-the-Sea in Massachusetts. "These things were not so much of like as of equally flushed complexion with two or three occasions of view, at the same memorable time, of Mrs. Fields' happy alternative home of the shining Massachusetts shore, where I seem to catch in latest afternoon light the quite final form of all the pleasant evidence."

Beginning in rather minor way the acquaintance between Miss Jewett and the Fields originally began when Mr. James T. Fields, long-time editor of the "*Atlantic Monthly*," published Miss Jewett's first story when she was only twenty years old. This mere contact provided a means of opening the door to the "house" as Mark A. DeWolfe Howe recalled, Miss Jewett "first entered the 'Atlantic Circle' in 1869 when Fields was still the editor of the magazine. The one story was the only one of Miss Jewett's that was published during his editorship since he retired two years later in 1871, but Miss Jewett's contribution increased as the years passed and other editors took up where Fields had left off.

The friendship of the two women had its basis in many things that they had in common. Both women were the daughters of medical doctors. In the second place they loved nature and the aristocratic traditions of the past, and both were engaged in projects of preserving old buildings for architectural and historical value. Likewise they had recently lost their best companions similarly, they were independently wealthy. Moreover they shared interest in reading aloud the current literature of their time to each other and listening to readings by Lowell, Aldrich, Holmes, Whittier, etc., at Mrs. Fields' Boston home on Saturday afternoons at what was known as Annie Fields' "Saturday Afternoon" of which Miss Jewett wrote to Annie Fields, "I love the Saturday companies dearly." In commenting on the meetings in a letter to Annie Fields, Miss Jewett told her, "You are like my monkey and the jack-in-the-box with your meeting." She then humorously warned her "Someday you will get up a big one that will scare you to death." In addition, the two women were interested in engaging in philanthropic endeavors, in attending the theater, in attending concerts and in viewing public art exhibits. Also they enjoyed entertaining and visiting friends from Boston and from the larger world-community of letters. They enjoyed collecting autographs from the famous.

William Dean Howells, in *"Literary Friends and Acquaintances,"* relates the visit of Mrs. Fields and Miss Jewett with Edwin Booth 'the prince of players' who had shown them the Players Club in New York. He tells about their attending a tea at an exhibition of Sargent's portraits, and that a local newspaper gave an account of Annie Fields and Miss Jewett and the 1300 others that attended the affair. The account noted a conversation between two other women when one said to the other, "Oh, don't hurry, pray don't. I have always wanted to see dear Mrs. Fields near to, and isn't Miss Jewett a picture."

The two women spent days and weeks together over a period of twenty-eight years at 148 Charles Street, Boston, at Annie Fields' summer home, Gambrel Cottage on Thunderbolt Hill at Manchester-by-the-Sea, and at Miss Jewett's home in South Berwick, Maine. The women usually spent each winter together in the fashionable home of Mrs. Fields where they watched the steamers on the Charles River, and at night saw the lights reflect across the river from the life along the other shore. Or when the river was frozen over in winter, they watched Boston move and work on ice.

William Dean Howells, a frequent visitor to the Fields' home, described a visit there and the house itself. He remembered, "We breakfasted in the pretty room whose windows look out through leaves and flowers upon the river's coming and going tides, and whose walls were covered with the faces and the autographs of all the contemporary poets and novelists." In further describing it, he observed its proximity to Dr. Oliver Wendell Holmes' home. Fields' address was 146 Charles Street and Holmes' was 164 Charles Street. And "I found an odor and an air of books such as I fancied might belong to the famous literary houses of London." Not only were the walls lined with portraits of famous men and the bookcases filled with books, but there were other mementos of the world of literature scattered throughout the house. Van Wyck Brooks said that the Fields' house "was a temple of busts and portraits, autographs and souvenirs of authors, drawings by Blake, heads of Pope, Dickens, Thackeray, Wordsworth, and Hawthorne." Ralph Waldo Emerson had written to the Fields, "Indeed we think your house should have that name inscribed upon it - - Hospitality." Louise Imogene Guiney, a friend of the women, always thrilled at the thought of turning the doorknob on which Emerson's hand had rested or some similar famous person, such as Longfellow or Thackeray, or Hawthorne or Kipling sitting in a particular chair, or standing by a window looking out it at the Charles River. Miss Guiney wrote that the "sapphire tidal basin of the Charles always full of sound and motion" was "particularly enchanting from the green carpeted, autumn-tinted drawing room" and that every picture and book in the house were "not only beautiful but an original, a token at first hand: pictures, autographs, books, almost too precious to breathe upon." The properly accessorized rooms tinted with literary colors made the right atmosphere where genial and intellectual minds could have equal intercourse with one another. Robert Collyer observed that "no one ever stood on stilts or sat on briers in their house, or was left neglected in a corner. Host and hostess had an eye to those who might be saying, 'I am nothing and nobody' and without seeming to be aware of it themselves, made such persons feel they were something and somebody." Henry James said that the most dominant thing about the Fields was their beautiful home and there chiefly that atmosphere and faultless womanly worth and dignity which fills it with light and warmth."

After the women returned to America, Miss Jewett wrote an article "An Afternoon in Holland" for the "*Atlantic Monthly*" describing their visit to Holland. The article appeared in the December, 1882 issue and is reprinted here since it does not appear in any of Miss Jewett's collected works.

"An Afternoon in Holland"

"To exchange the uneven surface of the English Channel for the level fields of Belgium was a great pleasure. The transition would have made the Great Desert itself seem a paradise; but even the attractions of Antwerp, and the delights of its pictures, and of a Sunday in its cathedral and the cheerful streets that lead to it, failed to content us, - we were in such a hurry to get to Holland.

"A constitutional dislike to climbing hills may have been attracted by the reported flatness of Holland, and a love for the sea even extended to a desire to make a voyage on a canal. And a fierce partisanship for Lombardy poplars naturally urged me out of my own country toward the peaceful asylum of those persecuted monarchs of the plain, - poplars, canals, and windmills.

"It was a great surprise to find the representative Dutchman, of the long pipe and mug of comforting drink, with moon-like face and ponderous bulk, apparently wanting in Amsterdam. Either the Knickerbocker's adopted home on the Hudson had favored his increase of size, or else the Hollanders of the present day are thinner and smaller than their ancestors. The universal right to the once monopolized trade with Japan may have led to the gradual impoverishment of society. Other glories which belonged to the older merchants of Holland have also been wrested from them. Both the land and the water highways of Amsterdam were busy, and crowded with rattling wheels or leisurely gliding boats, when I saw them; but one could not help thinking of the riches of the old days, and the industry of the present seemed to be less well rewarded than that of the past.

"It has been said that the Dutch language is like and unlike every other. It has a curious individuality of its own, and is full of surprises. A word which looks so familiar that you use it without hesitation proves to have a sound which is foreign to any idea ever known to you; and another visible sign of speech, which has so may double *o's* and *j's* in its spelling that you pass by it in horror and dismay, sounds, when spoken, like the easy little words which are familiar to a child of five.

"We had lingered in Amsterdam after the time set for leaving, in our never-to-be-relied-upon plan of travel, and, the day being fair, we had made up our minds to go to Broeck. We were told that the steamboat for Zaardam (which noted village proved to be not far out of our way) would leave at two o'clock; so we took breakfast at our <u>Bible Hotel</u>, and were in no hurry about it, being assured that the place of departure was round the corner, and understanding, from the backward gesture of the porter's thumb, that the steamboat's city home was in the canal, which lay just under our own windows.

"It had been a great amusement to us that the proprietors of our inn, seeming to recognize the discrepancy between the spiritual suggestions of its long-inherited name and the actual use of another kind of spirits that went on continually under its roof, had put a stained-glass window in the stairway, with an open copy of the Scriptures for its escutcheon. In distinct lettering on the page was the <u>admonition of St. Paul to Timothy</u> that he should drink no longer water, but a little wine. It was no unkind or unwise advice to the Timothys of Amsterdam in former years, for in that, like many another Dutch town, the water was not fit to drink.

"We loitered a good while longer than was necessary over our late breakfast, and were a little startled, at last, when we found that there were only a few minutes left before the boat was to go, and taking our wraps and the umbrellas which are the modern <u>pilgrims' staves</u>, we hurried out through the corridor and up the street. We turned the first corner toward the canal, but there was no craft in sight - this being one of the marine by-ways of Amsterdam - except some decrepit small boats and clumsy scows, or, as I heard a delayed and enraged stewardess on the Bergen steamer call them, mudhoppers.

"We stopped before a kind-hearted-looking market woman, who told us in a few stumbling English words that our wharf was beyond the railway station, three quarters of a mile away. There was no carriage visible, and it was within five minutes of two o'clock; we hurried along the street, keeping on after the bells had struck and chimed the hour with triumphant persistency, until we were not quite sure about our way. However, we came in sight of the Zaardam steamer at last, and waited fifteen or twenty minutes before she left the quay.

"It really was delightful weather; the canal was so full of boats and small shipping that it seemed like a parade, and the sharp-bowed steamer moved quickly out toward the country, leaving a broad white track of foam, and sending off waves to right and left that made the little boats within their reach bob up and down distractedly. The deck was a good place to rest. There were not many people on board. We took pleasure in watching a dutiful little old woman in a plain brown dress, who sat knitting beside the engine house. She seemed to be a well-known person, for she looked up with a smile, and had an eager little talk with most of the other passengers, and even with the solemn stewardess, who carried two tumblers of beer on a plate to some voyagers who were smoking astern. She was a very grumpy stewardess, we thought. She looked as if she had used every argument to keep the men from wasting their money in beer, and now would have nothing further to say. She held the plate in her hands, and stood in the low companionway, with long wisps of her hair blowing in the wind.

"Amsterdam had been a most delightful old city to stroll about in, but the suburbs of it pleased us even more. At last it was really Holland! And across the flat green fields and the dikes rose the sails of a vast company of windmills at Zaardam and Purmerend, and all the country side beyond and between. The air was thick with them, like a forest of great stumps and leafless branches. The mills near at hand were huge and round, with sails that <u>Don Quixote</u> would have fled from at first sight; but the farthest ones were like children's playthings, and seemed to beckon to us and to belong to our holiday. When we came nearer them we were gratified to find that the lower stories were often used for dwellings. It was a pretty picture to see children playing about the door, with the sails twirling slowly overhead, as if to frighten away some predatory fowl of the air, a gruesome hawk that was in quest of young Dutchmen. The thatch with which the tall round mills were covered was very smooth and fine, almost like fur, and of an exquisite color.

"We turned presently into a narrower canal, and soon reached Zaardam. We did not have a good first impression of it. We had felt we were adventurers, and almost as if no American travelers before us had bethought themselves to make such good use of a summer afternoon. We had felt ourselves remote from the beaten track of tourists, although we had found in the guide-book directions for going to Broek by way of Zaardam. And yet it was such a quaint and pleasant corner of the world that we had all the satisfaction of being the first discoverers, until we were fairly landed on the little pier.

"Then five men ran towards us in a great hurry. One claimed us for his own, and began to talk in fragments of English about Peter the Great's house, while his neighbors, in voluble Dutch, implored us to make arrangements to hire a vehicle of them, in which ti drive to see all the rest of the world; and he translated their threats and entreaties, when he could desist for a moment from telling us something we could not understand about Peter the Great. Dutch numbers are impossible for an American to recognize by ear, and it was a great relief when one of the men pulled a crumpled paper from his pocket, and pointed to a printed tariff, from which we learned that for certain gulden we could be driven to Broek, and afterward to the tollhouse, whence we could cross the ferry to Amsterdam. We were really tired when the clamor ceased, and four men turned their attention to putting in the horse, while the fifth walked quietly before us to the shrine of Zaardam.

"It was our first look at a Dutch village, except as we had hurried through a part of the country on the railway, a day or two before. We thought that Broek itself, the cleanest town in the world, could hardly be cleaner than this. The salt air blew across the sweet green fields, the casements were full of flowers, and the sunshine streamed in at the open doors. All the people looked comfortable, and nobody had seemed to take any notice of the excitement on the wharf. We followed our guide along the crooked thoroughfare; having suspicions that there might be treasures waiting to be discovered in the orderly small shops, and catching glimpses of the interior of the houses as we went by.

"We were fully convinced that we had not been the first strangers to come to the town, when we reached the home of the Russian Peter, if we had failed to be before, for it was so carved upon and written upon with names of pilgrims that it was like a page of the world's census. It was certainly well taken care of. The old house was warped and bent with age, but an outside shell and cover had been built over it, so that visitors could walk between the walls of the two houses. There had been not a few royal pilgrims, whose portraits and compliments, with their autographs appended, were hanging about the walls in frames, - a grander way of leaving one's name, but much the same thing as carving it with a jack-knife, that all the world may see. It was easy to fancy the young Russian coming home at night tired from his ship-building, and sitting in the three-cornered chair which is still part of the house's furniture. His thoughts must often have been far enough away from Zaardam; but I wonder that he ever lived to return to his people, if he slept in the low-storied cupboard of a bed, guarded with close doors and built in the wall of the kitchen.

"The house stood just at the edge of a field, quite apart from even the small activities of Zaardam. It seemed a pity to go to see it. It is the most tired-out little house I have ever seen. It can hardly hold itself up, yet there is no appearance of dustiness or decay. The people take good care of it, and prize it highly, as well they may, since it brings them so much money; but it appeared to me like some human being who had reached a very great age, and become an object of interest to curiosity hunters. There was a garden around the keeper's lodge. Children were strolling about, and sailing little boats in a very small canal, apparently made on purpose for them. As we looked up and down the wide canal, a sluggish and idle waterway, it was pleasant to see the doors opening directly upon it, and the little boat-landings; and as for the scarlet geraniums on the wide window-sills, they all leaned over to look at themselves in the water. The grass and weeds grew in a most luxuriant fashion, and all the vegetation was as vivid a green as it ever can be in Ireland. Wherever there was a bit of ground large enough a garden had been made, and with the children's voices chirping and calling, and the sound of laughter in one of the houses near by, it was all as charming a glimpse of village life as one would care to have.

"One of the four stable-men had driven to meet us, and we climbed into the heavy carriage, and began to laugh at the horse, which was as round as a dumpling, and nothing but a pony, at any rate. It seemed a brisk little creature, and we did not know how to suggest to our Dutch acquaintances that a larger one would have pleased us better. In some way or other we had learned that Broek was only a mile or two away, and so we rattled along the narrow paved street, with houses on one side and a canal on the other, until we were out in the open country. The road was at the top of a great dike; so we had a capital outlook. The wind came up a little, and the tall grass was waving about. The canals themselves could not be seen, but in every direction we could see brown or white sails gliding between the fields, and at some little distance, in the great sea canal, a large steamer was going slowly in to Amsterdam, its huge hull floating high above the rest of that level and sunken world, and looking strange and clumsy as it moved along.

"The fearfulness of a break in the sea dikes cannot be understood until Holland has been seen with one's own eyes; neither can the patience and toil of the Dutch. It is no wonder that the people are willing to take such care of their country, when such infinite pains have been given to its building and defense. They work at it as ants work, or as coral insects year by year add something to a reef. Their thrift and industry are marvelous, and it would be ungrateful grass that did no grow heavy as an arctic creature's fur over the fields, or heartless flowers that would not bloom by the way. All the streets of Amsterdam are on a lower level than the sea, though it is difficult to remember it in that solid and well-build city; but out in the country the sight of the sea canal, of the great ship high above the land, of the tremendously strong walls that were built to keep the ocean within bounds, was fairly amazing. The stories of the overflowing of the country became at once realities. I pictured to myself this green and fertile neighborhood at the mercy of an inundation; the havoc and desolation and sorrow that the sea any day might make.

"But the Holland men and women seemed to be sure of their safety and fearless of any trouble that day; there could not be a more peaceful country to look at. The next village was reached in course of time, and we rattled through it without stopping except to pay a turnpike toll at its entrance. The Dutch money and the coins of Belgium gave us great trouble. We were continually mistaking the shiny bits for silver, and the handfuls of nickel or base metal and copper that came to us, when we had to change even the smallest silver coin, were most surprising. We caught sight of another village, and pointed to it, and said "Broek?" inquiringly; but our driver shook his head and smiled, and pointed with his whip across the country, where the little hamlets were scattered about, half hidden, like birds' nests, under the clustered green trees. We could not tell which he meant, whether it was the nearest or the farthest, but were not impatient even to see Broek; it was so delightful a little journey we were taking toward it.

"Now and then we passed a solitary man mending the embankment, where a new piece of timber was to be fitted in, or where the filling of small stones was loosened and washing away. But the great dikes looked as if they would stand forever, so welded and clamped they had been, with such a solid weight of masonry and timber. The clean, well-scrubbed Dutch houses themselves are not better tended and kept than is all out-doors in Holland. One would think the rain that fell from heaven was soap and water, and that once a week, at least, the farms were swept and dusted and put to rights, and that even the little bushes had grown afraid to stir when a breeze came to play with them, lest they should rumple their leaves, and be called untidy.

"All the farms are surrounded by broad ditches, and the land is divided into squares of perhaps a quarter of an acre each. Sometimes there is a bridge, with a gate at the end, across from one field to the next. These gates looked very odd, standing stiff and straight by themselves, as if they had all the care and authority of miles of fence. Instead of fixed gates there was often a drawbridge hoisted up from the ditch, appearing as if it were meant for some kind of a trap, until you came near it. We were delighted with the beautiful cattle that were scattered about, half a dozen together, on the small green fields, and, as it grew later in the afternoon, men and boys pushed out from the kitchen doors of the farm-houses in flat-bottomed boats, with their milking-stools and white wooden pails, and followed the ditch-paths to the pastures.

"The shadows grew long, and we passed one village after another, and did not come to Broek; it was nearly six o'clock, and we had ordered our dinner in Amsterdam, at that time being certain in our ignorance that Broek could not be more than a long stone's-throw away. Our driver smiled, and kept on pointing with his whip.

"We had seen masts and sails always at a little distance, though we had met so many small boats hitherto in our drive, but at last the road led by a larger canal, and here we came close to the old-fashioned slug-like canal boats, where happy families lived in comfort and content, if not in splendor. Puffs of thin blue smoke were coming out of the chimneys of the little cabins, and yellow-haired children sat on the deck and watched us as we went by. Sometimes a little dog would stand with one foot on the rail and bark at us in a great frenzy, and presently we would overtake the larger dog, or the horse, and most surely the man who was tugging at the tow rope. It did not look very hard to pull even a large boat through the still water; the sloops were moved also by their sails, though there was not much wind, and no chance for beating or tackling. The little boats with their loads were drawn lightly along by a cord fastened to the top of their masts. All the people seemed to be on their way home, and we did not dare to think that the next village, also, might fail to be Broek.

"Suddenly, to our great distress, we were driven into the yard of a large farm-house which stood by itself among the fields. Could our driver mean that we should spend the night there and take the rest of the journey in the morning, or had he some important errand to his own to these acquaintances? In a few moments, however (the driver had meantime alighted and stood beside us with great patience, waving his hand toward the door of the house), the latch clicked, and an elderly woman came out to greet us, and we at once accepted her invitation to come in. This, to our surprise, was Broek, or, at any rate, its suburbs, for here was the famous stable where the cows' stalls were decked with colored tissue-paper cut in shapes, with muslin curtains at their little windows, and all manner of luxurious decoration and furniture. Having become world-renowned, there was an artificial splendor and bedizening. Specimens of delftware and china were hanging on the sides of the stalls; the floors were covered with clean pebbles and with painted cockle-shells arranged in patterns. It looked like a magnificent baby-house, and as if the elders of the family had never given up playing with dolls. The cows were living in their pastures: this was only their winter residence, and for my part, I would much rather see the stable when they were in it, and I have no doubt their housekeeping is carried on in unparalleled fashion, for the beautiful sleek-coated creatures looked dainty enough to be at large anywhere, even in Holland.

"The same great roof covered the stable and the house, and a door opened directly into a long kitchen, where some supper, which we should have been glad to eat, was set out on one of the tables by a latticed window, over which some vines were growing. In the next room was a great business of cheese-making, and in the next, which was walled with stone and cellar-like, were stored away a great number of cheeses, cannon-ball as to shape, and of a fragrance and yellowness impossible to describe. The point-lace lappets of our hostess's cap flapped as she walked before us and showed us room after room of her house, betraying pride only when she opened the door of one and said, "The salon!" It was the least interesting to us, being uncommonly stuffy, and carpeted and furnished in the most conventional and uncharacteristic way. We had noticed some superb pieces of furniture, heavy wardrobes and the like, of vast size and antiquity, but these were all in the living-rooms, fortunately, and not locked away from sight and use.

"It was only a little way farther to the cleanest town in the world, but Broek must have won its reputation by only a length in its race with the rest of Holland. The other villages may have followed its example until they became its rivals, however, so I will not try to steal its laurels, and it certainly is a most clean-faced and well-dressed little town. The houses are very pretty, and the flower-gardens were in gayest bloom. Flocks of children were playing about the streets; we came upon a dozen of them busy with some merry game or other in a little square near the church, which was shaded with trees whose foliage was so thick that it was damp and gloomy underneath. There were some stalls and booth, as if it were a fairground or market-place, or as if some wandering showman had arranged his much-battered properties for a performance.

"We could look between the houses out across the fields. The glimpses of the wide reaches of greenest grass, of the grayish willows and slender poplars, formed charming pictures. From the main street of Broek we could look far down the canal that led to Amsterdam: a delightful perspective of a tall white sail and a clump of willows, an idle windmill farther away, a blue sky that had not begun to fade, though the twilight had begun to fall, and white clouds that made the nearest stretch of water look like silver. It was dead calm on the canal; the breeze which had ruffled it a little all day had gone down with the sun. It was the Holland that Ruysdael painted, with its soft colors and its endless distances, where the earth and sky meet in a mist, like the blending of the sky and sea.

"We left the main street, presently, quite sure that it was true that the paving-stones of it were scoured every Saturday, and followed the only side street to where its houses ended. They were less pretentious than those we had just left. It was supper-time, and at each door a company of wooden shoes of various sizes were waiting for their owners. This was the pleasantest part of Broek to us, but one must see it for one's self on a summer evening, and I hope everybody will be fortunate enough to see, as we did, two young men who came hurrying up the narrow tow-path and got into a boat and rowed away as if they were belated. They certainly had been left behind by the fashions, for they both wore the amazing petticoat-trousers of a past age.

"It was not a long drive to the toll-house; we crossed the ferry and found a hackman who had, happily for us, finished his supper, and we were soon back at the hotel. The prim stateliness of the high-gabled roofs of Amsterdam delighted us more than ever by their contrast with that charming bit of the Low Countries we had just seen. The lights were shining out in the houses one by one and twinkling again in the canal underneath. I shall be glad to remember all my life how fresh the wind was, and how green the clover; how the people smiled at us, and said good-day as we passed them. I can always shut my eyes and see the sails moving this way and that among the green fields, and the round-topped windmills beckoning lazily with their long arms."

In the winter (1894-1895) Miss Jewett had pneumonia most of the winter and Mrs. Fields spent the winter in South Berwick with Miss Jewett. Other parts of the year found them together in different parts of the world. They stayed at the Hotel Ponce de Leon in St. Augustine, Florida, went to the Chicago's World's Fair and travelled several times to Europe. When the two women were apart they constantly thought of one another and kept up a lively correspondence. In one letter, Miss Jewett wrote to Annie Fields, "Oh, my dear, it is such a comfort to think of you in the dear house with the sea calling and all the song sparrows singing by turns to try and make you sing too."

In the course of several years Miss Jewett made four trips to Europe, two to the Caribbean and other trips into various places of the United States always in the company of Mrs. Fields and sometimes in the company of other friends and relatives. Miss Jewett took her first European trip in the summer of 1882 with Mrs. Fields, even though the older woman had made numerous European trips before. Miss Jewett had dreamed ten years earlier of taking such an excursion when she had expressed a desire to go by saying in a letter to Annie Fields, , "I wish very much to go travelling, and all the English history which I have been reading this winter makes me wish to go to England more than I ever have before."

The two women were seen off by Henry Mills Alden, editor of *"Harpers"* and after crossing the Atlantic Ocean without any sea trouble, they visited Ireland for ten days before going on to London and the countries of Holland, Norway, Belgium, Italy, France and Switzerland. In Ireland they enjoyed the beautiful old city of Dublin with its historic colleges and hospitals. There in Dublin they visited Dean Jonathan Swift's monument in St. Patrick's Cathedral. From Dublin they went to the original home of Dr. Perry, Miss Jewett's maternal grandfather in Enniskillen. They went on to Cork, Glengariff, Killarney and Belfast. After visiting London and exploring the coast of Cornwall, she and Mrs. Fields visited other places meeting with Tennyson, Charles Reade, Anne Thackeray Ritchie, and the family of Charles Dickens, with whom she had dinner.

After returning from her first European trip, Miss Jewett parted company from Mrs. Fields to return to South Berwick and renew life there. On October 6, 1882, Miss Jewett wrote Annie Fields about her grand reception on her return home. She wrote, "It was lovely in the old house and I wish you had come down too, it was all so sweet and full of welcome, and Hannah and Annie and John and Hilborn and Lizzie Pray all in such a state because I had got home!" The house itself was a welcome sight to her and she said "it all seemed to put its arms round me."

This trip in1892 was more meaningful since she was now an accomplished author going to visit places she had seen before but under new circumstances. The people she met on this trip were more receptive of her as a person since they had read her works and had appreciated them. Crossing the Atlantic in the Steamer, 'Werra," Miss Jewett was in the company of Mrs. Fields and Mr. and Mrs. Robert Underwood Johnson.

On this trip, Miss Jewett met several world renowned authors. In England they made a formal call on Alfred Lord Tennyson and his wife. Of this visit she wrote in enthusiastic terms, "But what can I tell you of going to see my Lord and Lady Tennyson, down among the Surrey hills! It meant a great deal more to me than when I saw them before. . . My Lord Tennyson was so funny and cross about newspapers and reporters that I feel his shadow above me even in this letter, innocent hearted as I be . . . his complete delight in my Japanese crystal, which he looked at over and over, and wondered much about, and enjoyed, and thought to find things in it. . . If I could have given it to anybody in this world, I could have given it to Tennyson then and there; but no! And now I like it more because he liked it, a shining in its silver leaves." Miss Jewett liked to quote Tennyson because of his great insight into the essence of things. In a letter to Mrs. Fields, she quoted Tennyson as saying about good books he had read "I love those large, still books." In another letter she likened Tennyson to a "King in captivity, one of the kings of old, of divine rights and sacred seclusions. None of the great gifts I have ever had out of loving and being with you seems to me as great as having seen Tennyson."

Other pleasures in London for Miss Jewett included a stroll through a charming old garden, viewing a cricket match, an eight hour visit to the House of Commons, a visit to the family of Matthew Arnold and Du Maurier and a visit with Mrs. Humphrey Ward, whom Miss Jewett described to Mrs. Fields as "very clear and shining in her young mind, brilliant and full of charm, and with a lovely simplicity and sincerity of manner . . . her life burns with a very fierce flame."

From London Miss Jewett and her companions went to Venice where they met Samuel Clemens and his wife, Olivia Susan Clemens. About that meeting of congenial friends, Edith Colgate Salsbury described it as being most delightful. She wrote in her book, "*Susy and Mark Twain: Family Dialogue*" "Sam was in high feather and gave an evening of readings from Browning at the Hotel Daniels for his friends." Robert Underwood Johnson, who accompanied Miss Jewett and Mrs. Fields on the trip, recalled delightful hours sitting in St. Mark's Square, with Mark Twain telling stories and how Susy, his wife, refused to join the group. He said that Susy Clemens stayed "in the hotel fuming and worrying!" Upon leaving Venice the party went to Aix-Les Bains where Miss Jewett's time and wits were taken away by the siege of mineral baths there. Even though one of her main purposes there was to seek physical comfort from the baths, all she could say of the bathtowns was "a foreign bath-town is a foreign bath town!" Further she visited the Grande

Chartreuse, gave candy to the peasant children, and went to Chamonix which she described, we went on up and up that dear, high green valley, passing cold little whit-silky brooks," and on up to the peak of Mont Blanc. Included in her French trip was a special pilgrimage to Barbizon, since Miss Jewett was such an admirer of Jean Francois Millet, a French painter and an outstanding member of the Barbizon School of Art. Back in Paris Miss Jewett again met with her longtime friend, Madame Blanc. The Jewett-Blanc meeting is more fully described in the section devoted to their friendship and association.

Back in America Miss Jewett attended the World's Fair in the company of Mrs. Fields and Sarah Chauncey Woolsey. For the special issue of *"Scribner's Magazine"* May, 1892, which was devoted to the Fair, Miss Jewett wrote a story in the November, 1892 issue, which was included in the World's Fair Edition of *Scribner's.*

In the winter of 1896, the two women went on a two month's cruise in the West Indian waters with Mr. and Mrs. Thomas Bailey Aldrich. The party cruised on the "Hermione," a yacht, which was owned by Henry L. Pierce, former mayor of Boston. The cruise events are recorded in the diary of Mrs. Fields, who "records discomforts and pleasures with an equal hand, and gives lively glimpses of island and ocean scenes.

At Santo Domingo, for example, the President of the Republic of Haiti dined on the "Hermione" on Valentine's Day 1896, and talked in a manner to which the impending liberation of Cuba from the Spanish yoke may now be seen to have added some significance." Miss Jewett later commented on the war as being a necessary evil. She said, "It seems like a question of surgery, this cure of Cuba - - we must not mind the things that disgust and frighten us, if only the surgery is in good hands."

In 1898 Miss Jewett and Mrs. Fields made their third trip to Europe. On this trip they were accompanied by Miss Mary Jewett and Theodore Jewett Eastman. After a successful sea voyage across the Atlantic and safe arrival in England, the party visited George Du Maurier, an English artist and novelist. During her stay in England Miss Jewett in a letter to Miss Ellen Chase wrote, "I remember also how I went about the streets of Whitby with Mr. Du Maurier and his little dog." The meeting with Du Maurier was completely successful for her. In enthusiasm she wrote, "You can't think of him at all until you see him and hear him sing his old French songs, and have him show you his drawings withal the simplicity of a boy with a slate and all the feeling of a great artist." It was a visit that Miss Jewett could not forget. In commenting about places and people she said, "Never mind people who tell you there is nothing to see in the place where people lived who interest you. You always find something of what made them the souls they were, and at any rate, you see their sky and their earth."

Next the party visited the home of Matthew Arnold, the famous English essayist who had died ten years earlier. In a letter to Mrs. Whitman, Miss Jewett reflected on her visit at the Arnold home. She wrote, "No, I am sure I have not told you about Mr. Arnold's favorite walks and his most interesting study, or how delightful I was to find your own rhododendrons hanging on the walls." Also in England the travelers visited the Bronte family shrine in Haworth, Yorkshire, and they met Rudyard Kipling who was an admirer of Miss Jewett's works.

In Paris on their trip, Madame Blanc showed them the sights of the city. Mme. Blanc also introduced them at the literary salons and to all her friends. During these rounds of the establishments, Miss Jewett met Violet Page whose friendship was dearly prized by Miss Jewett. As a result of her interest in the travelers' comfort and entertainment, Madame Blanc impressed Miss Jewett who wrote about her pleasure of their acquaintance and companionship. She said, "I am delighted to be with Madame Blanc, and it is almost like coming home. You would like the old walled-garden, with its 'pleached walks' and great fountains and prim box-borders, and dwarf fruit trees with young fruit." Further, she described the nightingales on their nests, basset hunting dogs, wide country views and brown villages nestled in the hills.

From cold and rainy Paris, the company of tourists went south into Provence where they visited the French poet, Mistral. According to Miss Jewett's account of their visit, the warm sunshine of Provence prevailed. Provence was beautiful with the fields of white poppies, the wild golden lilies that lined the roadsides, the old tile-roofed farmhouses, the snow-covered mountains on the horizon and the delightful visit with Mistral himself, made their stay in Provence a most pleasant one. From there the party went to St. Remy and to Avignon, where they stayed several days, and their visits in the quaint, foreign town was full of tours of ruined chateaus, of shopping in tiny market places, and watching of a farandole where all the dancers of different parishes had come together." The moats full of flowers and green bushes, the old bridges, and buildings with their marble columns kept the party's attention, always alert because of the great variety. Always on the alert to concrete details, Miss Jewett was aware of the sounds as well as the sights of her homeland.

One night she was apprehensive about sleeping in a convent's cell. She said of the experience, "I went to the Grande Chartreuse again, that lonely place in the mountains, and slept in a cold convent cell, and thought that the cliffs overhead might tumble down in the night." After several more days in France the party left the old country to come back to the new.

In January, 1899, Miss Jewett again took a Caribbean cruise on the yacht, S. Y. Hermione and again in the company of Mrs. Fields. While on the cruise the two women stayed a week at the Victoria Hotel in Nassau which Miss Jewett thought to be a charming place. Describing it to Mrs. Whitman, she said of it, "It is a charming little town along the waterside, with its square houses with four-sided thatched roofs. And down the side lane came women carrying things on their heads, firewood and large baskets of grapes. From Nassau the two women went to Kingston, Jamaica, "A most enchantingly beautiful country." In the islands of wild marshes they saw flocks of flamingos which delighted their eyes. Other stops on the cruise were Haiti and Puerto Rico.

Miss Jewett, in 1900, was again in Europe for a long spring and summer visit. With Miss Jewett and Mrs. Fields on this visit was Mary Elizabeth Garrett, whose father was the President of the Baltimore and Ohio Railroad and a founder of Bryn Mawr College. Miss Garrett was a dear friend of Miss Jewett and Mrs. Fields. Miss Jewett dedicated her book, "*Betty Leicester's Christmas*" to her. The voyage across the Atlantic was a hard one, but once across the waters the group set out to visit several European countries. They visited Italy, Greece, Turkey and France as well as England. On March 18, 1900, Miss Jewett wrote from the hotel Bristol in Naples to Miss Sara Norton about their stormy and difficult voyage and about the terrible gale that filled the floor of the stateroom of the ship. Miss Jewett told about staying two nights at La Cava with its pigeon towers and about visits to Paestum Pompeii, Ravalli, Brindisi, and Petra's. She described to Mrs. Whitman the late spring of Italy as being cold and wet even though she said of it, "It is wonderful old Italy though I accuse it so cheaply of cold and bleakness."

In March, 1900, staying in the Hotel Grande Bretagne in Athens, they viewed the old marbles of the Parthenon. Miss Jewett described the sunset as it high-lighted the Parthenon against the sky, and she reflected on the great Greek heritage of the world, "when I remember what my feelings have been toward the Orpheus and Eurydice and the Bacchic Dance, and then see these wonderful marbles here, row upon row, it is quite too much for a plain-heart to bear." She continued, "It isn't the least bit of use to try to write about these marbles, but they are simply the most human and affecting and beautiful things in the world. The partings, the promises, are immortal and sacred, they are life and not only lives and yet the character of them is almost more than the art to me, being a plain storyteller, but full of hopes and dreams.' They also saw the Marathon as well as viewing the natural wonders in that part of the world: olive trees, wildflowers, the Apennines and the Gulf of Corinth. They spent a week in Constantinople where they saw turbaned men and veiled women with their trays of sweetmeats for sale. They saw the Mosques, minarets, beautiful homes, and the wild dogs of the streets. The party also passed by the cities of Megalopolis, Nauplia, Mycenae, Epidaurus, Tripolitza and Sparta.

Back in Paris, Miss Jewett saw for the last time her old friend Mme. Blanc. The visit occurred at Chateau d' Acosta in Mme. De Beaulaincourt's out-of-town residence ten miles north of Paris. Miss Jewett said that she thought often of Mme. Blanc and her son after she had returned to America and settled back into her old familiar life with Mrs. Fields and her other friends. There is no record of any further trips abroad or cruises.

In her book, *"A Writer's Recollections"* (1918), Mrs. Humphrey Ward, a niece of Matthew Arnold, recalls the companionship with Miss Jewett and Mrs. Fields. She recollected, "Mrs. Fields and Sarah Orne Jewett - - a pair of friends, gentle, eager, distinguished, whom none who loved them will forget." The blessings of the close companionship were cherished more and more as time went on. Miss Jewett wrote to Mrs. Fields about their maturing relationship, "We only understand the blessing of older friends and 'somebody to go to' as we grow older and older and put our hearts more and more into what we find to do." An early poem by Miss Jewett entitled, "Together," applies to any separation that occurred between the two women. The poem is collected in *"Verses."*

Together

I wonder if you really send
These dreams of you that come and go!
I like to say, "She thought of me,
And I have known it." Is it so?

Though other friends walk by your side,
Yet sometimes it must surely be,
They wonder where your thoughts have gone,
Because I have you here with me.

And when the busy day is done
And work is ended, voices cease,
When everyone has said good night,
In fading firelight then in peace

I idly rest: you come to me,—
Your dear love holds me close to you.
If I could see you face to face
It would not be more sweet and true;

I do not hear the words you speak,
Nor touch your hands, nor see your eyes:
Yet, far away the flowers may grow
From whence to me the fragrance flies;

And so, across the empty miles
Light from my star shines. Is it, dear,
Your love has never gone away?
I said farewell and—kept you here.

Mrs. Fields, fifteen years the senior of Miss Jewett,
survived her by six years. During Mrs. Fields' years of
solitude she collected as many letters of Miss Jewett as she
could and published a volume of them in 1911. Mark, A.
DeWolfe Howe remarked about the collection, "The
selection and publication of Miss Jewett's letters was a
labor of love which continued the sense of companionship
for the first two of the remaining years." And after Mrs.

Fields' life was over, Henry James looked upon Annie Fields' very long life as "all of infinite goodness and grace, and, while ever insidiously referring to the past, could not help meeting the future at least half-way." Annie Fields' life was enriched by her years of companionship with Miss Jewett, a woman whose life, too, was "all of infinite goodness and grace."

Deephaven, James R. Osgood, 1877

The thirteen stories that are collected in "*Deephaven*," are "*Kate Lancaster's Plan*," "*The Brandon House and the Lighthouse*," " *My Lady Brandon*," "*Deephaven Society*," "*The Captains*," "*Danny*," "*Captain Sands*," "*The Circus at Denby*," "*Cunner-fishing*," "*Mrs. Bonny*," "*In Shadow*," "*Miss Chauncey*," and "*Last Days in Deephaven*."

Because she was already established as a short story writer and because she had many points of strength such as "lightness of touch, humor, pathos, perfect naturalness," she persuaded William Dean Howells, editor of the "*Atlantic Monthly*," to publish her first book, "*Deephaven*." She was to use the sketches that had already appeared in the magazine. In a letter dated December 29, 1876, she gave permission to James Osgood to publish her first book. She wrote, "I have a letter from Messrs. Houghton and Company telling me that they have been thinking of reprinting some of the "*Atlantic*" stories and should have chosen the Deephaven sketches for one of the little books.

But they have no wish to keep me waiting since there is uncertainty about the time and cheerfully give their consent to my reproducing them in book form as proposed by Messrs. Osgood and company—'with their best wishes for my success.'"

In 1877, the James R. Osgood Company of Boston published *"Deephaven,"* and it immediately received favorable comment by E. L. Godkin in *"Nation"* where it was said to be "more like a graceful vacation letter than a novel."

It is a bundle of thirteen local-color sketches,--a "loose-leaf novel," and it is the first of twenty volumes produced in her lifetime. Some of the sketches in the book Miss Jewett wrote especially for the collection since Mr. Howells had advised her "that it is much better to have the book partly new."

"Deephaven, which is "a series of figures, landscapes, and interiors" of a small Maine town, was written to make the people of Maine better acquainted. It was an immediate success with the public. The book went through twenty-four editions in its first fifteen years. The story which is told by a female narrator involves two Boston girls, Helen Denis and Kate Lancaster, who spend a summer in the Brandon House in a small Maine sea-coast village, where they discover an interesting history in the antiques and mementos that they find.

As a result of her literary modesty, Miss Jewett attributed the success of the book to the fact that it was written by such a young girl. "Through the eyes of a young girl visitor to Deephaven, she reveals the beauty of the civilization proud even in its decay, and uncompromising with progress."

In the 1877 preface to *"Deephaven,"* we find that "this book is not wholly new, because several of the stories had already been published in the *"Atlantic Monthly."* Miss Jewett wrote, "It has so often been asked if Deephaven may not be found on the map of New England under another name, that, to prevent any misunderstanding, I wish to say, while there is a likeness to be traced, few of the sketches are drawn from that town itself, and the characters will in almost every case be looked for there in vain."

Annie Fields, the editor of the *"Letters of Sarah Orne Jewett"* wrote in the introduction, "Many years later, in 1893, when an illustrated edition of her first book, *"Deephaven,"* was published, we find affixed to the volume a new preface which contains some of her very best and most autobiographical writing. After speaking of the changes creeping over the old village life she says: "Old farmhouses opened their doors to the cheerful gayety of summer; the old jokes about the respective aggressions and ignorances of city and country cousins gave place to new compliments between the summer boarder and his rustic host.

The young writer of these Deephaven sketches was possessed by a dark fear that townspeople and country people would never understand one another, or learn to profit by their new relationship. It seemed not altogether reasonable when timid ladies mistook a selectman for a tramp, because he happened to be crossing a field in his shirt-sleeves. At the same time, she was sensible of the grave wrong and misunderstanding when these same timid ladies were regarded with suspicion and their kindnesses were believed to come from pride and patronage.

There is a noble saying of Plato that the best thing
that people of a state is to make them acquainted with one
another. It was happily in the writer's childhood that Mrs.
Stowe had written of those who dwelt along the wooded
seacoast and by the decaying, ship-less harbors of Maine.
The first chapters of 'The Pearl of Orr's Island' gave the
young author of 'Deephaven' to see with new eyes, and to
follow eagerly the old shore -paths from one gray, weather-
beaten house to another, where Genius pointed her the way.
. . . There will also exist that other class of country people
who preserve the best traditions of culture and of manners,
from some divine inborn instinct toward what is simplest
and best and purest, who know the best because they
themselves are kin to it. Human nature is the same the
world over, provincial and rustic influences must ever
produce much the same effects upon character, and town
life will ever have in its gift the spirit of the present, while
it may take again from the quiet of the hills and fields and
the conservatism of country hearts a gift from the spirit of
the past.'"

Throughout her lifetime Miss Jewett counted her
mother and her father as her two best friends. The
dedication of her first book, "Deephaven" (1877) was
dedicated to them. She wrote, "I dedicate this story of out-
of-door life and country people first to my father and
mother, my two best friends, and also to all my other
friends, whose names I say to myself lovingly, though I do
not write them here." With her mother she felt a deep sense
of security every time she was in her presence for the forty-
two years they lived together. She wrote a letter to Thomas
Bailey Aldrich, "As long as one's mother lives the sense of

being lovingly protected never fails, and one is always a child."

In "*The New York Times*," 28 April 1877, the reviewer summarizes and criticizes the book. It is about two young women who are going to spend their summer observing the lives of the people of a Maine seaside community. "They are going delightfully and refreshingly to an old house in Deephaven to observe the habits of small seaside boys, angular country folk, and decrepit fishermen, and even to lure from the sides of wharves that prickly and very indigestible fish called a cunner. It need hardly be said that the tale is not a thrilling one. Such well-regulated young women do not even need a yachtsman with a brown moustache to enliven their summer. They go to a dreary circus performance, and listen to the prudently circumspect yarn of the superannuated sailor, gossip about the musty remains of good society still lingering in the ancient town, and indulge in other harmless amusements."

Upon the publication, she ordered twenty-five copies for herself and requested that a copy be sent to her uncle, John Taylor Perry, editor of the Cincinnati "Gazette." In response to the gift, he wrote his praise of her talent. He said "Your forte lies in description. You hardly improve there. Invention, on the other hand, is not your strongest point."

Several years after "*Deephaven*" was published, in a letter to Theophilus Parsons, a Harvard law professor, Miss Jewett explained, "I think that was the reason people liked '*Deephaven*'—it was a book written by a girl, which is perhaps a rarer thing than seems possible at first thought. I am beginning to like it myself in a curious sort of way, for I am not the one who wrote it any longer and in this last year since my father's death, though I have learned many new things, I have outgrown a good deal else." She said the book was 'made up" before she knew about the people in York, a nearby town, but she confessed that everything in "*Deephaven*" could be found in York even though she explained in her Preface to "*Deephaven*" that she had invented the seaport town. In "*The Cambridge History of American Literature*" it was said that with her first work, "*Deephaven*," she "struck the new note of the decade, concreteness, geographical locality made so definitely and so minutely real that it may be reckoned with as one of the characters of the story," and that she wrote "of the ebb, not despairingly like Miss Wilkins and the depressed realists, but reverently and gently," and that "her delight was in the simple and the idyllic rather than in the dramatic."

Horace Scudder, in his review of her next book reflected back to "*Deephaven*" by saying that its charm "lay chiefly in the sympathetic delineation of character, and in the pictures of homely life seen from the side of this fresh, unspoiled, and reverent girlhood," and that "nothing could be purer than the relation between young and old which 'Deephaven' disclosed." The next year, 1878, she published her second book, "*Play Days*."

Play Days, Houghton, Osgood, 1878

"*Play Days*" was a collection of stories for children. It was published by Houghton, Osgood and Company and reached the eighth edition in 1889. Commenting about these stories, Jay Martin in "*Harvest of Change*," said that they "dramatize the conventional virtues of the weakened later nineteenth-century Protestant ethic: self-reliance, individualism, honesty, thrift, hard work, and prudence."

The contents of *"Play Days"* are "The Water Dolly," "Prissy's Visit ," "My Friend the Housekeeper," "Marigold House," "Nancy's Doll ," "The Best China Saucer," "The Desert Islanders," "Half-done Polly," "Woodchucks," "The Kitten's Ghost ," "The Pepper-Owl," "The Shipwrecked Buttons," "The Yellow Kitten," "Patty's Dull Christmas," and "Beyond the Toll-Gate."

To honor her father's influence in her life, Miss Jewett dedicated *"Play Days"* (1879) to him. Appropriately the dedication of the book to him happened in the year of his death. The inscription reads: "To T. H. J. – My dear Father; my dear friend—the best and wisest man I ever knew, who taught me many lessons and showed me many things as we went together along the Country-By-Ways." Her father's influence was even stronger than her mother's. She wrote in *"Looking Back..."* "I cannot help believing that he recognized, long before I did myself in what direction the current of purpose in my life was setting. Now, as I write my sketches of country life, I remember again and again the wise things he said, and the sights he made me see. He was only impatient with affectation and insincerity." Annie Fields, who was the dearest friend that she had during the last twenty-eight years of her life wrote, "After her father's early death she loved to go into his office to consult his diary; she knew his papers, his books, his medicines—nothing that belonged to his mind or his work was foreign to her."

Horace Scudder reviewed *"Play Days"* for *"The Atlantic Monthly"* in the December 1878 issue. He wrote: "The qualities which made Miss Jewett's *"Deephaven"* so agreeable could not fail to appear in any book which she might write for children, and '*Play Days*' is characterized by the same temper of gentleness and good-breeding which gave distinction to the earlier book. We are old-fashioned enough to like good breeding, with all that the homely, significant word intends, and we like its mark in '*Play Days*' because it is so genuine and native. It is, we hasten to say, not modeled upon the type which we recognize instantly in the literature which young English masters and misses receive with apparent docility. There is not a governess in the book. There is no lad there either, -- that singular being whom Chauncy Wright so well described as 'a boy with a man's hand on his head.' There is no slang introduced for the purpose of shocking the governess or older sister, and giving the boy who uses it the reputation of an abandoned swearer and awful example; in effect, that conventional good-breeding which is founded on class distinction, and not on Christian democracy, is refreshingly absent from '*Play Days*.' The element which we find there is conspicuous also by its contrast with the noisy, ungrammatical, and boisterous type of young America which gets recognition enough in books for young people. The suggestions are of home life and the sweet sanctity of a protected childhood. Even the pathetic and lovely story of '*Nancy's Doll*' makes the misery of poverty to be but the dark background on which to sketch one or two golden figures; and '*The Best China Saucer*,' which comes as near as any to the conventional type of moral tales, is relieved by a grotesque humor and a charity which never fails. There is a refinement in the book which is very grateful, as we have said, but it does not take the form of a disagreeable fastidiousness. The humor is always spontaneous and simple, and not above a child's enjoyment; 'The Shipwrecked Buttons' shows this in a very charming manner, and is the cleverest story in the book, from the originality of the frame-work, in which a number of little stories are set. There is a facility of writing which possibly misleads the author, for while all the stories are written with apparent ease, the writer does not always distinguish between what is essential to the story and what is mere graceful decoration. If Miss Jewett always had a story to tell, her charm of manner would add to the agreeableness of the story; but her interest in writing sometimes leads her to forget that children want a story, and will be indifferent to many graces which please a writer. A more positive story would add greatly to the pleasure which Miss Jewett's book gives, and we trust that she will cultivate the power of invention. She needs the development of that side of a story-teller's gift to make her work singularly good; it is too good now not to be better."

Old Friends and New, **Houghton, Osgood, 1879**

In 1879, she saw her third book published, "*Old Friends and New*" by Osgood Company. H. E. Scudder reviewed the book in the May, 1880 issue of the "*Atlantic Monthly*" and praised Miss Jewett's "womanly kindness" that pervade her stories, and stated that "Miss Jewett has already begun to appropriate an audience, and may, if she choose, whisper to herself of her readers as a clergyman openly speaks of his people." Specifically, Mr. Scudder praised her for not picturing her old maids as "pieces of faded sentimentalism" but as women with dignity in their quaintness. He noted her use of the first person point of view which, he said, caused her to carry her characters around with her clinging to her skirts. His only criticism was that he thought that her characters lacked motive, especially the motive of love as a passion between young people.

Country By-Ways, **Houghton-Mifflin, 1881**

In 1881 her *"Country-by-Ways,* was published by Houghton-Mifflin and Company. It is another collection of short stories. The stories are;

> *"A Lost Lover"*
> *"A Sorrowful Guest"*
> *"A Late Supper"*
> *"Mr. Bruce"*
> *"Miss Sydney's Flowers"*
> *"Lady Ferry"*
> *"A Bit of Shore Life"*

In *"Country by Ways"* she declared, "From this island town of mine there is no seafaring any more. It is only a station on the railways, and it has, after all these years, grown so little that it is hardly worthwhile for all the trains to stop." She hated the discordant times, the coarse life of immigrants that moved to Berwick to work the mills and the factories, and she disliked the ugly scars left in the woods where the trees had been removed, for she was the poet of the gentle, the beautiful and the harmonious.

She was well acquainted with the out-of-doors in all seasons of the year and she thought that the open sky, the farms, and the spruce-filled country villages produced a stronger character than the more sophisticated civilization of larger cities. Based on her love of nature and nature's God, she is quoted in her obituary in *"The Nation,"* "I have always liked my outdoor life best and in driving about ever since I can remember with my father, who is a doctor; I have grown more and more fond of the old-fashioned country-folks."

Breathing the wind from the sea was like wine to her and every aspect of nature gave her constant delight. Sometimes she would sit in an old boat as it rested on the pebbles and watch the waves of high tide and the lonely gulls along the misty sea shore. In September 1876, she told Annie Fields of some delightful times spent out-of-doors, "I am having such a good time just now out of doors; this morning I have been rowing down river, yesterday I went up Agamenticus and could see seventy miles of seacoast and all the White Hills, and two days ago I went to the Cliff, which is a place you ought to see." The winter cold, she said, made the grey sky appear as a great block of clear shining ice which gave the whole world a beautiful appearance.

In 1889, she was taking a drive around South Berwick and saw a lovely hillside covered with the right amount and quality of snow, decided to borrow a sled and slide down the hill. In her letter to Annie Fields, an account of the incident was given by a small boy who said, "There were two fellows that said Aunt Sarah was the boss, she went down side-saddle over the hill just like the rest of the boys!"

Sailing with her friends made her placid and serene. It made her forget that she were "ever a girl who couldn't go to sleep at night." She enjoyed sailing with the Higginsons of West Manchester, Massachusetts and yachting with the Forbes family and several other friends from time to time. The sea with its misty fogs, its gulls, its great waves at high tide, the harbor lights and its plashing waves on rocky shores gave her reason to be near it.

The river was just as meaningful. Especially did she like to row close to the bank or close to the shore and by the islands where at sea or on the river she could hear the singing birds, the bleating lambs, and the other sounds of land life. Capturing the beauty of such a boat ride in her mind, Miss Jewett wrote a poem, "*Boat Song*," collected in "Verses," which expressed her love for the water and a ride upon it.

Boat Song

Oh, rest your oars and let me drift
　While all the stars come out to see!
The birds are talking in their sleep
　As we go by so silently.
The idle winds are in the pines;
　The ripples touch against the shore.
Oh, rest your oars and let me drift,
　And let me dream forevermore!

The sweet wild roses hear and wake,
　And send their fragrance through the air;
The hills are hiding in the dark,
　There is no hurry anywhere.
The shadows close around the boat,
　Ah, why should we go back to shore!
So rest your oars, and we will float
　Without a care forevermore.

Oh, little waves that plash and call,

How fast you lead us out of sight!
And we must follow where you go
　This strange and sweet midsummer night;
The quiet river reaches far—
　The darkness covers all the shore;
With idle oars we downward float
　In starlight dim forevermore.

In her poem entitled *"Top of the Hill"* which is
collected in *"Verses"* she expressed her delight in autumn
fields, the winding river and her steepled town.

Green slope of autumn fields,
And soft November sun,
And golden leaves—they linger yet,
While tasseled pines new fragrance get,
Though summer-time is done.
The hedge-rows wear a veil
Of glistening spider threads,
And in the trees along the brook
The clematis, like whiffs of smoke,
Its faded garland spreads.

Miss Jewett enjoyed long solitary walks into the
country to explore new regions in the woods, beside some
stream or to see sights such as the round-headed windmills
that were busily supplying water for the oxen who stood
like rocks from the pastures, to make new friends and visit
old ones, to find new treasures and to enjoy new pleasures
that the full land had to give her. She said the experience
made her one with nature, "like an atom of quick-silver
against a great mass." With delightful heart, she strolled

across the quiet, green fields in the company of her dog who sometimes chased little birds and crickets across the moor-like pastures.

Once she found a solitary place that gave her peace like "one goes to on the way to sleep." In her letter to Annie Fields she wrote "I have found such a corner of this world under a spruce tree, where I sit for hours together, and neither thought nor good books can keep me from watching a little golden bee, that seems to live quite alone, and to be laying up honey against cold weather." The seasons were like seeing the seasons of mankind. The autumn's sadness was like "that of elderly people," and she reflected, "We have seen how the flowers looked when it was ripe, the questions have had their answer, the days we waited for have come and gone." In winter the snow and mud covered hills were "like big leopards and tigers ready for a pounce at something with their brown and white spots."

Nearly all the south side of Portland Street across from her home was farmland and it rose up the slope of Butler's Hill to the southeast of her home. In a story, "*Country By-ways*," named "*A Winter Drive*," she remembers on old oak tree and the population growth that put pressures on the character of the town. The growth was at the big brick shoe factory that created Jewett Avenue near Thomas Jewett's old farm. She wrote in the story: "I think it [the old oak] is likely to live until the new houses of the town creep over to it, past Butler's Hill, and the march of improvement reaches it and dooms it to be cut down because somebody thinks it would not look well in his yard, or because a street would have to deviate two or three feet from a straight line. However, there is no need to grow angry yet, and the tree is not likely to die a natural death for at least a hundred years to come, unless the lightning strikes it, -- that fierce enemy of the great elms and pines that stand in high places."

She describes driving in her hometown in winter: "A drive in a town in winter should be taken for three reasons: for the convenience of getting from place to place, for the pleasure of motion in the fresh air, or for the satisfaction of driving a horse, but for the real delight of the thing it is necessary to go far out from even the villages across the country. You can see the mountains like great stacks of clear ice all along the horizon, and the smaller hills covered with trees and snow together, nearer at hand, and the great expanse of snow lies north and south, east and west all across the fields. In my own part of the country, which is heavily wooded, the pine forests give the world a black and white look that is very dismal when the sun is not shining; the farmers' houses look lonely, and it seems as if they had crept nearer together since the leaves fell, and they are no longer hidden from each other. The hills look larger, and you can see deeper into the woods as you drive along. Nature brings out so many treasures for us to look at in summer, and adorns the world with such lavishness, that after the frost comes, it is like an empty house, in which one misses all the pictures and drapery and the familiar voices."

The Mate of the Daylight, and Friends Ashore,
Houghton, Mifflin, 1884

"The Mate of the Daylight" is a collection of eight of her short stories. The stories are typical of stories that appear in her other works. All the stories are studies of the people who lived in her world but who are kin to everyone else who has ever lived. These stories are universal. They reflect upon the truth of human nature itself.

The stories have the charm and brightness that distinguishes all her stories and which have that strength and grace of tone that place her among the foremost short story writers of her day. The book was published in 1884 by Houghton-Mifflin Company of Boston and sold for $1.25 per copy. It is dedicated to "A.F." (Annie Fields). "*Good Company*" magazine says about the purity of her sentiment in her stories, "The unstrained felicity and naturalness of her style, the thorough likableness of all the people to whom she introduces us, all conspire to render her stories about as nearly perfect in their way as anything in this world ever gets to be." G. F. Lathrop, author of the popular "*Five Little Peppers*," reviewed the book in the May, 1884 issue of the "*Atlantic Monthly*." In it he explained that these short sketches are written in the same style as her other books and that they "reflect sundry quiet phases of American life with far greater precision." He said that her stories approach the "real occurrences" of life and that "people are introduced, sitting in their quiet New England houses, or going about their small affairs, or living along-shore, with as little preparation or grouping as if we had come unawares upon the originals themselves; a single incident suffices for the machinery; and everything proceeds to exactly as it would in fact that when the quaint veracious talk, the hopes and fears and little quarrels or joys centering upon that incident, have all been detailed, the story comes to a close because it could not go on without being a different story." Lathrop praised her faculty of recording the conversation of her people. "They talk idiomatically, with just a hint of dialect, which is hardly dialect and does not become a stumbling block." He liked her thoroughness and her unstrained command of materials. He wrote, "to read Miss Jewett is like listening to the casual reminiscences of a lady, say, in a fire-lit study; until the half-seen speaker gives place the figure she calls up, and we find that there is a little drama going on."

Lathrop recognized the moral impulse behind her realism. An unsigned review of "The Mate of the Daylight" in "The Dial" was less generous to her. The reviewer criticized her "surface" treatment of life and said that one cannot "gain much insight into the deeper recesses from a perusal of her work." However, this was not the consensus view of her contemporaries.

The first story in "The Mate of the Daylight" carries the same title as the book. The story "The Mate of the Daylight" reaffirms the triumph that young love can have over the objections of elders. In a decaying New England setting, the story opens with three ancient sea-captains in an old fish-house discussing the rainy weather. The captains, Captain Joe Ryder, Captain Jabez Ryder, and Captain Peter Downes, are "like some old driftwood at the harbor taking all the comfort they can get from their pipes full of strong black tobacco and their companionship bred of long years of kinship and friendship." All three have had their day at sea, and they bemoan the conditions of present-day shipping. The worm-eaten ships with their rusty anchors lying in the harbor remind them of better days and of better men. When their conversation turns to the present, they think of a group of young men who had gone out early that morning is a fishing smack to risk their lives in the foggy "Scotch" mist.

At first, "The Mate of the Daylight" seems to deal with the conflict of man against the sea, but as it progresses the conflict of man against man gradually stands out. The conflict exists between a young couple and the older generation. The young couple, Dan Lewis and Susan Downs, is deeply in love, and few of the economic considerations of life seem to stand in the way of their marriage. At least is seems to their elders. Her grandfather, Captain Joe Ryder, thinks that Dan Lewis is a high-strung young fellow and wishes that Dan had a better start than being second mate of the Daylight and not having as least $5,000 already in the bank. Captain Joe says, "Young folks thinks that love's the main p'int, and I don't say but what it is; but there's a good deal more chance for it to hold out when there's means to make things comfortable." Even the other captains think that young Lewis is marrying Susan for her grandfather's property. They also judge Dan to be all talk and no cider.

But the young couple really is in love and they are not as unmindful of their responsibilities and of their relationship to their elders as it first appears. There is a hot argument between Susan and her grandfather and tempers flare. The other captains really want to see "who'll beat, her or Joe." The tension, though, in the family is relieved by an evening visit of Susan's aunt and uncle who come to help clear the air between the feuding two. They say, "They'll be glad to have us drop in if they ain't feelin' comfortable among themselves".

The visit of the old couple helps resolve the conflict but the main thing that calms the animosity is the sea voyage of Dan to the East Indies. Several months later when he returns, Dan comes back as Captain of the Daylight and has a stable financial future to offer Susan to the relief of her family. "So the Mate of the Daylight returned to his unbelieving friends a shipmaster, and when he sailed on his next voyage having gained the owner's permission to carry her, he had his wife for his company.

In addition to the conflict and its resolution in "The Mate of the Daylight", interesting bits and pieces of several people's lives are related. One of the most interesting bits concerns Susan's Aunt Melinda Downs. In her youth Melinda had fallen in love with a young sea-captain who was lost at sea. All her life she remained faithful to his memory and visited the "burying ground" often to read the slab erected in his memory and to reflect on what might have been. When Susan's young man went to sea, Aunt Melinda prayed that Susan would not have to suffer a similar sad farewell. Aunt Melinda was coming from the cemetery when she heard the noise "welcome back" to Susan's young Dan'l. And she was glad for his safe return.

Miss Jewett again reaches to a general and genteel audience by portraying the various characters in this typical New England village. She does not draw an expected moral. On the other hand the story has its connections to reality, to the concrete, and much of its importance is in its impressions, the atmospheric qualities. And the natural environment beyond the pleasantness of the simple and the ordinary is shown as a shaper of culture and character. The promise of new life and freedom for Dan and Susan in the bosom of the sea is the expression of an authentic poetic gift and takes on the aspects of timelessness.

In this sketch Miss Jewett presents the essential qualities of the quaint maritime villages of eastern Maine, the rare character of a remote New England people who fancy themselves living at the center of civilization, and the sometimes harsh atmosphere in which hardy men and women labor and love and live. She causes anyone, who reads her stories, to fall in love at first sight with the people who live along the unchanged rocky shores in their "tree-nailed" houses, and face the sea at high tide and at low. Anyone who has walked through the bits of garden with their flowers and herbs and vegetables, who has breathed the salt air from the steamboat wharves, who has looked to the far sea-line from the background of dark spruces and pointed balsam firs, and who has observed the elaborate conventionalities of each neighborhood, through the eyes of Miss Jewett, cannot do ought but admire her art and the object of her art, nor fail to let that love mature into a true friendship for that New England which was sacred to her mind.

The second story in *"The Mate of the Daylight,"* "A Landless Farmer", is a New England version of Shakespeare's *"King Lear"*. The story has about the same plot-line, but, of course, the characters and the scenes are far different. In this case, one old farmer has two daughters who stay close to his situation and a prodigal son who comes back from his wanderings at the end to rescue his father from the clutches of the loyal girls.

The story begins and ends at the same location with approximately the same characters in reflective conversation. On a beautiful spring Sunday after church, three men meet on the bridge that crosses Cranberry Brook to engage in friendly chatter. The day is the first pretty day after a typical New England winter and the people at church and these men look pale "as if they had been hidden or lost for months." Life is being reborn all around. The frogs are croaking along the new green willows lining the brook's edge and the air is full of spring smells. Melting snow has filled the brook to its brink. As the three men, Ezra Allen, Henry Wallis, and Asa Parsons argue about the height of the flood waters and the depths of snows now compared to the time of their youth, the main subject of "*A Landless Farmer*" comes up in their conversation.

Ezra Allen introduces the subject by condemning his cousins, Serena Nudd and Mary Lyddy Bryan who forced their old father, Jerry Jenkins, to sign away his property to them. Ezra tells the men on the bridge that he himself spent the previous night "watching" with his sick uncle, Jerry, and that the old gentleman was really being "put upon ". Ezra describes Serena as a "grasping creatur'" because she got twice as much of her father's holdings than her sister did, and that their brother, Parker, had been left out altogether. He describes the other sister, Mary, as a "poor dragging creatur'" because she "sheltered her laziness behind various chronic illnesses, which had excused her from active participation in the world's affairs."

From the bridge, the scene shifts to Serena and Aaron Nudd's farm the following summers. Mr. Jenkins who has given his farm, his bank stocks, and his money away to his two daughters still tries to boss the affairs of the farm. He "was always calling Aaron, or the man who had been engaged to help him, and demanding strict account of the potatoes and corn and beans." But he was treated like a child. He became so upset that he was "like a distressed New England Lear" similar to Shakespeare's character King Lear who did a foolish thing and gave his kingdom away before he died. Mr. Jenkins said that he would go live with his other daughter where he would be better treated. Before he left Serena's house, he told her that he was not going to be "pulled about by the nose in this way another day." And that "it's a hard thing for a man o' my years to see another master over his own house, and live to see himself forgotten."

At her house Mary Lydda treated his as a welcome guest for a time, but her "meeching" ways soon returned, and Mr. Jenkins' life with her was as miserable as his life had ever been. Folks wondered how long he and his daughter would keep their "horses hitched together". Our new England Lear stayed a year in his hitch, when he was rescued by his wayfaring son, Parker. The prodigal returned with $25,000 he had gotten from selling a western mine. With the money he restored respect to his father in the eyes of the church and in the eyes of the community. Parker also succeeded in righting the wrongs of his sisters and finding mutual forgiveness and respect. In the end Parker fell in love with his neighbor's daughter and old Mr. Jenkins found respite in the Indian summer of his life.

The story ends with a fine quotation which shows that the tragedies and comedies well known in literature are enacted again and again in unknown ways in lonely New England houses. "Stranger dramas than have ever been written belong to the dull-looking, quiet homes, that have seen generation after generation live and die. On the well-worn boards of these provincial theatres the great plays of life, the comedies and tragedies, with their lovers and conspirators and clowns; their Juliets and Ophelias, Shylocks and King Lears, are acted over and over and over again."

"*A Landless Farmer*" is characterized by a certain simplicity and directness. "King Lear is adequately translated into the experience of ordinary New England folk. Though Mr. Jenkins is Lear and must receive the most sympathy for his self-inflicted tragedy, the two characters, who win most respect, are Ezra Allen (Kent) and Parker (Cordelia). Both of these men are sketched as individualists with a propensity for quiet reflection, a sense of some inward sorrow, and a fighting spirit against all that is wrong in this world. Both characters are developed as fully as they need to be and each represents a value system, a basic attitude toward life.

The theme of "*A Landless Farmer*" revolves around the problem of old men "giving up" and "giving in" too soon, before they die. A person is responsible for who he is and for what he has until he loses his life or his senses. Both Lear and Mr. Jenkins learned this lesson in a very painful way. The clue to this theme of Miss Jewett is found in the title itself, and she unfolds it gradually until it becomes sharply defined through the actions and responses of the several characters and incidents of the short story. It is necessary to withhold judgment until the story is understood as a complete whole. Miss Jewett, like Shakespeare, offers a penetrating comment on the human condition. On the surface level we have a simple tale with three principle characters, but its implications can be as profound as the reader has insight.

The third story in *"The Mate of the Daylight," "A New Parishioner"* shows that appearances are deceiving. In this story Miss Jewett makes a thoughtful and to some extent a skeptical assessment of the situation and the characters that she has created. Her qualification to make such assessment comes from her temperament, her experience, and her outlook. This is a story of many precious parts and well-settled judgments. Miss Jewett does not allow her free expression of ideas to interfere with the reader's amusement, though she steps out of the story from time to time in order to drive some point home to the reader. The characters are never obscure or ambiguous by the intruding author who has almost unlimited opportunities for expressing her ideas through this method of a single plot and the omnipresent personality of the author.

"A New Parishioner" is set in September in the busy New England kitchen of the principal character, Miss Lydia Dunn, who has lived by herself for many years. She has self-respect, for in matters of caring for her physical comforts, she "always treated herself as if she were a whole family." Miss Jewett goes to some length to tell of her energy in helping neighbors in time of sickness and death, and of her warm-hearted disposition and generous nature. The little old woman is the granddaughter of a Walton minister and she stands for clean living and hard work in keeping with her heritage.

Lydia Dunn's first encounter with another human being in the story occurs after eight pages of description. Old Jonas Phipps comes to see if she has any domestic chores for him to perform. Jonas is Walton's handyman, but a conflict of outlook and temperament occurs each time

Jonas and Lydia Dunn are together. He is lazy and she is not. On this particular Friday, Jonas brings her news that Henry Stroud has returned to Walton, after having been gone for forty years, to live out his last days in his old hometown. Henry Stroud becomes the new parishioner.

Henry Stroud, a world traveler and a seemingly wealthy man, soon establishes himself in the good graces of the community and of the First Parish Church, all that is except Lydia Dunn. Lydia cannot believe that this man's character has changed from what it was when she knew him as a youth, forty years ago. Her opposition to him causes Lydia to be somewhat isolated from her neighbors. Henry Stroud appears to be such a good man. Even the minister, Mr. Peckham, is proud of the man's presence in the town. Mr. Stroud listens intently to each sermon; he prays "long and eloquently, greatly to the approval of his hearers." He makes expeditions to the burying ground to have it fenced, graded, and the stones made straight; he promises funds to build a new vestry for the church and arranges for the foundation stones from Beckett's quarry; he gives money to the poor and the old and the needy. He is a true member of the church and is treated like a king by all, all except Miss Lydia. She abides by her father's saying, "When you see anybody too good, look out for 'em" and Miss Lydia concludes "It seems to me as if he was kind of buying his way into heaven out of his pocket."

Miss Lydia, however, almost gives in to his goodness, when he comes to see her. He comes to give her a note for six thousand dollars in restitution of an old account that his grandfather owed her grandfather. After he leaves she entertains thoughts of forgiveness, and even of possible marriage. But she is saved from such notions when her doubts about his character prove true. When he is arrested in an evening church service, his whole story is told. He is a bigamist and a financial imposter. Nearly everything is in promise only, even the church has to finance their new vestry. In the end, all those who were taken in by Mr. Stroud praise Miss Lydia for her perception of his character and her unwillingness to go along with the crowd. And Jonas Phipps had to conclude that Lydia "in the long run" had done more good than Mr. Stroud.

Miss Jewett in *"A New Parishioner"* sustains a desirable colloquial ease and naturalness as she presents Miss Lydia Dunn. Early in the story she establishes with her readers a form of mutual compliment and admiration for this wise old soul whose character continually rejects the affected and artificial.

The fourth story is *"An Only Son"*. The story involves a father's struggle to keep faith in his only son when every indication seems to prove the boy untrustworthy. The plot line is easy to follow though it includes several people, several locations, and several situations. More than a mere sketch, it is a well-told story.

The tale begins in the New England village of Dalton where the town's three selectmen gather to conduct the town's usual business of paying the bills for the town poor, of discussing school matters and of reviewing the requests of the county commissioners for a new road. Also the three are waiting for the tax-collector to bring to their meeting a sum of money to help them meet the town's obligations. When the money is brought, the July meeting is adjourned. Deacon John Price, one of the selectmen, carries the $735 home with him to keep it safe until he can take it to the bank in South Dalton the next day.

Deacon Price returns home in time to wish his cousin and housekeeper, Eliza Storrow, a good journey to a nearby town to help celebrate a golden wedding anniversary. Upon first returning to his farm, the Deacon hides his leather wallet with the town's money in it under his bed pillow. As he looks up his son, Warren is standing in the doorway. The old man rebukes the young man for not mending the pasture fence that morning. The old man is so gruff, that Warren cannot bring himself to tell his father about some good news and his trip next day to Lowell. While the Deacon repairs the fence himself, he wonders why Warren is walking across the pastures toward the railroad tracks.

Later the Deacon remembers his responsibility about the town's money, checks on the hiding place of the money, and is surprised to find it gone. He jumps to the conclusion that Warren took the money for some unknown reason. Warren likes to tinker with mechanical contrivances trying to invent some machine that is better than another already in existence. The father knows his boy is like the moon "always with one side hidden and turned away." And the father mistrusts the boy who has "odd notions" and is "kind o'crazed" about machinery. The story uses excellent detail about the father's restless night worrying about Warren, about his visit next day to Captain Stones' house to borrow $800, about his trip to the bank to pay the town's creditors, and about his return to his empty house to await his housekeeper and his son's reappearance and explanation.

Through all these experiences, Deacon Price acts as though the world is about to end, and the shame and sorrow weighed him down. He looked to one neighbor, as "if he'd had a stroke." Miss Jewett delays the resolution of his conflict just long enough until the reader can wait no longer and must demand an explanation. Before long, his housekeeper returns with the news of the golden wedding anniversary and a report on all their kinsmen at the celebration. While she is putting on her apron to begin the evening meal, she discovers the Deacon's leather wallet in her deep pocket. She explains how it came to be there. The Deacon is relieved to find it again, but even more he is greatly relieved to know of his son's innocence. When Warren returns later that evening, he tells his father of his trip to Lowell and the selling of his invention and its prospects for manufacture. His father could not be more pleased and satisfied with his son who was not bent "in a practical direction."

The father in "*An Only Son*" becomes a symbol of isolation. The father lives in the world essentially alone. Even though Deacon Price has a housekeeper and a son living with him on the farm, he is a solitary figure who fights this biggest battle of his life with himself. He cannot share it even with his closest friend. Miss Jewett does not present his experience as a curse, but as a blessing. His character is further hammered out on the anvil of inner suffering, and he becomes a part of the human race at last. Deacon Price's struggle has serious implications.

One incident in the story reveals the New Englander's reluctance to let go of the status-quo. It is about the shoemaker who complained to one of the selectmen that his business had fallen off considerably because folks had gotten into the habit of paying five dollars for two pair of factory-made shoes rather than pay four dollars for a pair of well-built, hand-made shoes.

The next incident begins with a seamstress who bemoans people "buying cheap ready-made-up clothes" at stores rather than use her services. These two references to craftsmen and the changing times reflect on the peaceful village society being swept away in part by the torrent of social change at the beginning of the Twentieth Century. In a way, Miss Jewett suggests that important values are lost when men prefer change to stability and are ready to sacrifice everything even the homes of their fathers—to material progress and speculation in land and investments. Miss Jewett was seriously concerned about the direction American life was taking and deeply regretted the material orientation of her countrymen.

"*Miss Debby's Neighbors*" is the fifth story in "*The Mate of the Daylight.*" It is a fragile little sketch about an old woman, Miss Debby, telling her unidentified visitor about a family that had been her neighbors for years. Their conversation is interrupted occasionally by Miss Debby having to re-thread her needle for she was a seamstress by vocation and "kept at her task regardless of her visitor and their conversation." The sketch includes a comment about the elderly women of New England in Miss Jewett's day. The story begins with these words: "There is a class of elderly New England women which is fast dying out:-- those good souls who have sprung from a soil of true New England instincts; who were used to the old-fashioned ways, and whose minds were stored with quaint country lore and tradition. The fashions of the newer generations do not reach them; they are quite unconscious of the western spirit and enterprise, and belong to the old days, and to a fast–disappearing order of things."

In the process of their conversation, Miss Debby insisted that the railroads were causing the people "to look and act of a piece" and that the young people were "more alike than people of her day." Miss Debby found fault with the desire for more and more material goods by condemning the folks for having "the same chromo pictures hung up" and by commenting that the luxuries of the present time and "makeshifts o' splendor" would make the people of her youth "stare their eyes out o' their heads."

Miss Debby is a shrewd person who knows about the character and nature of her neighbors, the Ashbys. She tells her listener that the Ashbys were cursed by their inability to keep the peace among themselves. The Ashbys were always at war with themselves, especially after Grandmother Ashby's death. One fight caused one of the Ashbys to pull a practical joke on another Ashby that was funny in a way and pathetic in another.

While one Ashby was gone from his home, his brother came with teams and men, hitched their horses to the house of his brother and pulled it over the icy road to a crossroads where they left it. The reaction of the offended brother was one of mixed laughter and rage and it resulted in a feud that took years to resolve.

Miss Debby told of another house moving escapade of the Ashbys. They had decided to move the old home from its quiet environment to a more convenient spot on another nearby farm. They had trouble pulling it over the hill, but when they tried to cross the railroad tracks the house stuck and two passenger trains were stranded by the strange event. Eventually they dragged the house off the side of the tracks and gave up on their endeavor. Later that winter, it burned to the ground, much to the relief of all the neighbors.

Miss Debby finally judged the Ashbys in this way: "Them Ashbys never was like other folks, and yet some good streak or other there was in every one of 'em. You can't expect much from such hindered creatur's..."

The sixth story in *"The Mate of the Daylight"* is *"Tom's Husband,"* which first appeared in *"Atlantic Monthly"* in February 1882. It is a story which reverses the traditional roles of husband and wife. By the end of the story, Miss Jewett shows that Tom Wilson who has been a househusband for several years comes to realize "that his had been exactly the experience of most women." In the process of telling the story, Miss Jewett contrasts marriage to the ideal during the courtship days with marriage in the real after the wedding. The young couple after they were married had to assume new responsibilities and establish a new household. This change brings about "a little feeling of disappointment." There is the "loss of eagerness that is felt in pursuit," and Miss Jewett notes that hunger is more satisfying in the long run than satisfaction.

When Mary proposes to take over the mill and make it profitable, Tom agrees to let her try. He also agrees to be the domestic husband and keep the house. He said, "I've a great mind to take it off your hands, I always rather liked it, to tell the truth, and I ought to be a better housekeeper, - I have been at it for five years; though housekeeping for one is different from what it is for two, and one of them a woman. You see you have brought a different element into my family. Luckily, the servants are pretty well drilled. I do think you upset them a good deal at first!"

Mary's response was positive and she said, "Tom! I'm going to propose something to you. I wish you would really do as you said, and take all the home affairs under your care, and let me start the mill. I am certain I could manage it. Of course I should get people who understood the thing to teach me. I believe I was made for it. I should like it above all things. And this is what I will do: I will bear the cost of starting it, myself, - I think I have money enough, or can get it; and if I have not put affairs in the right trim at the end of a year I will stop, and you may make some other arrangement. If I have, you and your mother and sister can pay me back."

From the first of their different kind of marriage, both have to face the laughter and ridicule of neighbors, relatives, friends, and business associates. They understand that their life is something like women smoking, "it isn't wicked, but it isn't the custom of the country." But as time passes, the community and business men learn to respect the role each has accepted for himself. Mary proves a success with hard work and practical sense. At the end of the second year of running the reawakened enterprise, Mary declares a small dividend and at the end of the third year she makes money faster than most other people do. Even though at the start, Tom thinks Mary is going to make "dricks and drakes" of his money, he comes to accept the situation philosophically when this "unnatural state of things" becomes well established, Tom settles into the comfortable role of househusband, and for diversion collects coins and medals and becomes "a numismatologist of great skill and experience." And so the relation, strange as it may seem for the nineteenth century, lasts without a bobble for several years.

But Tom starts feeling that he is dependent on his wife for his livelihood, though she doesn't feel as though she were head of the family. Still he has "an uneasy suspicion that she could get along pretty well without him." He becomes rusty in social affairs and the thought comes over him that he is a failure. His depressed feelings get the better of him; he goes to the family burying ground to think things over, and he decided that their marriage would be better if they could both escape from their roles for a while. He persuades Mary of this remedy for his melancholy and they set sail for a six-month vacation to Europe and the story ends. It is assumed, though, that on their return they will pick up again where they left off and will live somewhat happily ever after.

"*Tom's Husband*" is a modern drama reenacted periodically by couples whose personalities and temperaments demand that their life style be somewhat the reverse of the traditional. One function that both Tom and Mary serve in the story is to provide a measuring stick for the changes that took place in the last of the nineteenth century. Also what happens to Tom in the story may be taken as a symbolic account of the fate of such men in a society where only success matters. Both are more attractive as human beings because they were willing to accept themselves as they were.

The next story in "*The Mate of the Daylight*" is "*The Confession of a Housebreaker*," which first appeared anonymously in "The Contributors' Club" column of *The Atlantic Monthly* (September 1883) it is most likely the record of one of Miss Jewett's own personal experiences. The author tells of ending a restless night indoors by getting up at the first tinge of light from the eastern sky, stealing out-of-doors while the rest of the household is asleep, and enjoying the beginning of a fresh June day as she watches it arrive from her garden seat. The delight with which she greets the day is a poetic one. She describes the sounds of the birds, the presence of a bat that in the semi-darkness was a creature of mystery and horror, the appearance of the bright little waning moon through the branches of an olive tree, and of the fragrances of the dew-covered roses, the white petunias, and the old-fashioned honeysuckle.

As she revels in nature, she remembers other places and other people, personal and historical. And as she thinks about one friend in particular through the dreamlike experience, her mind's eye sees the present and the past in one grand view. Sitting on her garden bench she listens to the grand chorus of pewees, song-sparrows, bobolinks, and golden robins; she observes a sober-minded toad who seemed a philosopher, and she sees the trees and distant fields in the uncanny light of the early morning. A cock crows, and the day dawns as she steals home again to the comfort of her bed where she sleeps again. The ringing of the mill-bells wakens her for another ordinary day. Through this personal experience she achieves her heart's desire, and she reveals her love of nature, her delight in escaping from the house for a secret encounter with nature, and her recreation of this image of peace and security is in print.

"*A Little Traveler*," the last story in "*The Mate of the Daylight*," is a mere sketch told in first person. Most likely, it is another personal experience of Miss Jewett; though it doesn't have to be. This sketch has more possibilities for fiction than the "*Confession of a House-breaker.*"

The narrator takes a train trip and is comfortably settled in a section of sleeping car with twelve or so other people. Among them are a newlywed couple, three elderly women, four or five businessmen, a Catholic priest and a little girl with a doll. The narrator soon becomes interested in the little girl who is traveling alone. After the narrator becomes acquainted with the little traveler, she finds out that the girl's father was killed two years ago in a train accident and that her mother had died of pneumonia only last Sunday. The girl, who is going to live with her aunt in Boston, is the object of much inquiry and much sympathy by the conductor and her fellow travelers. Nelly, the little girl, wins all their respect by her pretty manners, her quaint dignity and reserve.

Everyone on the passenger car takes Nelly into their hearts. The bride gives her candy and hugs her to her breast. The priest gives her bits of money and fixes the loose strap on her hat. One old lady who has a tame robin in a cage lets Nelly see and talk to the bird. Others give her picture paper and fruit. When the girl is delivered to her aunt in Boston, all the passengers are relieved to see that the woman is a kindly, motherly person.

A Country Doctor, Houghton, Mifflin, 1884

In the same year that "*The Mate of the Daylight*" appeared, "*A Country Doctor*," Miss Jewett's biographical novel of her father, was published. She wrote the book in the conventional novel form but some say that it does not hang together. The novel was written "to clear up some misconceptions about the medical profession." The critic in *"The Nation"* noted that the book would delight young people because of its New England flavor, its instinctive refinement and its graceful workmanship. The critic wrote, "Her *'Country Doctor'* is a living portrait from life." It is a portrait of her father in the character of Dr. Leslie and of herself in the character of Anna Prime. Arthur Quinn said that the novel was a better study of the woman physician than Howells' *"Dr. Breens' Practice"* or Mrs. Ward's *"Doctor Zay."* Willard Payne in *"The Dial"* when the book was first published said that the book was "one of the most satisfactory books of the season." He wrote that the book was found satisfactory because of the "close and accurate observation, delicacy of touch, genuine discrimination, firm and sympathetic grasp of character, and instinctive refinement."

Horace Scudder, editor of the *"Atlantic Monthly"* wrote that "the task which Miss Jewett has thus had to accomplish has been the faithful portrayal of a character ripening under favorable conditions, and this task exactly fits her powers." He was struck with its "serene good sense," and its wisdom, its delicate shades, and its gracefulness. He further praised the book by saying, "It is such to be in company with such genuine high breeding, such unfailing courtesy. There are touches, moreover, of something higher; quiet passages which glow with a still beauty." He concluded his review by saying, "we speak of her treatment as feminine, and the merit of it is that the womanliness of the work is of a thorough healthy sort. Heaven be praised for a handling of the theme which is absolutely free from hysterics, and regards men and women in a wholesome, honest fashion! The very seriousness with which the author regards her task is sweet and fragrant seriousness." He continued to like her work for he labeled her ten years later, "one of our most happily endowed writers."

In her twenties she had ironically exclaimed to Horace Scudder, "It's a dreadful thing to have been born very lazy, isn't it, Mr. Scudder? For I might write ever so much; it's very easy for me and that I ought to study—which I never did in my life hardly, except reading, and I ought to try harder and perhaps by and by I shall know something I can write really well."

In *"Looking Back on Girlhood"* in *"The Youth's Companion"* she wrote: "I have tried already to give some idea of my father's character in my story of *"The Country Doctor,"* but all that is inadequate to the gifts and character of the man himself. He gave me my first and best knowledge of books by his own delight and dependence upon them, and ruled my early attempts at writing by the severity and simplicity of his own good taste.

"How often my young ears heard these words without comprehending them! But while I was too young and thoughtless to share in an enthusiasm for Sterne or Fielding, and Smollett or *Don Quixote*, my mother and grandmother were leading me into the pleasant ways of *"Pride and Prejudice,"* and *"The Scenes of Clerical Life,"* and the delightful stories of Mrs. Oliphant."

Her father was a country doctor who had graduated from history-steeped Bowdoin College in Brunswick, Maine. Next he earned his medical degree at Jefferson Medical College in Philadelphia. In addition to his academic studies he also studied medicine with Dr. William Perry of Exeter, New Hampshire.

Miss Jewett wrote that Dr. Jewett was "unconscious of tonnage and timber measurement, of the markets of the windward Island or the Mediterranean ports. He had taken to his books, as old people said, and gone to college and begun that devotion to the study of medicine which only ended with his life." He married Dr. Perry's daughter, Caroline and they lived a harmonious and happy life together. To them were born three daughters: Mary, Sarah, and Caroline. Doctor Jewett became the most distinguished doctor of the region. For three years during his country practice, he took time off to teach obstetrics at the Maine Medical School at Bowdoin where he was professor of obstetrics and diseases of women and children.

He was elected President of the Maine Medical Association, and he delivered a speech to the Association on June 18, 1878, a few months before his death. His general practice in his community, his lectures before medical students, his printed presentations to the medical society, and an exemplary life as a husband, father, and friend led Alpheus Spring Packard in a brief biography of Dr. Jewett in "The History of Bowdoin *College*" (1882) to say that Dr. Jewett "enjoyed more universal confidence, respect, esteem and love, whether in professional or social life."

As a country doctor, he gave Miss Jewett much knowledge of the medical profession, especially information about the behavior of patients and the necessity of will power and attitude needed for speedy recoveries. Once she wished she had been a doctor herself though she confessed in "*Looking Back on Girlhood*," "though very likely I am enough of one already to get the best of it for myself, and perhaps I have done as much as ever I could for other people." He taught her about the wild birds of the region, about the piney woods, wild flowers, and woodland animals. He taught her "to observe, and to know the deep pleasures of simple things, and to be interested in the lives of people." She wrote, "I had no consciousness of watching or listening, or indeed of any special interest in the country interiors. In fact, when the time came that my own world of imaginations was more real to me than any other; I was sometimes perplexed at my father's directing my attention to certain points of interest in the character of surroundings of our acquaintances."

Dr. Jewett taught her to observe the country people that lived on the scattered farms of the Berwick region. She declared, "I knew many of the patients whom he used to visit in the lonely inland farms or on the seacoast in York and Wells. I used to follow him about silently, like an undemanding little dog, content to follow at his heels."

She was his constant companion in her youth; and in her adult years, father and daughter remained close friends. She delineated the relationship she had with her father in a letter that described the value of older men, "I believe that their best teaching may be given then to those who are fortunate enough to be their nearest friends and they may give the golden value of their lives into a few fit hands. It is the loveliest inheritance, this character and the sense of true values, with the power of appreciation, makes its best treasures."

In her novel, "*The Country Doctor*" (1890), she honored her father by making the book essentially a biography of his life as she wrote in "*Looking Back...*" "I have tried already to give some idea of my father's character in my story of "*The Country Doctor*' but all that is inadequate to the gifts and character of the man himself. He gave me my first and best knowledge of books by his own delight and dependence upon them, and ruled my early attempts at writing by the severity and simplicity of his own good taste." The country doctor was credited by his daughter as being a good literary critic as well as being a good man. But his life had larger implications than the influences on family. His character was expressed in his medical profession, in his active membership in the Maine Historical Society, and in his religious contributions as a member of the Congregational Church of South Berwick.

Dr. Jewett died suddenly while staying with the Crawfords in the White Mountains of New Hampshire in September 1878. The next day after his death, Miss Jewett wrote to Theophilus Parsons, a Harvard law professor, "My dear father died suddenly yesterday at the mountains. It is an awful blow to me. I know you will ask God to help me bear it. I don't know how I can live without him. It is so hard for us."

Miss Jewett missed her father deeply and in a letter to Annie Fields four years later wrote on his birthday, "I wonder if people keep the day they die for another birthday in heaven? I have been thinking about him a great deal the last day or two. I wonder if I am doing all the things he wishes I would do, and I hope he does not get tired of me." His influence on her is immeasurable. She wrote a poem about him in her collected book of "*Verses*" (1916). It was "*To My Father*" in which she wrote: "A thousand times across the land and sea / Your loving thoughts straight to my heart have flown, / Returned from that far country of the stars. / Again you find me in the quiet room,-- / Your angelhood has lent your love fleet wings / To make the journey through the evening's gloom." One poem is not in "Verses" but is entitled "Missing." "You walked beside me, quick and free; / With lingering touch you grasped my hand; / Your eyes looked laughingly in mine; / And now—I cannot understand. / I long for you, I mourn for you, / Heavy the weight the pall men left, / And cover silently with flowers."

Miss Jewett recorded in "*The Country Doctor*" some of her beliefs in Christ. Among these beliefs was her belief in the powers of Christ that could be received by a person if he could come to know those powers and to understand them. She wrote, "It depends upon our degree of receptivity, and our using the added power that comes that way; not in taking our few tools, and our self-esteem and satisfaction with ourselves, and doing our little tricks like dancing dogs; proud because the other dogs can do less than we, or only bark and walk about on their four legs." She believed that worship should be directed toward God and that worship is "something different from a certain sort of constant church-going, or from even trying to be conformers and to keep our own laws and our neighbors." She believed that religion should be an accepted reliance and guide rather than a basis for argument and that "if we can only keep our faces toward the light and remember that whatever happens or has happened, we must hold fast to hope!" In closing a letter to her friend, Anna Laurens Dawes, she blessed the girl by saying, "God bless you dear and help you to keep close to Him, and give you His peace and His strength always."

In an article published in memory of her life entitled *"Sarah Orne Jewett"* in July, 1909 issue of *"Outlook,"* Miss Jewett's religious spirit is classified. "Miss Jewett expressed the spirit of the Pilgrims rather than that of the Puritans. Her vision of righteousness was merged in a larger view of life than fell to the lot of the Puritan, and was tempered by a sweetness and breadth of sympathy which made her the recorder, not only of the judgments expressed in character and fate, but of those qualities which redeem the hardness of life and modify its cruel fortunes." In addition, the article says "she was never infected by curiosity concerning morbid things; the passion for psychology which had brought confusion and weariness into art, and distorted and wasted many a talent, never touched her." She was interested in the humanity and fellowship and a deep moral sense she trusted in God, a hope in the future life, a helping hand for the needy, and a loving heart for her neighbor.

In a fitting tribute to her character, Carroll Hollis, in an article for the *"Colby Library Quarterly"* in September 1968, reflected on the loving protection through life that she received from her background, her setting, and her associates. He wrote, "Protected by her family and friends, and in fact by society itself, not only from what might corrupt her innocence but even from what might disturb her candid yet solidly Christian view of herself and the world, she represents a certain perfection of type of the genteel society."

A Marsh Island, Houghton, Mifflin, 1885

In 1885, after much grumbling and groaning, she said, got *"A Marsh Island"* to the printer. Louis Auchincloss in *"Pioneers and Caretakers"* called this novel "a charming, concentrated, well-balance little novel of rustic love in the haying season." A. C. Quinn called the novel "a prose poem of earth and water." The story involves a conflict among three young people, Dick Dale, a rich young artist, Doris Owen, a farmer's daughter and Dan Lester, a neighbor boy.

William Payne in the September 1885 issue of *"The Dial"* said that besides being a simple and exquisite story of country people, that "it is in a high sense, an artistic production. Miss Jewett has little invention, but she has a rare delicacy of touch, and the American fiction of today shows no more healthful sign than that which is given by her stories and sketches."

A White Heron and Other Stories, Houghton, Mifflin, 1886

The book is dedicated "To My Dear Sister Mary." The contents are: *"A White Heron," "The Gray Man," "Farmer Finch," "The Dulham Ladies," "A Business Man," "Mary and Martha," "The News from Petersham," and "The Two Browns."*

The first story is *"A White Heron."* Its appeal centers in its modern ecological theme. The story is about a little country girl named Sylvia who overcomes the temptation of revealing the secret hiding place of a white heron to a charming lad who wants the stately bird, stuffed and preserved, for his bird collection. The conflict of choosing between keeping nature's secrets and winning human companionship, which takes place in her heart, is a conflict with which the reader is in full sympathy. "Alas, if the great wave of human interest which flooded for the first time this dull little life should sweep away the satisfactions of an existence heart to heart with nature and the dumb life of the forest!"

Having lived her first eight years in a crowded manufacturing town, Sylvia is alive to nature for the first time. "There never was such a child for staying about out-of-doors since the world was made." Since Sylvia has no playmates and she is "afraid of folks," she looks to the animal and bird kingdom for friendship. Her grandmother's milk cow is her valued companion. Nearly every day "the horned torment" plays hide-and-seek with Sylvia when it is time to come home. Other life, too, affords her many comforting relationships. The grandmother says of Sylvia, "There ain't a foot o' ground she don't know her way over and the wild creatur's counts her one o' themselves." Sylvia's heart is filled with pleasure when squirrels eat from her hand, or when twilight moths strike softly against her, or when the old cat "fat with young robins" rubs against her legs, or when she listens to the thrushes in the deep dark woods.

As a June sun sinks in the West, Sylvia, the nine year old girl drives a milk cow from a wooded, New England pasture to her grandmother's isolated farmhouse. As the girl and the cow make their way along a familiar path toward home they hear an unfamiliar whistle and a friendly "halloa." A tall young boy carrying a heavy game-bag and a gun on his shoulder joins her, asking his whereabouts and wondering is Sylvia's folks might keep him for a couple of days. After they get to the house and introductions are made, Sylvia's grandmother invites the boy to stay. The supper that night is the "best supper he had eaten for a month," and he is surprised "to find so clean and comfortable a little dwelling in this New England wilderness."

After supper the boy tells of his mission to find the nest of a white heron that he has spotted three miles away. When he describes the "queer tall white bird" with soft feathers and long thin legs "Sylvia's heart gives a wild beat; she knew that strange white bird." The boy offers a ten dollar reward to anyone, who can find the nest, and Sylvia's mind spends a sleepless night going over the "wished for treasure" that she could buy with the money, and trying to discover a way to find the nest.

Next day before sunrise, Sylvia slips out of the house and goes one-half mile to a great pine tree, "the last of its generation." With brave and beating heart, she makes the perilous and hard climb to the top of the pine were she spots the white heron's nest. There, too, she saw the sea for the first time. With trembling hands she descends the tree and runs home with the secret. But she does not tell the boy the secret. "No, she must keep silence." "She cannot tell the heron's secret and give its life away. Her loyalty, that suffered a sharp pang as the guest went away disappointed later in the day, which could have served and followed him and loved him as dog loves!" So the story turned out as we said. Sylvia could not bear the thought of the bird dropping silently to the ground with its feathers wet with blood and its songs hushed forever. "Were the birds better friends than their hunter might have been, - who can tell? Whatever treasures were lost to her, woodlands and summer-time, remember! Bring your gifts and graces and tell your secrets to this lonely country child!"

It is gratifying to note in this day of ecological emphasis that Sylvia's loyalty to nature wins out. In the last lines of the story, Miss Jewett writes that the little girl has withstood the test, that nature's secrets will not be revealed by her for a paltry consideration of money or friendship.

The second story in the book is "*The Dulham Ladies.*" This story also appeared in "*The Atlantic Monthly*" in April 1856. In this story, Miss Jewett shows the absurdity of two old maids completely absorbed in the exaggerated triumphs and dignities of their parents' past. Miss Jewett becomes amusing in presenting Miss Harriet Dobin and Miss Lucinda Dobin as they consider themselves the leaders of the Dulham society simply because their father, dead for many years, had been an eminent minister of the First Parish Church. She presents them without becoming overly serious or tediously involved. The women's claim to high social position also rests in their mother's Boston breeding. The "claims of pedigree" of Hightrees and Greenaples, cause the ladies "to hold the standard of cultivated mind and elegant manners as high as possible." Miss Jewett describes them as "much influenced by such an unnatural prolongation of the filial relationship, and they were amazingly slow to suspect that they were not as young as they used to be."

By assuming various degrees of emotional detachment, Miss Jewett shows the young people of Dulham making fun of the ladies' mincing steps and the shape of their parasols, and the new people of Dulham

scoffing at their eccentric behavior and caring little for
Greenapples and Hightrees. Because of this lack of respect
for the Dobin sisters, openly shown at the social gathering
when the mistake is made "in treating Harriet as if she were
on a level with the rest of the company" and a child's
reference to their thin grey hair, the sisters "take steps to
retrieve their lost ascendency." The paralleling of
atmosphere in the treatment of their character and the social
plane on which they live tends to interfere one with the
other in the reader's imagination and suggests both specific
and a general connection between them.

The Dobin sisters go to nearby Westbury, in the
guise of buying Christmas gifts, but really to buy hairpieces
to "replace their lost adornment." The story centers on this
incident and shows the pathetic predicament of the older
women who "try to keep up with the times." After buying
their trifling Christmas gifts, the sisters attend to the serious
commission of the day, but in their modesty they pass
several shops with only fleeting glances at the "frizzes"
displayed in the windows. Finally they get up enough
courage to enter a shop and tell the middle-aged Frenchman
of their need for some "little arrangements." The wig
merchant with glib voice pushes them into buying frisettes
that had long been out of fashion. The frisettes almost
cover their eyebrows and do not match the color of their
hair, but the ladies "tripped down the main street of
Westbury confident that nobody would suspect them of
being over thirty," and "the spirit of youth flamed afresh in
their hearts and they were very happy."

The reactions of friends to their new-found youthful
looks end the tale. When the old railroad conductor sees
them "he affected not to notice anything remarkable in their

appearance." When one of the passengers, Mrs. Wollden, who always mispronounces their names, sees them, she comments, "I expect they wanted to get thatched in a little before real cold weather; but on't they look just like a pair o' poodle dogs." When Hetty, their maidservant and general protector sees the sisters, she laments, "I knew somebody would be foolin' of 'em - - - they believe them front pieces has set the clock back forty years."

Miss Jewett in this story comments upon the changes in society and how those changes affect the aristocracy of New England of which she herself was a member. She gets involved with the humorous aspects of the ladies' predicament. She shows the ladies intentions and innocent inability to comprehend reality and their charm and mistakes and amusing miscalculations. The story has the feel of cultural density, of complex community relationships and of an intricate involvement with the past. The continuity of style, setting and characters informs and adds dimension to the story and each is inextricably linked and intertwined with the overall atmosphere of the story. The social concerns of caste and character have made this story a favorite one; it has proven more fascinating to the general reading public than nearly anything else she wrote. We find "*The Dulham Ladies*" is a variation on one of her themes: the thwarted New England spinster.

The Story of the Normans, G. P. Putnam's Sons, 1886

After two years of work on "*The Story of the Normans*,' Miss Jewett wrote to Annie Fields of having her table "so overspread with the story of the Normans that I can hardly find room to put my paper down on it." In 1886 she published her first non-fiction book, a compact history of the Normans from the 9th to 11th centuries, entitled *"The Story of the Normans, Told Chiefly in Relation to their Conquest of England."* It was written for young adults. A critic of the book in *"The Dial"* praised its blended symmetry, its earnest spirit and scrupulous veracity, its charm of a romance, and its picturesque force.

The critic in *"The New England Magazine"* in April, 1887 wrote, "A large number of American readers should be interested in the history of the Normans, since in their veins runs a rill which, in some degree, had its source in Normandy in times antedating William the Conqueror. In her history of this people, Miss Jewett has treated an important as well as an interesting subject in a sprightly and in a worthy manner. In their own land they are brought to our view in the persons of the first seven dukes, the successive rulers of Normandy, who were "typical of their time and representative of the various types of the national character." The author regards these Normans as the foremost people of their day, "the most thoroughly alive, and quickest to see where advances might be made." This is observed to be true in regard to their methods and skill in government, and in the extension of their power and their national growth. It is shown in their very striking and original architecture, which has had so wide an influence, and whose beauties are constantly reproduced in modern structures. The same eminence is perceived in the social field; for it is admitted that this people were gifted with sentiment and with good taste, together with intellectual cleverness. Yet as with others there is a dark side to this picture,--failures in point of noble action, and misfortunes that involved much privation. These were owing, as usual, to a blindness to the inevitable results of certain courses, and the accompanying unwillingness to listen to their best teachers. In order that we may understand the old Norman beauty and grace, their manly strength, courage, and courtesy, the author would have us go now to the shores of Norway, where in the country of the saga-men and the rough sea-kings, beside the steep-shored harbors of the Viking dragon-ships, linger still the constantly repeated types of our earlier ancestry, and where the flower of the sagas blooms as fair as ever. This is a rather romantic view of the subject, but in a certain sense, it is probably a true one."

To honor his active and useful life, Miss Jewett dedicated her book, "The Story of the Normans" "To my dear grandfather, Doctor William Perry of Exeter."

The King of Folly Island and Other People, **Houghton, Mifflin, 1888**

This book of stories is dedicated with grateful affection to John Greenleaf Whittier. Its contents include: "The King of Folly Island," 'The Courting of Sister Wisby," "The Landscape Chamber," "Law Lane," 'Miss Peck's Promotion," "Miss Tempy's Watchers," "A Village Shop," and "Mere Pochette." The book was published by Houghton Mifflin.

A. C. Quinn noted the variety of the stories in "King of Folly Island and Other People" when he said, "There is more variety than is generally appreciated in Miss Jewett's short stories." Even though, she states that "there are no new plots to the comedies and tragedies of life." The critic of the book in "*The Nation*" severely criticized the book but added a note of praise for her ability to retain images. The critic said that these sketches contained the same old people but with new names on them. And he said that there was little need to present them again. The reviewer in "*The Critic*" criticized her for her limited scale of coloring, her avoidance of picturesque situations, and her lack of the dramatic and humorous. The reviewer did, however, praise her artistic touch, her close fellowship with nature, and her "poetic insight into to human side of it...The impression of New England life, of the faded, sad, hungry-featured women, the narrow hard-spoken men, the scrimping, weary farm work, the uneventful village life, the faint, meager romances of youth and maidens remain distinctly in one's mind long after the last page is turned and the book is laid aside. Any bright surface may reflect back an image, but to retain, to fix it, is the special prerogative of art."

William Dean Howells said of the book, "It is not only the delightful mood which these little masterpieces are written but the perfect artistic restraint, the truly Greek temperance without one touch too much, which render them exquisite, make them perfect in their way."

"*Miss Tempy's Watchers,*" is one of Miss Jewett's most often anthologized stories, in which she gives two old women's estimate of a dead friend, Miss Temperance Dent. The story is set in a remote New Hampshire town. During an April night, Mrs. Crowe and Miss Sarah Ann Binson, from different stations of life, watch with the body of Miss Dent on the night before her funeral. While they watch in Miss Tempy's kitchen with her body lying in a cold upstairs bedroom, the two neighbors engage in steady conversation which reaches an "unusual level of expressiveness and confidence." Their talk helps to lessen the burden of the long night hours, and it gives them another chance to voice their mutual feelings about their old schoolmate and dear friend.

The two women affirm that Miss Tempy's life, which appeared without pleasure to outward view, was really brimful of pleasure to herself. Miss Tempy's generosity is praised by both women. Though they reveal that she took "a lot o' trouble to please a child," her biggest mercy was the time she helped a poor young schoolmistress, who had "overdone herself getting her education," to go on a health-reviving vacation to Niagara Falls. The mercy had cost Miss Tempy $60.00, or two-thirds of her yearly income. A profound reaction follows. "The women looked at each other in silence; the magnitude of the generous sacrifice was almost too great for their comprehension."

After listening to the clock tick, to a mouse gnaw at dry closet boards, and to a distant brook that tried "to make the watchers understand something that related to the past," and after ascending the creaky stairs for another look at the dead form, the two come back to the warm kitchen, eat a small meal of bread and butter spread with quince preserves, and a cup of tea. After a few more reflections about Miss Tempy's life, they fall asleep in their chairs. When they awaken, the day has dawned, and Sarah Ann Binson says as the story ends, "'Twill be a beautiful day for the funeral."

Miss Jewett takes a serious subject and makes it a commonplace reality by focusing on the individual women in their relations with each other rather than by highlighting their relation to society at large or to God. Her selection of detail again is one of her greatest strengths. Though the story has no tough realism in it, the story is realistic. With a typical situation in a New England village, and by relating a conversation that could very well have happened, Miss Jewett helps to achieve her illusion of reality. She used the two women's dialogue and the scene of the dead woman's house to get one to see and feel and hear as she had seen and felt and heard similar happenings in South Berwick. In the story, she celebrates a unique and heroic type of person found only in rural New England, but who has cousins in all parts of the world.

Generally, Sarah Orne Jewett is classified as a local colorist, which means that she presented the idiosyncrasies and peculiarities of a specific locality and its people, namely Maine and its sea-faring farmer folk. Edward Wagenknecht says that "few wise readers doubt that in her sphere she is one of the best of American writers." In fact, she said of her New England emphasis, "my local attachments are stronger than any cat's that ever mewed." She became a true New England nun. Since she did write of a place that was declining economically and socially, her field of observation was extremely limited. She, along with other local colorists of her day, had few exciting details and incidents to convey, but she attempted to picture the people and their situation in a realistic manner. Her sketches rest for their value not upon dramatic qualities but upon their pure tone and singleness of effort. Her engaging modesty and admirable self-restraint show through. She stressed the eccentricities of her subjects rather than their conventional usual characteristics. In a sense then, her realism is an unusual realism. It is a realism in which certain aspects of the common are accentuated and still others are not emphasized at all. Her romantic quaintness colors the realism of the country tales with their note of the idyllic. She was limited in her subject area dealing with people without much color or vitality in their lives. Her handling of these subjects was, as one person wrote, "a miracle in pastel shades."

Tales of New England, Houghton, Mifflin, 1890

Three of her books were published in 1890: "*Betty Leicester*" a children's book, "*Tales of New England*" a collection of stories, and "*Strangers and Wayfarers*," another collection of stories. The reviewer of "*Tales of New England*" in "*The Critic*" placed Miss Jewett alongside Hawthorne and Mrs. Stoddard as an excellent teller of New England Tales. In the review Miss Jewett's closeness of observation was again praised. The critic said, "There is an art, too, of which the reader is unconscious - - until all is said - - in the way in which she presents the slight happenings of some quiet neighborhoods, an art which is not mannered, though it is distinctly that of the 'New England School!'"

Four short stories, named in the review as being especially noteworthy in presenting character are "*The Dulham Ladies,*" "*Miss Tempy's Watchers,*" *Marsh Rosemary,*" and "*a White Heron.*" The critic concluded by praising her power to plant in the minds an impression from nature, "More often we jog along by hedgerow and grey farm to find at the end that some exquisite bit of nature has made a lodgment in our memory."

Strangers and Wayfarers, **Houghton, Mifflin, 1890**

The twelve stories in "Strangers and Wayfarers" are "A Winter Courtship," "The Mistress of Sydenham Plantation," "The Town Poor," "The Quest of Mr. Teaby," "The Luck of the Bogans," "Fair Day," "Going to Shrewsbury," "The Taking of Captain Ball," " In Dark New England Days," "The White Rose Road," and "By the Morning Boat."

In the review of *"Strangers and Wayfarers,"* in the *"Atlantic Monthly"* H. E. Scudder placed Miss Jewett alongside Mary E. Wilkins Freeman because Miss Jewett too recognized the "subordinate value of dialect." He claims, "They give just enough to flavor the conversation, but rely more on the homely phraseology of the ordinary New England speech than on very sharp accentuation." He said that her delicacy of picturing her ancient townswomen was the result "of very careful study and clear perception of artistic values," and that her stories are not mere recitals of incident, but are interpretations of life.

Scudder wrote, "We are glad, therefore, that Miss Jewett has tried her hand at a picture of New England Irish life, as she has done in this story of '*The Luck of the Bogans;*' and singularly enough, as soon as she steps out of her familiar field she acquires an access of dramatic power, as if the exercise had stimulated her and given a new freedom to her imagination. The same charity which lights all her stories illumines this, but beyond there is recognition of sharp passages in the drama of life, as if the author needed to go away from familiar scenes to discover what others have found in her own domain. Be this as it may, she shows an insight, an appreciation, of the Irishman's nature which intimates a possible new vein in the quartz which she has worked so industriously hitherto."

The story, *"Going to Shrewsbury,"* which uses a single incident to reveal the pathetic history of a seventy-five old country woman and to picture her present uncertain situation, the great crisis in her simple existence. With pale face and tear-stained eyes, Mrs. Peet boards the train at a way-station while our narrator remembers her as a woman once renowned for her good butter and fresh eggs and that she always made the most of her farm's slender resources. The narrator is seated beside Mrs. Peet, who is taking her first train ride. The narrator has known Mrs. Peet for several years and she gives the antecedent action that is not revealed in their conversation. The narrator also tells of another event that concludes the story and writes the final word of Mrs. Peet's biography. Opening the conversation with a look of good humor in her tired old eyes, Mrs. Peet comments on this new experience, "So this 'ere is what you call ridin' the cars! Well, I do declare!"

In looking for her ticket, Mrs. Peet shows the contents of her bundle-handkerchief, a few battered books, singed holders for flatirons, her faded little shawl, an old tin matchbox, and a much-thumbed "Leavitts's Almanac." In her basket she carries her old cat, and she comments, "but I expect we're both of us goin' to miss our old haunts. I'd love to know what kind o' mousin' there's goin' to be for me."

After the old creature, who has "a look of tragedy about her," gets her basket and bundle situated, she lets it be known that she's "broke—up" and that she, a childless widow, is moving to Shrewsbury to live with relatives. Thereupon she launches into the story of the method whereby the farm was taken away from her by an "unrighteous claim." She tells that her nephew, "Is'iah Peet," with fox blood in him, had over persuaded her husband on his deathbed to sign the place away. Mrs. Peet says, "It's hurt me to have the place fall into other hands." After a few more comments about losing all her savings on a spool factory that "come to nothin'" and about Isaiah not giving her a chance to remain on the farm "without hurtin' my pride and dependin' on him," the topic of talk changes to the train ride and their fellow passengers.

Getting caught up in the spirit of the moment; Mrs. Peet looks around and critically observes several people. She says on one, "Jest see that flauntin' old creatur' that looks like a stopped clock." But she cannot take her eyes off herself for very long. She blurts out about her own miserable situation, "An uprooteder creatur' never stood on the airth," "Everybody know me to home, an' nobody knows me to Shrewsbury;'t won't make a mite o' difference, if I take holt willin'." "I ain't goin' to sag on to nobody."

The train arrives at Shrewsbury and deposits Mrs. Peet who has no one to meet her. To our narrator, "The sight of that worn, thin figure adventuring alone across the platform gave my heart a sharp pang as the train carried me away."

The scene shifts abruptly to the following spring

and back to a country road near Mrs. Peet's old place. Our narrator and another person ride along talking about their mutual friend and her stay in Shrewsbury. They tell that Mrs. Peet enjoys her life with her nieces and that Mrs. Peet insists that Isaiah did her a good turn. At that moment the two ladies meet Isaiah Peet on the road who tells them that Mrs. Peet died that very morning. The narrator believes that she had known Mrs. Peet better than anyone else had known her.

"Strangers and Wayfarers" was dedicated to Miss Sarah Wyman Whitman, "to S. W., Painter of New England men and women, New England fields and shores." Miss Whitman had designed the cover for the new book as she had designed the covers for "The King of Folly Island," "Betty Leicester," and "The Queen's Twin." After Miss Whitman's death, Miss Jewett, as an honor to her, edited the "Letters of Sarah Wyman Whitman" (Cambridge, 1907) and wrote the preface to the book.

A Native of Winby and Other Tales Houghton, Mifflin, 1893

In 1893, "A Native of Winby," a collection of stories was published. The book consists of nine short sketches or stories. They are "A Native of Winby," "Decoration Day," "Jim's Little Woman," "The Failure of David Berry," "The Passing of Sister Barsett," "Miss Esther's Guest," "The Flight of Betsey Lane," "Between Mass and Vespers," and "A Little Captive Maid.

Miss Jewett dedicated "The Native of Winby," to Caroline with these words: "To my dear younger sister. I have had many pleasures that were doubled because you shared them, and so write your name at the beginning of this book."

One story, "*The Flight of Betsey Lane*," had already been published in "*Scribner's*" in August, 1893. While the story pictures life at a New England poor-house, the story has an intriguing plot about an old woman who runs off to the 1876 Centennial in Philadelphia and about the people who believe she had drowned herself in the farm pond. Three principal characters, Miss Peggy Bond, Aunt Lavina Dow and Betsey Lane, possess a most interesting past, though there is not much hope to their future. The story involves an incident that happens to one of the three that gives them a new topic for many future conversations.

The story begins on a May morning, when three old women, dressed in stout brown gingham dresses and faded blue aprons, sit in a shed at Byfleet Poor-house picking over a bushel of cranberry beans. As they work the beans, the women pass the time of day by "croaking" hymns, by gossiping about the people at their rustic institution, and by listening to the thump of bees on the windowpanes. There is an air of comfort and a cheerful feeling of activity surrounding their work and lives.

Miss Peggy Bond, in her eighties, is introduced as being "upsighted," a name given to the cataracts crowding out her vision. She cocks her head "as if she were first cousin to a hen." Aunt Lavina Dow, in her late seventies, is afflicted with plain rheumatism. And Betsey Lane is the youngest at 69. She has spent "most of her life as aid-in-general to the respected household of old General Thornton." Betsey Lane is the center of the story. She has always wanted to see the world and she wishes to go the

Centennial. She says, "It seems to me as if I can't die happy 'less I do."

While the women are working, a stranger from London arrives at the farm and inquires for Betsey Lane. Betsey finds out that the visitor is a granddaughter of Old General Thornton, and the visit is highly enjoyable to both parties. The visitor, as she leaves, puts a roll of money in Betsey's hand, $100 in new bank bills, which Betsey immediately conceals in her dress.

A few days later, Betsey Lane mysteriously disappears. At first her friends think that she has gone visiting but after a few days, futile inquiries are made of her relatives and friends on the nearby farms and in the village. Finally, curiosity gives way to the fear that she may have put an end to her life. The belief is justified by the facts that she had no money, that she didn't buy a train ticket at the South Byfleet Station, and that she cannot be found in any place within reasonable distances of the poor-house.

But the reader is told what actually happened. Betsey, on the day of her disappearance, rises early, dressed in her old straw bonnet and black gown, and steals away "like a plunderless thief." She cuts across the fields to the train track where she finds a freight train on a siding. When she asks the men, passage is given her free on the condition that she sews buttons on the coat of one of the men. Triumphantly she goes to Philadelphia and to the Centennial, which is "like the day o' judgment" to her. There, she delights in the holiday spirit by visiting with folks from "Chiny an' the back o' Pennsylvany," by seeing hogs that weighed "risin' thirteen hundred," by filling her pockets with trinkets for her friends back home, and by finding an eye surgeon that promises to come and give

Miss Bond's sight back to her. Her adventure was exactly what she had always wanted.

On the ninth day of Betsey's disappearance, Miss Peggy Bond and Aunt Lavina Dow decide to go to the farm pond to see if Betsey's body has surfaced since bodies are supposed to float after nine days in the water. The rheumatic and the upsighted make a pathetic sight as they stumble along. Mrs. Dow, the captain of the expedition, knows that Betsey "hove herself in. It run in her family." But as they reach the pond and survey the glittering water and pond-lilies, Betsey Lane appears, "following the short way homeward from the railroad." The two friends are pleasantly surprised to find their old friend full of life and of stories about the Centennial. Betsey Lane says, "I guess I've got enough to think of and tell ye for the rest o' my days." The two women don't tell why they went to the pond, and the three go triumphantly toward the poor-house, "full o' dust, an' pretty nigh beat out."

In "*The Flight of Betsey Lane*" Miss Jewett includes just the right amount of indirection in narrative technique and a suggestiveness of style that goes so far to reflect the action of a given scene in the rhythm and cadence of the sentences. The story itself is simple enough; it is an episodic account of the exploits of the three women. And the reversal of the reader's expectations at the end of the story emphasizes the distinctness of her ability to write unusually good fiction. Again, her love of the gentle and the peaceful is evident here. She is dealing with life, and therein lies a philosophical and moral scope that is too comprehensive to be contracted into a few easy generalizations.

Betty Leicester's English Christmas, Privately Printed, 1894

"*Betty Leicester's English Christmas. A New Chapter of an Old Story*" was published in Baltimore and was privately printed for the Bryn Mawr School students, Board of Managers and graduates. 150 copies were printed to hand out as Christmas gifts. A trade edition of the book was published in 1899 and was given a slightly different title, "Betty Leicester's Christmas."

Miss Jewett begins her story in the first person, in the role of the narrator, and writes of Betty as if she were a dear friend. She opens the story: "There was once a girl named Betty Leicester, who lived in a small square book bound in scarlet and white. I, who know her better than anyone, and who know my own way about Tideshead, the story-book town, as well as she did, and have not only made many a call upon her Aunt Barbara and Aunt Mary in their charming old house, but have even seen the house in London where she spent the winter; I, who confess to loving Betty a great deal, wish to write a little more about her in this Christmas book for the girls of the Bryn Mawr school. The truth is that ever since I wrote the story I have been seeing girls who reminded me of Betty Leicester, of Tideshead. Either they were about the same age or the same height, or they skipped gaily by me in a little gown like hers, or I saw a pleased look or a puzzled look in their eyes which seemed to bring Betty, my own story-book girl, right before me."

The Life of Nancy, Houghton, Mifflin, 1895

"*The Life of Nancy*" is a collection of several short stories bound together in one volume. There are ten selections: *"The Life of Nancy," "Fame's Little Day ," "A War Debt," "The Hiltons' Holiday ," "The Only Rose," "A Second Spring ," "Little French Mary," "The Guests of Mrs. Timms," "A Neighbor's Landmark ," and "All My Sad Captains."* It was published by Houghton, Mifflin & Co. and it sold for $1.25.

The reviewer in "Literary World" in 1895 says the stories are first rate. The reviewer writes: "Some of Miss Sarah Orne Jewett's most delightful work is to be found in the stories which make up the volume entitled '*The Life of Nancy*.' The one from which it is named -- the tale of Nancy, the fresh, dimpled country maid, on her first visit to Boston, counting all things as delight, and accepting each small kindness as evidence of a real, underlying friendliness, and the same Nancy years after lying helpless on her bed in the country neighborhood which she has done so much to cheer and elevate, and still feeding on the thought of that happy visit -- is simply and pathetically beautiful. Even better, perhaps, is the story of "*A War Debt,"* with its picture of the picturesque, half-ruined Virginia manor house, the shadows of the Civil War still brooding over it; and we are grateful to Miss Jewett for the hinted hope of the last sentence, added since the tale appeared in the "*Century*." But it is difficult to choose where all are so good. The gentle drollery of "Fame's Brief Day," the homely but no less genuine pathos of "The Only Rose," the charm of childhood in "Little French Mary," the delicious New Englandism of "The Guests of Mrs. Timms" -- each and all are admirable in their way. And it is a way that is Miss Jewett's own, the ripened fruit of a lifetime of experience and observation, and widely distinct and distinguishable from the way of other people, from the gaunt, sordid, painful, crotchety New England which we find in some other novels and stories; for Miss Jewett's keenness of vision is tempered with a tenderness no less discriminating, her records are as kind as they are accurate, and her own sweetness of good breeding finds a way into the recesses of the true courtesy, honor, and worth which often underlie the rugged exterior of her country people."

The reviewer in "*The Nation*" for February, 1896, writes that "Miss Jewett is content, and most heartily contents us, with the American at home, almost restricted to the New Englander working his unproductive farm, fishing on the more responsive sea, and gossiping up and down the village streets. The incidents in the volume entitled '*The Life of Nancy*' are simple almost to bareness, but they are exalted by a sympathetic revelation of human nature and by an exquisite literary representation. The fussy old maids, kind or cross, the unconsciously humorous and self-complacent sea-faring men, the taciturn husbands and loquacious, irrelevant widows, all are in a way characteristically of New England, but Miss Jewett goes deep enough to link them with a wider world and to insure them greeting as kin, irrespective of geographical limitation and local accident. When a thing is perfectly well done, it is profitless to try to explain how and why. Nature's special endowments defy analysis, and those curious about seemingly wonderful achievements are restricted to guessing what has been added by care and industry to the original, inexplicable faculty, the unknown and incalculable quantity. What Miss Jewett appears to have gained by her sincere and loving application to letters is facility of expression which shows neither haste nor waste, and a classic beauty of form and serenity of manner. She has certainly proclaimed that beauty and truth are not antagonistic, and that the real and the ideal are inextricably woven in the warp of human life."

The story "*The Only Rose*" appeared in the January 1894 issue of "*The Atlantic Monthly.*" The humor of Miss Jewett surfaces again in the story when a thrice-widowed woman of property tries to decide on which of her husbands' graves she is to place a bouquet of flowers which contains a single red rose. The story, told in two parts, reveals the biography and character of Mrs. Bickford. The first part consists of a conversation between Mrs. Bickford and a neighbor, Miss Pendexter, while Mrs. Bickford divides flowers for her husbands' graves into three piles as nearly alike as could be. In the second part, the act of driving to the graveyard and the deed of placing the bouquets on the graves is told.

The story begins on a bright summer day when Miss Pendexter visits Mrs. Bickford, who lives alone in a large house on the edge of Fairfield. Mrs. Bickford is a solitary housekeeper since she has buried three husbands and has "neither chick nor child." Though she has "no gift of entertaining" and she is "subject to fits of untimely silence" with visitors, on the day of this story she is open in her conversation with her sprightly, cheerful, little neighbor. Through dialogue they present and interpret themselves with little comment from the author.

Mrs. Bickford, who is "bent upon a visit to the burying ground" sorts flowers into three heaps, one for each husband's grave and recalls each husband's character. She remembers Albert Fraley, the husband of her youth and their life together as a time when they were "dreadful happy." But Albert died of a fever early in the marriage. In this reflection, Miss Jewett understands the value of affection, of communication among men and that love is necessary to self-realization and simple dignity to the end.

Next, Mrs. Bickford reviews her life with Mr. Wallis, who was always inventing impractical gadgets instead of making a living. In a forgiving spirit, she says "Life was very disappointing with Mr. Wallis, but he meant well." She characterized him as "a dreadful notional man" though he was "splendid company for winter evenings."

To Mr. Bickford, who did "everything by rule an' measure," she felt obligated because he left her so comfortable. So she tries to be absolutely impartial in dividing the flowers for the three graves, until she decides to pick her only rose and place it on the grave of her favorite husband. She says, "I don't seem to know which of 'em ought to have it." "I do so hate to make a choice between 'em; they all had their good points, especially Mr. Bickford, and I respected 'em all."

Mrs. Bickford worries all night about the decision that she thought she had to make. Who was to get the rose, the "definite symbol and assertion of personal choice?" But when her young nephew, John, drives her to the graveyard, he takes her mind off her problem until they reach the graveyard by telling her about his love for Mary Lizzie Gifford. When they reach the graveyard, John leaps to the ground and, before Mrs. Bickford can stop him, takes the three bouquets. "To leave the matter of the rose in the hands of fate seemed weakness and cowardice, but there was not a moment for consideration." As Mrs. Bickford wonders which husband gets the rose, John returns, much to her relief, with the rose in his own button hole. He tells her that it fell out of the bouquet, and he thought he would give it to Lizzie. All Mrs. Bickford can say is, "Well, well! I guess the rose was made for you." And the story ends. Miss Jewett desires that one participate in the story's action but not to the extent of losing oneself in an emotional reaction. And despite the humor and lightness, the story has its measure of pathos. Miss Jewett uses a rather slight closed plot which runs the customary course of conflict, complication, climax and resolution. The story is an excellent example of how the basic elements of a story work together to produce an important interpretation of some aspect of life.

"*The Only Rose*" gives a fresh insight into a human personality. Mrs. Bickford deals with the conventional necessities of life; she has material comforts and she thinks orthodox thoughts. Like other writers of fiction, Miss Jewett has created Mrs. Bickford, a character, placed her in an ordinary situation, and caused her to behave as an ordinary human being. The story does depend on plot, but the significant action and conflict actually lie with Mrs. Bickford herself, which means that Miss Jewett is using her plot to reveal character. In turn she used both plot and character to reveal her theme in which she is deeply involved with the quality of experience. It is apparent that

Miss Jewett has written a serious story, a thoughtful interpretation of one aspect of humanity. Her interpretation emerges from her own world view and her philosophy of life. Miss Jewett has a scale of values, and above all she makes a distinction between quantative and qualitative values in *"The Only Rose."* And her evaluation of Mrs. Bickford's experience is Miss Jewett's own truth.

The Country of the Pointed Firs, Houghton, Mifflin, 1896

In 1896 *"The Country of the Pointed Firs,"* with its tales from a city boarder's visit to the coastal Maine village of Dunnet Landing is her masterpiece which first appeared in serial form in the *"Atlantic Monthly."* It was immediately heralded as one of the great works of American Literature. In a letter to Miss Jewett, William James, the great psychologist, wrote to her, "Having just read your *'Country of the Pointed Firs'* I can't hold in from telling you what exquisite pleasure it has given me...The proper reaction upon it is the uncontrollable expression of pleasure in one's face and not a pretense of analytic words from one's pen—and the expression is on my face whenever I think of it. Most gratefully yours..."

Rudyard Kipling said of her novel, "It's immense - - it is the very life. So many of the people of lesser sympathy have missed the lovely New England landscape and the genuine New England nature. I don't believe even you know how good that work is!" Another New England author, Annie Trumbull Slossum, praised her novel. She said, "I have just laid down your *"Country of the Pointed Firs"* and want to say a few words about it. I tell you frankly that is may be partly because of my strong feeling as to the present condition of literature that I have taken this book so to my heart. This day, Breathings, Sighs, Cameos, Silhouettes, Clots of Bloody Bravery, etc., etc. makes me tired. I'm dreadfully old, but I am young again for the hour as I read your story, and I want to thank you for doing and being all this I recognize."

Hamilton Mabie reviewed her book in "*Review of Reviews*" and compared her to Jane Austen. He stated, "It is a pleasure to add that Miss Jewett's latest story, "*The Country of the Pointed Firs,*" shows her true and delicate art in all its quiet and enduring charm. This unaffected and genuine artist will have a place in our literature as distinct and secure as that which Jane Austen fills in the literature of our kin beyond the seas."

Willa Cather placed the book in the top three of American novels, alongside "*Huckleberry Finn*" and "*Scarlet Letter.*" Cather believed that the book would enjoy a long life. She said, "I like to think with what pleasure, with what a sense of rich discovery, the young student of American literature in far distant years to come will take up this book and say 'A Masterpiece!' as proudly as if he himself had made it. It will be a message to the future, a message in a universal language, like a tuft of meadow flowers in Robert Frost's fine poem, which the mower abroad in the early morning left standing, just skirted by the scythe, for the mower of the afternoon to gaze upon and wonder at - - the one message that even the scythe of Time spares."

F. O. Matthiessen, her first biographer, said that the book has universal applications. He compared her to Thoreau who also saw the classical present in their surroundings. "We were no more a New England family celebrating its own existence and simple progress; we carried the tokens and inheritance of all such households from which this had descended, and were only the latest of our line."

Charles Thompson in *"The Atlantic"* for October, 1904, showed how delicate and rare her art of scarching out virtue is. He wrote, "I always think of her as one who, hearing New England accused of being a bleak land without beauty, passes confidently over the snow, and by the gray rock, and past the dark fir tree, to a southern bank, and there, brushing away the decayed leaves, triumphantly shows to the faultfinder a spray of the trailing arbutus. And I should like, for my own part, to ask this; that the fragrant, retiring, exquisite flower, which I think she would say is the symbol of New England virtue, is the symbol also of her own modest and delightful art."

George Baker in his review in *"The Bookman,"* said that the work was very fine and very true, that it "is a story of wholesome, simple, rural life with the breath of the sea for tonic and the sunshine of summer for warmth. The picturesque delineation of character, the writer's close contact with nature, and her appreciative insight, all contribute a reality and charm to the book which are very convincing."

Her novel or novella has a loose structure that is claimed by some to have no plot. Her genius in the book is to use literature to paint a picture. The narrator has come to Dunnet, Maine, to finish writing her book. When she gets there, she stays with Mrs. Todd. Mrs. Todd's herb garden is one of those well painted pictures. Her reputation is in her knowledge of herbs. It is a delight to go through her garden and learn the names of the herbs, their smells, and their medicinal uses.

Miss Jewett divides the novel into twenty-four short stories, and she gives each story a name. The first one is entitled "The Return." In it, the writer-narrator, already a lover of Dunnet Landing, returns for a summer visit to the Landing because of her first visit there two or three summers earlier. She had stopped by on a yachting cruise, and had fallen in love with this maritime village of eastern Maine. Now, her admiration focuses equally on its setting and on its people. The seaward-pointing houses with their flower gardens and fir trees watch her steamboat dock at Dunnet Landing. A young crowd of spectators follows her up a narrow street. This first section sets the story in time and place, and it gives the narrator's attitude toward the town. Her love affair with the village is shown in the twenty-three stories that follow.

The second story is entitled "Mrs. Todd" and it introduces the main character of the novel. The narrator hires a room from Mrs. Todd where she is treated as a guest and friend. Mrs. Todd's house, though physically secluded from the busier parts of town is actually a gathering place. Her friends and neighbors come to her for her human kindness and for her herbal wisdom. She gathers her herbs from her own herb garden and from nearby fields and woods. And she cooks them on her kitchen stove until they turn into healing elixirs for all kinds of human ailments and needs. Also she is quick to give medical advice to her customers. Even the village doctor knows the value of her knowledge to the community, but he persists in poking gentle fun at his medical rival. The newly-arrived narrator quickly fits into this busy scene. She helps Mrs. Todd with her daily sales of herbal potions, and in the cool evenings the two women talk.

In the third story, "The Schoolhouse," the narrator, needing time to write and a private place to collect her thoughts, hires the little white schoolhouse on the brink of a nearby hill from the Selectmen of Dunnet Landing. There she retires from Mrs. Todd's busy world to work. Since the narrator had come there to write and because Mrs. Todd's increased summer business brought too many loud and cheerful gossips to distract the narrator, she had to get away. She says, "One afternoon, when I had listened, it was impossible to not listen with cottonless ears, and then laughed and listened again, with an idle pen in my hand, during a particularly spirited and personal conversation, I reached for my hat, and, taking blotting-book and all under my arm, I resolutely fled further temptation, walked out past the fragrant green garden and up the dusty road."

The fourth story, "At the Schoolhouse Window" takes the narrator to the schoolhouse and to her writing. It is early July. She is late in her arrival at her writing desk, because she had attended the funeral of Mrs. Beggs, a friend of Mrs. Todd at one o'clock. After the funeral she excuses herself and comes to the schoolhouse, where she stands at the window and watches the funeral procession walk its way to the burying ground. She sees Mrs. Todd walking slowly and "keeping the after-part of it back," she sees Captain Littlepage, an old mysterious man, walking beside Mrs. Todd. "He looked like an aged grasshopper of some strange human variety," and she watches "that Mari' Harris," the housekeeper of Captain Littlepage, following the pair. She watches and thinks for an hour, but finally she sits down to work. But bees are attracted to her ink pot because it is scented with bergamot and she spends too much time swatting them with the teacher's stick. Her wits also wander and so the sentences fail to come. She begins to yearn for a companion. She has only to wait an hour before her yearning is realized in the form of old retired sea captain, Captain Littlepage, who makes his first appearance in the novel. In the midst of a funeral procession "...I recognized the one strange and unrelated person in all the company, an old man who had always been mysterious to me."

Fifth story is named, "Captain Littlepage." They introduce one of the most interesting characters in the novel. After the funeral of Mrs. Beggs, Old Captain Littlepage makes his way to the schoolhouse for a little visit with the writer. In their conversation, the Captain gives "his time to the poets" and that Milton's *Paradise Lost* is his favorite poem. He somewhat objects to Shakespeare by saying that even though Shakespeare copied life, "You have to put up with a great deal of low talk."

The eighty year old captain has been at sea for forty-three years, has visited hundreds of ports around the world, and he realizes that life is more than "the battle for town clerk here in Dunnet." He describes other sea-captains and their peculiarities. He says that Captain Tuttle was so intrigued about bees and beekeeping that people nicknamed his ship, "Tuttle's Beehive." Another one, Captain Jameson, "had notions of Solomon's Temple," and had meticulously made a little model of it using "Scripture measurements." Then Captain Littlepage bemoans the loss of shipping out of New England ports. He thinks that "large-minded ways" of thinking are also lost.

The sixth story is "The Waiting Place." With a little encouragement from the narrator, Captain Littlepage launches into telling about a strange experience that a friend of his had had near the North Pole. Littlepage was captain of a ship named "Minerva" which was carrying general merchandise from London to Ft. Churchill at Hudson Bay when contrary winds, winter weather, and a fever stranded him in a small Moravian Mission post for the winter.

The Captain found himself rooming with an old Scotch seaman named Gaffett in a small but warm cabin where they "lived like dogs in a kennel." But it was a dreadful place, frozen and insolated. They had no books and the poetry in the Captain's head sustained him with a measure of comfort. There, he says, Shakespeare reigned as king over Milton, because the accurate sea terms of Shakespeare and "some beautiful passages were calming to the mind."

Gaffett, though, was affected in his mind and he brooded and talked to himself until he decided he could reveal his "Discovery" to Captain Littlepage. "To hear old Gaffett tell about it was something awful." It was a tale of snowy travel with dogs and sleds, but it had a strange twist. The travelers to the north found a warm flowing current that flowed into an open sea. The men rode the current to a rocky shore where strange things happened. The place was not charted on the maps and was farther north than anyone had been. On the coast they found a place that looked like a town, but it was soon found to be a waiting place for souls that were caught somewhere between life and death. The inhabitants were just "shapes of folks." The fog-shaped men came at them like bats, but they never came near them. The men were scared away but they were forever affected by the cobweb shapes and weird events. The men decided that the shapes caught between life and death could be seen because of "some condition o' light and the magnetic currents that let them see those folks." Gaffett made a believer of Captain Littlepage, and now the Captain tries to convert the narrator to the truth of his tale. His story did have a ring of truth to it. The story reminds one of Coleridge's 'The Rime of the Ancient Mariner" and James Hilton's "Lost Horizon."

In story seven, "The Outer Islands," the narrator and Captain Littlepage stand looking at a wall-map in the school-house which troubles the Captain for a moment, and then he turns to the writer and asks "We were just speaking of – and he stopped. I saw that he had suddenly forgotten his subject.'" As soon as the narrator gets back to Mrs. Todd's home, they talk about the Captain and his great narratives. Mrs. Todd says, "Funerals always sets him goin'. Some 'o them tales hangs together toler'ble well."

As Mrs. Todd and the narrator face the sea, they look at the outermost island as rays of sunshine hit it. Mrs. Todd says that her 86 year old mother lives on that island and that her mother is a "spry, light-footed little woman, always was, and light-hearted too." Then Mrs. Todd invites the narrator to go with her to visit her mother, Mrs. Blackett, and her brother, William.

Story eight is entitled "Green Island" and it tells of their visit to Green Island. Mrs. Todd wakes up thinking of her mother. And since the wind is light from the northeast, it is a good day to take a handy dory and Johnny Bowden with them. They don't want to take any men, "having to be considered every minute an' takin' up all our time." As they go across the water, they stop at Mrs. Todd's brother's trawl line to choose a proper haddock to take to her mother. Mrs. Todd keeps up a delightful commentary about the islands as they pass by them, including comments on a mean sheep owner who lived on one, and the houses of two farmers on another island who had not spoken to each other during their lifetimes because of past hostilities.

A favorite passage appears in this context when Mrs. Todd explains her need for variety. She says, "I must say I like variety myself, some folks washes Monday an' irons Tuesday the whole year round, even if the circus is goin' by."

Then they catch sight of Mrs. Todd's mother and a "tiny flutter in the doorway" which sends a quick signal from the heart of one to the heart of the other. Immediately they see smoke pouring from a chimney which indicates that the mother is brightening up her fire because of her expected company. Next, they land and exchange greetings and introductions, and present the haddock for one of her mother's famous chowders.

Story nine is entitled "William" and is portraiture of William, Mrs. Todd's peculiar brother, who lives with their mother on the island. As the narrator goes out to dig a few more potatoes for the chowder, William comes up to give her a hand. He is an older man, gray headed and clean shaven with bent shoulders and a timid air. "With William it was the first step that cost" and then he was as sociable as could be expected of one who was more acquainted with the sea than with mankind. While dinner is cooking, William takes his guest out to a great ledge, one of his favorite spots. He tells her "There ain't no such view in the world, I expect."

They are a little late getting back to dinner. But after being seated at the table, William asks "a blessing in words I could not hear" and they eat their chowder with delight and thanksgiving. Mrs. Blackett and William have the ability "to make themselves and their houses belong entirely to a guest's pleasure."

Story ten is "Where Pennyroyal Grew." After the meal, Mrs. Todd and the narrator set off to the pastures to where the pennyroyal grew, a sacred place to Mrs. Todd, because it was the spot where she and her husband had courted. Mrs. Todd also points out the location at sea where her husband was drowned. After gathering their herbs they go back to the house for tea with her mother, and then set sail for home.

Back at the house, right after tea-time, William and Mrs. Blackett entertain the visitors in story eleven which is entitled, "The Singers." The narrator is pleasantly surprised at the true and sweet tenor of William as he and his mother sing "Home Sweet Home." It is a time of great pleasure.

In story twelve, "A Strange Sail," Mrs. Todd's friend, Mrs. Fosdick, comes to visit and Mrs. Todd greets her with "I declare if you ain't the same old sixpence."

The narrator soon finds that Mrs. Fosdick, in her time, had been to sea and was full of curiosity about the world too. Susan Fosdick tells her life's history to the narrator about her large family of sons and daughters, their fortunes and their misfortunes. The section is full of reminiscences and personal news. And they conclude with "yes'm old friends is always the best 'less you can catch a new one that's fit to make an old one out of.'"

Story thirteen is "Poor Joanna." The summer flies by and it is time to light the fire in the Franklin Stove. The narrator catches a reference one evening from Mrs. Todd about Shell Island and Poor Joanna who used to live there. Miss Joanna Todd was a cousin of Mrs. Todd's late husband, who lived as a nun on the island. She lived that way because she had been crossed in love. She retired from the world, "though she was a well-off woman." People used to go by her island and leave provisions for her of one kind or another. One time Mrs. Todd took the minister of the church with her to see poor Joanna but it was a big mistake because the minister "was a vague person...Well meanin' but very numb in his feelin's." Poor Joanna kept her hens as companions and let the world do as it pleased.

In story fourteen, "The Hermitage" Mrs. Todd continues telling Mrs. Fosdick and the narrator more about her visit with Joanna. She describes the lonely woman's bare house and its furnishings and she tells how she entreated Joanna to come live with her or with her mother, but all Joanna could say was, "I haven't got no right to live with folks no more, you must never ask me again, Almiry." When Mrs. Todd and the minister got back to Dunnet Landing they went their separate ways, but Mrs. Todd still resents his character and his manner. She is so fed up with him that she makes this comment about his sermon the following Sunday. She said that "he seemed to know no remedies, but he had a great use for words."

In the story fifteen called "On Shell-heap Island," Mrs. Todd finishes her reflection upon the sad lot of Joanna who lived there. She says, "There is something in the fact of a hermitage that cannot fail to touch the imagination:

the recluses are sad kindred, but they are never commonplace. The narrator persuades Mrs. Todd to take her where Joanna used to live and where she died twenty-two years earlier. Mrs. Todd is convinced, so the two women make the trip to her shrine of solitude. Looking at her grave, they know that "there was the world, and here was she with eternity well begun."

In story 16, "The Great Expedition" the narrator sees that Mrs. Todd has some great adventure on her mind when they greet each other at the breakfast table. One can always tell when Mrs. Todd has something up her sleeve by the way she repeats her visits to her store room, and by the way she pounds the stairs as she climbs. Today she becomes agitated when she learns that they have to take the grocery wagon instead of Mrs. Begg's best chaise on their trip upcountry to the Bowden reunion, and she worries whether her mother will get there in time to go with them. Of course, the grocery wagon is not half bad and Mrs. Blackett, the mother of Mrs. Todd, arrives just right so that the trip has all the assurances of a successful time. The reason that Mrs. Todd kept the trip a secret is because she doesn't think it is prudent "to wear a day all out before it comes." Besides, bad weather has to be considered as a real possibility, and she didn't want her plans to be spoiled.

Story seventeen is "A Country Road" which follows. It is the record of the trip to the reunion by Mrs. Todd, Mrs. Blackett, and the narrator. It is a descriptive passage with a few actions and reflections. The party, as they go along the country roads, smells donuts frying all along the way, but they only get to eat some when a checkrein comes loose from the horse forcing them to stop at a stranger's house where the stranger turns out to be a distant kinsman who tells them that she is going to the reunion too. They pass on through narrow slots in the woods until they come to the upper bay area where the landscapes spreads out before them and they realize that they are nearly there. Several others appear on the road before them: kinsfolk going to the reunion too. "Mrs. Blackett's eyes are bright with excitement, and even Mrs. Todd showed remarkable enthusiasm."

Story eighteen is "The Bowden Reunion" which occupies several pages and is one of the important passages of the novel. The reunion itself "has transfiguring powers and easily makes friends of those who have been cold-hearted, and gives to those who are dumb their chance to speak, and lends some beauty to the plainest face." People have come by wagon and by boat and the place is filled with people. All of a sudden they get quiet to listen to the instructions of a "soldierly" man named Sant Bowden who orders them to line up in ranks of fours in order to make the long procession around the field over a recently mowed path and back to the grove. The narrator says. "We might have been a company of ancient Greeks going to celebrate a victory, or to worship the god of harvests in the grove above." Mrs. Todd is somewhat choked up to see her mother marching at the head of the procession alongside the ministers. After engaging conversation with Mrs. Caplin, they sit down at long tables to mounds of food and more conversation. A cousin by marriage that Mrs. Todd despised, passed by and the narrator gets to see another side of Mrs. Todd that she had not seen before.

Story nineteen is entitled "The Feast's End." The most amazing piece of artistic food is in the form of the old Bowden house "made of durable gingerbread, with all the windows and doors in the right places, and sprigs of genuine lilac set at the front." Of course, the house falls at the end of the feast to the hands of the Bowden family who eat it with a general seriousness. The feast is followed by religious speeches and by the recitation of "a long faded garland of verses," that sounded pretty to Mrs. Todd. The leave-takings are then made with the words "next summer" used to indicate that more reunions would follow. And they retrace their way back to Dunnet Landing.

Story twenty, "Along the Shore," begins with an essay on four fishermen of Dunnet who had grown up together, worked together and struggled together against the sea, and who had a common bond that held them fast to almost a silent brotherhood. The narrator says, "I often wondered a great deal about the inner life and thought of these self-contained old fishermen; their minds seemed to be fixed upon the nature and the elements rather than upon the contrivances of man, like politics and theology." One of these fishermen, Mr. Elijah Tilley, invites her to visit him sometime, so that afternoon she makes her way to his place where she discovers a carefully painted house of yellow and white and a neatly kept yard and pasture, and once inside his kitchen, she recognizes what a good housekeeper he is. He says, "I try to keep things looking right, same's poor dear left 'em." After a lengthy talk about how pretty his wife was and how he misses her, he takes the narrator into the "best room" where she sees the unworn carpet, the glass vases on the mantelpiece, and the tea things that Mrs. Tilley thought so much of. He remembers the summer before "poor dear" died, that she told him that she couldn't think of anything else she needed to furnish the best room and he says, "it kind o' chilled me up when she spoke so satisfied." In the end, the narrator finds out that Elijah Tilley is also an excellent knitter, and that Mrs. Todd thinks he is "a ploddin' man."

The last section, number twenty one, in the 1896 edition is called "The Backward View" and is a reflection of the author's attitude toward Mrs. Todd, and her friends of Dunnet Landing as she prepares to leave the small coastal town and return to the busier world of Boston. Her goodbyes are said and she departs with considerable nostalgia in her looks and in her words. Her farewell is like a death. So she concludes, "So we die before our own eyes; so we see some chapters of our lives come to their natural end."

In the 1910 edition of "The Country of the Pointed Firs" are three stories inserted between "Along the Shore" and "The Backward View." They are "A Dunnet Shepherdess," "The Queen's Twin," and "William's Wedding." The first of these three stories is included in "The Queen's Twin." Only "William's Wedding" is added here. The other two are included in the next book.

In the 1910 edition "William's Wedding" is story twenty three. It is about the wedding of William and Esther after a forty-year courtship. William and Esther are free to marry soon after her invalid mother's death. Just a week after her death, on a clear day, William strikes his sail for Dunnet Landing, arrives under the notice of all of Mrs. Todd's friends and goes up country to find Esther to bring her back to Dunnet Landing and to the minister's house for a private wedding ceremony, not allowing anyone present except the minister. During the ceremony, Mrs. Todd and the narrator bake a cake and open an old bottle of wine for their wedding reception at Mrs. Todd's home.

The day of the wedding is mostly a day of waiting for Mrs. Todd and her companion. First they wait for the white sail to show on the horizon, next they wait for William's return with Esther at his side. Then they wait for the married couple to emerge from the minister's home. The narrator comments on waiting. She says, "It is very solemn to sit waiting for the great events of life – most of us have done it again and again – to be expectant of life or expectant of death gives one the same feeling." While they wait, a stream of friends curious to know the details of William's wedding pour through her door but Mrs. Todd is slow to reveal anything that she knows, lest it upset the delicate balance of her own emotional struggle of the moment.

After the couple is married and returns to Mrs. Todd's home, Mrs. Todd's feelings are released and she takes Esther into her arms and holds her there, and she takes William's hand and they give each other "the kiss of peace." "We took the cake and wine of the marriage feast together, always in silence, like a true sacrament, and then to my astonishment I found that sympathy and public interest in so great an occasion were going to have their way." After the reception and after the departure of the newlywed couple, Mrs. Todd and the narrator retire for the day with the precious memories of the day lingering on their hearts.

The town where Miss Jewett grew up influenced her life. She characterizes it in her novel, *"The Country of the Pointed Firs,"* with these words: "In that handful of houses they fancy that they comprehend the universe." In her youth, the town was already two centuries old. It was settled by English people in 1627. Its first church was organized in 1702. Writing of the 200th anniversary celebration of the old village church in 1902, Miss Jewett humorously wrote in *"Looking Back on Girlhood"* "that was the time, 1702, when we were converted by missionaries from Harvard, and before we had been only a little royal colony with Church of England preaching." Being one of the oldest Maine towns, South Berwick on June 9, 1713 became the ninth town to be incorporated in the State of Maine. Because of its antiquity the town had had time to establish traditions which Miss Jewett notes in these words, "Being one of the oldest colonial settlements, it is full of interesting traditions and relics of the early inhabitants, both Indians and Englishmen." From her birth and throughout her life, the town gave her rich heritage of personal experiences and historical considerations.

"About the hidden fire of enthusiasm in the breasts of her fellow New Englanders," Miss Jewett further reflected that "in quiet neighborhoods such inward force does not waste itself upon those petty excitements of every day that belong to cities, but when, at long intervals, the altars of patriotism, to friendship, to the ties of kindred, are reared in our familiar fields, then the fires glow, the flames come up as if from the inexhaustible burning heart of the earth; the primal fires break through the granite dust in which our souls are set." Gladys Hasty Carroll in *"New England sees it Through"* wrote that Miss Jewett "had the artistic wisdom never to touch material which she did not thoroughly know." Miss Carroll praised Miss Jewett's art of characterization, "her gentle narratives of the elderly, of herb gatherers and shepherdesses, of retire seamen, cheery invalids, and tranquil lighthouse-keepers are carved with the delicate precision of cameos; never an ill-chosen word; never a blurred stroke, always an extraordinary skill and a loving care and an abiding tenderness."

In their own quiet and quaint ways the country people fascinated Miss Jewett. She visited their farmhouses and the fisher cottages by the sea, but she never as an intruder, but always as an affectionate sympathetic friend of these people that she loved. She ate at their tables, and helped care for their sick alongside her father. She knew the hidden sorrows, the secret hopes and the glad happenings of them all. She knew their customs, their ways of speech and their incredible strength. In the last paragraph of "The Landless Farmer" she looked deep in the lives of the silent people. She wrote, "Heaven only knows the story of the lives that the gray old New England farmhouses have sheltered and hidden away from the curious eyes as best they might. Stranger dramas than have ever been written belong to the dull-looking, quiet homes, that have for generation and generation live and die. She knew the people in their quiet homes, and she saw some of these dramas that were enacted in their lives. She knew, and she understood.

The Queen's Twin and Other Stories, Houghton, Mifflin, 1899

Before her carriage accident which virtually stopped her writing career, Miss Jewett produced three more books. She collected her stories for *"The Queen's Twin and Other Stories"* in 1899, which she dedicated "To Susan Burley Cabot," whose home at Pride's Crossing was described by Miss Jewett in a letter to Sara Norton in 1896, as "a house unlike any other, with a sense of space and time and uninerruptedness, which as you know isn't easy to find in this part of the world." Mrs. Cabot received Miss Jewett's annual visits for several years.

Miss Jewett begins *"The Queen's Twin"* with a story of the same title. The collection of stories is about the people of the coast of Maine who had travelled the high seas, "rounded the Cape of Good Hope" and "braved the angry seas of Cape Horn." Included in this group of seafarers is Mrs. Abby Martin, the main character of the first story who also made a sea voyage to London on her brother's ship. Miss Jewett reflected that these people knew something of the wide world, and that they did not mistake "their native parishes for the whole instead of a part thereof."

The first story is "The Queen's Twin" and is set at Dunnet Landing in the month of September. The narrator's landlady, Mrs. Almira Todd, a main character in *"The Country of the Pointed Firs"* has returned from visiting Mrs. Martin. When the narrator hears of Mrs. Todd's friend, she asks Mrs. Todd to take her to see the woman. So in a couple of days, they take an old Indian trail across the heron swamp to a "dreadful out-o'-the way place" to visit Mrs. Martin. Mrs. Martin's home is separated from neighbors by distance and by the bog. Their visit to Mrs. Abby Martin "seemed in some strange way to concern the high affairs of royalty." Mrs. Todd called her "The Queen's Twin" because her old friend fancied herself to be the twin of Queen Victoria, since the two women were born on the same day and a number of other things that had corresponded in the lives of Abby and the Queen.

When they arrive at her low grey house they see the bent-shouldered woman waiting with an air of welcome about her. She is sort of "ceremonious" but gentle mannered and sprightly. Immediately she introduces her favorite topic by mentioning what it would be in London. She then launches into her one trip abroad and how she came to see the queen as she rode forth from Buckingham Palace. In remembering this event she says, "'twas a moment o' heaven to me." She identified with the queen because they both were born at the same hour of the same day, both married men named Albert, both had children named Edward and Alice, and both lost their child, Alice. After she got to look the queen in the face she said, "I don't know how to explain it, but there hasn't been no friend I've felt so near to me ever since," and that "she's been the great lesson I've had to live by."

Mrs. Martin shows her guests the mementos she has saved in her best room. Her devotion to her fantasy made her place a vase of flowers before a framed newspaper of the queen and to read from the Queen's book about the Highlands every Sunday. In fact, she confesses to a time when she got the notion that the Queen was coming to see her, and she straightened the house, put fresh sheets on the bed, placed pretty flowers about the house, and fixed supper for her. Of course, the Queen didn't come, but a cousin, who was not all there, came stepping by, and Mrs. Martín invited the "dreadful willin'" soul in to eat the meal.

Mrs. Todd comments that many people have such fantasies and says "Don't it show that for folks that have any fancy in 'em, such beautiful dreams is the real part o' life."

After viewing the pictures of the Queen and drinking tea, Mrs. Todd and the narrator leave to go home again through the "birdless and beastless" swamp, but they know that they had not left Abby Martín alone.

The second story in "The Queen's Twin" is "A Dunnet Shepherdess." The story brings William Blackett, Mrs. Todd's brother, from his island home to her door. He is going to go trout fishing up country and Mrs. Todd prepares his breakfast and spreads a pennyroyal lotion on him to ward off mosquitoes. But after going a ways, he returns to the white school-house and invites the narrator to go with him. She accepts and so with "pleasure at the helm" she goes out into the happy world of adventure with a man who has a hard time putting three sentences together on a single occasion. Next the two adventurers arrive at a farmhouse where they leave the team of horses and where they present to the housewife a stack of dried fish and a few live lobsters. They hike off across the pastures and to the woods to find their brook, cut their fishing poles and to cast their lines for trout. They divide up, with William going upstream and the narrator going downstream. After fishing all morning without success, they meet back at their beginning point for lunch and a quiet time of peace on the green banks. After a while, William declares that he's going over to the Hight's farm and to inquire about

Thankful Hight's folks since it would please his sister, Mrs. Todd. As they cross the poor pastures, the narrator tells William that the owners of the land ought to raise more sheep, and he replies, "That's what she always maintains." The narrator is inquisitive about who "She" is. As they proceed, they come into a bright clearing where they can look up the way to a large flock of sheep. William tells the narrator that the sheep are doing so well because they are "shepherded." It turns out that they are watched by a shepherdess, the "she" of William's earlier remarks. When they arrive at the farmhouse, they meet cross old Mrs. Hight who is confined to life in a chair during the day and in a bed at night. After a few introductory words, Mrs. Hight gives William permission to go search for Esther, the Dunnet Shepherdess, and he leaves the young companion and the complaining old woman to review the gossip of the day on the streets of Dunnet Landing. As time passes and the conversation begins to lag and William has not reappeared, they begin to wonder what has happened to him in his search for Esther, and all of a sudden it dawns on our narrator that she has "fallen upon a serious chapter of romance." Mrs. Hight begins to worry about William and Esther, and sends her guest to the door to see if she might see them in the pasture. She sees them near the house sitting on a long grey ledge engaged in pleasant conversation.

Before long the two friends return to the house and after William unloads his gift of fish, they say their goodbyes and return to Dunnet Landing.

Following "The Dunnet Shepherdess," are "Where's Nora?" "Bold Words at the Bridge," "Martha's Lady," and "The Coon Dog."

The seventh story in "*The Queen's Twin*" is "Aunt Cynthy Dallett," which concerns the interrelationships of three elderly women, again Miss Jewett turns to the lives of those around her for her material. Her own town and surrounding country was filled with the kind of women that she places consciously and deliberately into this New England story. The story is a study of character and personal relationships drawn from a philosophical and psychological point of view.

The story begins in the warm but bare kitchen of Miss Abby Pendexter as she and her well-to-do friend, Mrs. Hand, exchange ideas about the customs of observing Christmas and New Year's Day. The Yankee propensity to talk about their neighbors and to question each other about their beliefs leads them to a discussion of Aunt Cynthy Dallett who is said to keep New Year's Day as "an extra day." The two kindhearted women reflect upon their years of association with Abby's aunt and the aunt's present lonely life in a farmhouse on a mountain road some distance from the town. Together the women vow to make a trek to the old woman's farmhouse for a New Year's Day celebration. While they talk, the reader learns of Miss Abby's kinship with Aunt Cynthy and of Abby's present poverty. Abby has had to sell all her chickens except one to pay her last quarter's rent, and now she has no means of making a living. Abby's situation allows Miss Jewett to add a significant dimension to the story, a dimension of human need met by human compassion.

The second part of the narrative involves the women's preparations for the walk to Aunt Cynthy's home. The cold weather causes them to dress sufficiently for their walk up the mountain road. Under their wraps each woman keeps her gift for Aunt Cynthia hidden from sight. Miss Pendexter with her roast hen and Mrs. Hand with her two mince pies walk along the road, again in unhurried conversation. This time, more details of Miss Abby's financial predicament are revealed. Finally Mrs. Hand suggests a remedy to the Aunt's problem, a remedy Abby had already thought of. Mrs. Hand advises Abby to move in with her Aunt to save on rent and food and to provide companionship for both lonely souls.

The third section of the story tells about their arrival at the aunt's home, her warm reception, and their enjoyable visit together. During the course of their visit, Abby tries to persuade her aunt to come to town and live with her. But Aunt Cynthy, refusing to budge from her home, invites Abby to come live with her on the farm; Abby accepts, and the story ends.

Miss Jewett presents Aunt Cynthy's farm as a place of peace, plenty and happiness, and everything in the story is conducted calmly and leisurely; no hurry, no bustle, no struggling and scrabbling for existence once the solution is proposed by Aunty Cynthy and accepted by Abby Pendexter. And yet for all the pleasantness of the visit and its outcome, the story has its somber side.

The collection ends with the story, "The Night before Thanksgiving."

Although many contemporary writers of Miss Jewett praised her work, some thought that she was limited in what she was doing. Edith Wharton criticized her for looking at New England through "rose-colored glasses." In this story, Miss Jewett was certainly looking at life unrealistically. Her instinctive refinement and her graceful workmanship might be mistaken as a weakness of realistic writing, but it shouldn't be. The critic in *"The Nation"* praised her art and said that her style was more distinctive than that of any other American woman.

The Tory Lover, Houghton, Mifflin, 1901

Another literary acquaintance was Charles Dudley Warner. According to the book, *"Charles Dudley Warner"* by Annie Fields, he advised her to write a historical romance about her hometown of South Berwick, Maine. Since Warner was contributing editor of *"Harper's"* and was the co-author of Mark Twain's *"The Gilded Age,"* Miss Jewett felt that his advice was sound. Miss Jewett, therefore, set out to write something entirely different than the stories and tales of New England that had become her trademark. She worried about the novel being a complete success, and she expressed her doubts to Warner who wrote back to her, "I am not in the least alarmed about the story, now that you are committed to it by the printing of the beginning, only this, that if you let the fire slow down to rest for a week or so, please do not take up any other work, but rest really." He further advised her to "hold the story always in solution in your mind ready to be precipitated when your strength permits. That is to say, even if your fires are banked up, keep the story fused in your mind."

"The Tory Lover' presents a sympathetic picture of the people and their lives. Warner continued his praise by saying that her stories breath "forth an air of calm leisure that in its avoidance of hurry or catastrophe suggests the almost forgotten note of Goldsmith and Irving."

The exchange of letters between Miss Jewett and Warner was merely an indication of the friendship that existed between the two. For years she had been a regular and frequent visitor at the Warner's home in Hartford, Connecticut, with the Warners reciprocating with visits to South Berwick. On one occasion Mr. Warner wrote to Annie Fields, "If SOJ is not with you I might run up to South Berwick and see her." Again in a letter to Miss Jewett, Warner said, "I want to see you ever so much and talk to you about your novel, and explain to you a little what I tried to do with Evelyn in my own." In another letter to her, he thanked her for some pointed fir that she had sent him, "The Pointed Firs in your note perfumed the house as soon as the letter was opened, and were quite as grateful to me as your kind approval. . ." The friendship ended with his death, October 20, 1900.

According to F.O. Matthiessen in his book "*Sarah Orne Jewett*" she wrote "*The Tory Lover*" against her better judgment, but that she was pleased that she wrote it, for she said to Horace E. Scudder "I can't help hoping that you will like this last one, "*The Tory Lover*," which has taken more than a solid year's hard work and the dreams and hopes of many a year beside. I have always meant to do what I could about keeping some of the old Berwick flowers in bloom, and some of the names and places alive in the memory, for with many changes in the old town they might be soon forgotten. It has been the happiest year of work that ever came to me as well as the hardest."

And so Miss Jewett set to paper a dream that she had for a long time when she wrote "*The Tory Lover*." The work was hard and professionally dangerous as she confessed in a letter to the wife of "The Century's editor, Katherine McMahon Johnson, "It is certainly a dangerous thing to try to write something entirely different after one has been for years and years making stories as short and sound as possible, but I have long had a dream of doing this, as you know, and I suppose I had to do it."

"*The Tory Lover*" was serialized in the "*Atlantic Monthly*," from November 1900 to August 1901. It was in response to the Atlantic's request for something long. According to F. O. Matthiessen in "Sarah Orne Jewett" that Miss Jewett said that everything in the book was from her heart, even more so than "*The Country of the Pointed Firs.*" She said though that "the two together hold all my knowledge, real knowledge, and all my dreams about my dear Berwick and York, and Wells - - the people I know and have heard about: the very dust of thought and association that made me!"

In a letter to Sara Norton, she judged "*The Tory Lover*" as falling somewhat short of the dreams she originally had for it. She wrote, "*The Tory Lover*" got itself done at last. . . I grow very melancholy if I fall to thinking of the distance between my poor story and the first dreams of it, but I believe that I have done it just as well as I could."

Her last novel, "*The Tory Lover*," was written in 1901. It was a historical romance about her hometown of South Berwick and about a young American officer from South Berwick who struggled with his loyalties to the King and to his country. The young man served aboard the "Ranger" under the command of John Paul Jones who had gathered his crew from South Berwick. The action takes place in South Berwick, in France, in England and back again. The book was dedicated to her nephew, Theodore Jewett Eastman, who had just completed four years at

Harvard with an A. B. degree, cum laude, and with honors in French. The critic of the novel in the *"Outlook"* said, "Her method is unchanged; her refinement, delicacy, and trained skill are on every page, she has simply varied her method." The critic also gave a general assessment of her art by saying, "She has never been diverted from her vocation as painter of New England traits and life—a painter of sensitive feeling, clear insight, and a finished, reposeful, but individual and vital style...Her quiet fidelity to high standards, wholesome methods, and the realities of character have evidenced that quality in her nature and in her art which stamps her as one the writers of our time whose place is secure."

M. H. Vorse, reviewed the novel in *"The Critic"* and said *"The Tory Lover"* is a graceful story, and attractively written, and that Miss Jewett has been very merciful in that she has spared us descriptions of the horrors of war—she has so far departed from precedent that not every one Tory is tarred and feathered by indignant patriots."

The story was praised by other critics in a variety of periodicals. The critic in the *"Boston Herald,"* wrote: It is one of the most pleasing, dignified, and artistic historical novels of the last five years. Indeed, one would be at a loss to point to a modern historical romance that equals it in all those qualities and features that make a book worth reading twice." The editorial in the *"Boston Journal"* said, "It is a book which will bring especial delight to New Englanders, but its characters and the treatment of them are great and broad enough to win admiration anywhere. It will long outlive the year of its appearance." In the *"Beacon"* (Boston) the critic wrote: "It is the emphatic verdict of all who have learned to admire the subtle imaginative power, the refined humor and exquisite literary form of the writings of Sarah Orne Jewett, that she has put her best work thus far into "*The Tory Lover.*" The story as a story moves with stately grace; the historical setting is perfect." In the "*Cambridge Tribune*" the reviewer said, "The story is told with great spirit, and the atmosphere of the period is well preserved." "*The Portsmouth Journal*" praised the book: "The reader is bound to recognize in "*The Tory Lover*" a faithfulness of incident, locality, and character which makes it a novel of unusual merit, easily ranking among the very best productions of its class."

Included in the novel is the Jewett home which was built in 1774 by John Haggins. She described their home that faced "the southern country just where the two roads joined from the upper settlements. A double stream of travel and traffic flowed steadily by the well-known corner, toward the upper and lower landings of the tide river," and "in the winter the two roads were blocked as far as a man could see with the long processions of ox teams laden with heavy timbers, which had come from fifty or even a hundred miles back in the north country." In those days living on the corner of heavily travelled streets was an indication of one's social position.

Their mansion was a landmark in South Berwick. It was a pre-revolutionary, Colonial-style house of two and a half stories with shuttered dormer windows, a high-peaked roof, Corinthian porch pillars and two chimneys that were overshadowed by Lombardy poplars. Its tall, solid stance, with the appropriate yard accessories gave the house a permanent appearance. Attached to the house at the entry way in the nineteenth century was a Doric portico with fluted columns. Its exterior as well as its interior was appointed with the proper furnishings. The house had white clapboard siding and was surrounded by green lawns, terraced gardens of flowers, vegetables, herbs, and fruit trees. White paling fences and hedges of high box enclosed the house.

The house was described by her friend Willa Cather. Miss Cather wrote that Miss Jewett lived "within scent of the sea but not within sight of it, in a beautiful old house full of strange and lovely things brought home from all over the globe by seafaring ancestors." Miss Cather loved to visit the Jewett home because of what it looked like and contained, but more so for the writer who lived there. Miss Cather admired her above all other women in American literary circles.

The family mansion was an old Colonial house in the center of South Berwick where she was born and where she lived her life. The wealth and position of her family show in their home, one of the principal homes of South Berwick. It was the old Haggins' mansion which stood at the northeast corner of Main and Portland streets. The house was a historical showpiece having been handed down from older generations. She would have had many memories of the Portland Street where she played with her young cousins, children of Thomas Jewett and the Elisha Jewett families.

Six years after Miss Jewett's death, Henry James described the setting of the Jewett home where he had visited. "Other amplified aspects of the whole legend, as I have called it, I was afterwards to see presented on its native scene – whereby it comes back to me that Sarah Jewett's brave ghost would resent my too roughly

Bostonizing her: There hangs before me such a picture of her right setting, the antique dignity—as antiquity counts thereabouts—of a clear colonial house, in Maine, just over the New Hampshire border, and a day spent amid the very richest local revelations." James and Cather described the setting of her life accurately and sympathetically.

The Jewett home was a fitting place for Miss Jewett to receive the sensory impressions of country and town. In her home she could hear the loud noise of the Piscataqua River Falls as they "came beating into the room and echoing back from the high pines across the water" from her bedroom she could hear the cry of herons and the mocking laugh of a loon from far down the river, and she worked in her own garden where she smelled the fragrance of upland pastures and the salt scent of the sea tide.

The Jewett's were honored when their house was included in Mark Anthony DeWolfe Howe's, *Who Lived Here? A Baker's Dozen of Historic New England Houses and Their Occupants"* (1952). At the death of Mary Jewett, the last of the sisters, the house was bequeathed to her sister's son, Theodore Jewett Eastman, who in turn gave the house in 1931 to the "Society for the Preservation of New England Antiquities" who opened the house for public viewing. An early photograph of the home appeared in the October 1901, issue of *"The Critic"* along with pictures of Miss Jewett and her study.

Another citizen of South Berwick and a writer herself, Gladys Hasty Carroll said, "Sarah Orne Jewett's home is the heart of our village. It has long been and will always be the priceless heritage of countless generations of the town's young people. It has encouraged and inspired others to write as well as possible of what we know. Miss

Sarah has proven to us that what we have can be of inestimable value to the world if we find the way, as she did, to interpret and thus to share."

An Empty Purse: A Christmas Story, **privately printed, 1905**

"*An Empty Purse: A New England Tale for Christmas and Holiday Time*" first appeared in the *Boston Evening Transcript* (Saturday 21 December, 1895, p. 14) and in *Philadelphia Press,* (21 December, 1895). It was later collected in *The Fireside Book of Yuletide Tales* edited by Edward Wagenknecht (Bobbs Merrill, 1948, 172-179) and again in Richard Cary's *Uncollected Stories of Sarah Orne Jewett.* It was also privately printed by Merrymount Press (Boston 1905). It was the last book to be produced in her lifetime.

Verses.

Miss Jewett wrote and published many of her poems in various magazines of her day. Some of them have been collected in a volume of poems called, *"Verses."* The book was printed for her Friends and it was dedicated to her nephew, Dr. Theodore Jewett Eastman (1879-1931). He was the son of Caroline Jewett and Edwin C. Eastman.

The first poem was devoted to her father and is titled, "To My Father: I." The first seven lines show how precious her memories of her father were. She wrote:

"To My Father: I."

"When in the quiet house I sat alone,

Sometimes I heard your footfall drawing near;
And with a thrill of gladness open wide
I flung my door to bid you welcome, dear.
Sometimes you did not even speak to me,
But left me quickly when our eyes had met
And you had kissed me -- ah, how tenderly!"

A second poem was also written about her father and shows how much she missed him when she contemplated the beauties of nature.

"To My Father: II"

"And in my mind there was no longer room
For any thought but of that dearest friend
Who taught me first the beauty of these days—
To watch the young leaves start, the birds return,
And how the brooks rush down their rocky ways,
The new life everywhere, the stars that burn
Bright in the mild, clear nights. Oh! He has gone,
And I must watch the spring this year, alone.

Other poems in "*Verses*" were: "*Assurance,*" "*The Gloucester Mother,*" "*Flowers in the Dark,*" "*Boat Song,*" "*Top of the Hill,*" "*At Home from Church,*" "*Together,*" "*A Caged Bird,*" "*Star Island,*" "*The Widows' House,*" "*Dunluce Castle,*" "*Discontent,*" "*A Four-Leaved Clover,*" "*A Child's Grave,*" "*The Spendthrift Doll,*" "*The Little Doll That Lied,*" and "*The Fallen Oak.*"

Many of her poems were children's poems. One was

"The Little Doll That Lied."

'Why, Polly! What's the matter, dear?
You look so very sad:
Has your new doll been taken ill?
It cannot be so bad!'
Nine of the dolls sit in a row,
But there is one beside-
See in the corner, upside-down,
The little doll that lied!

Out in the corner, all alone,
The wicked doll must stay!
None of the rest must speak to her,
Or look there while they play.
All her best clothes, except her boots,
Are safely put aside
(Her boots are painted on her feet)-
The little doll that lied!

Oh, lying's such a naughty thing!
Why, she might swear and steal.
Or murder someone, I dare say;
Just think how we should feel
To have her in a prison live,
Or, worse than that, be hung!
What won't she do when she is old,
If she did this so young?

And now the silver mug and spoon
Come into use again,
And down the faces of the dolls
The tears run fast as rain.
Three have tipped over in their grief,
Their tears cannot be dried;

Their handkerchiefs are dripping wet-
The little doll has lied!

In her poem, *"At Home from Church,"* she described her enjoyment of the flowers' fragrances, the silence of the empty house, and the busy bees in the apple trees. She said that she watched the robin in the elms, and listened to the Sunday morning stillness broken by the slow sweet drone of the church organ.

About a similar occasion, Miss Jewett wrote a poem entitled,

"Flowers in the Dark"

Late in the evening, when the room had grown
Too hot and tiresome with its flaring light
And noise of voices, I stole out alone
Into the darkness of the summer night.
Down the long garden-walk I slowly went;
A little wind was stirring in the trees;
I only saw the whitest of the flowers,
And I was sorry that the earlier hours
Of that fair evening had been so ill spent,
Because, I said, I am content with these
Dear friends of mine who only speak to me
With their delicious fragrance, and who tell
To me their gracious welcome silently.
The leaves that touch my hand with dew are wet;
I find the tall white lilies I love well.
I linger as I pass the mignonette,
And what surprise could dearer be than this:
To find my sweet rose waiting with a kiss!

Miss Jewett wrote poems in honor of her fellow poets, John Greenleaf Whittier and Ralph Waldo Emerson. The poem on Whittier is included in another place in this book, entitled *"Literary Acquaintances."*

A Sonnet on Meeting Ralph Waldo Emerson

RIGHT here, where noisiest, narrowest is the street;
Where gaudy shops bedeck the crowded way;
Where idle newsboys in vindictive play
Dart to and fro with venturesome bare feet;
Here, where the bulletins from fort and fleet
Tell gaping readers what's amiss today,
Where sin bedizens, folly makes too gay,
And all are victims of their own conceit;
With these ephemeral insects of an hour
That war and flutter, as they downward float
In some pale sunbeam that the spring has brought,
Where this vain world is revelling in power;
I met great Emerson, serene, remote,
Like one adventuring on seas of thought.

F. O. Matthiessen in his *"American Renaissance"* said that Miss Jewett admired Emerson and his philosophy and in one of her books by Emerson, she had underlined this statement of his: "I value qualities more and magnitudes less."

Final Thoughts

Two important events mark the turning point in Miss Jewett's life and literary career. One event was happy while the other was tragic. The tragic one followed the other like winter follows harvest time. The happy event involved a signal honor when Bowdoin College, the state's oldest college and the Alma Mater of her father, bestowed a Litt. D. degree upon her at the graduation exercises of that all-male school in 1901. She was the first woman to receive a degree from Bowdoin. The college numbered among its former graduates Nathaniel Hawthorne, Henry Wadsworth Longfellow, Horatio Bridge, and Franklin Pierce. Because the school had such a fine reputation as an educational institution, Miss Jewett counted the honorary degree a highlight in her life, and she was pleased to be called "the Daughter of Bowdoin." In a letter to Mrs. Field, she recounted her experiences at the graduation exercises and her delight over the occasion. She wrote, "I have so much to tell that my pen splutters. You can't think how nice it was to be the single sister of so many brothers at Bowdoin, walking in the procession in cap and gown and Doctor's hood, and being fetched by a Marshall to the President, to sit on the platform with the Board of Overseers and the Trustees, also the Chief Justice and all the Judges of the Supreme Court, who were in session in Portland, or somewhere nearby! And being welcomed by the President in a set speech as the only daughter of Bowdoin, and rising humbly to make the best bow she could, and what was most touching was the old chaplain of the day who spoke about father in his 'bidding prayer,' and said those things about him which were all true and your SOJ applauded twice by so great an audience."

The second event marking the turning point in her life, the one of tragedy, occurred the next year on her birthday, September 3, 1903, during her habitual afternoon ride. Her horse that was pulling her carriage stumbled and fell as it was going downhill. Miss Jewett was thrown from the carriage. The injuries to her spine and to her head and her extremely slow recovery forced her to give up writing as a profession. She was still able to write letters to her friends until her death seven years later. Following the terrible blow on the head, a strange loss of balance, blurred wits, and continual pain in her back occurred. Writing about her accident a month after it happened, she told Thomas Bailey Aldrich about her slow recovery, "Perhaps you haven't heard what bad days I have fallen upon—or rather that I fell upon too hard a road the first of last month. I was thrown out of a high wagon and hurt my head a good deal and concussioned my spine, so that I am still not very well mended, and have to stay in bed or lie down nearly all the time." A year later on September 3, 1903, she penned these sad words, "I can write very little." Having a "hunted feeling like that last wild thing that is in the fields," Miss Jewett attempted a recovery by going to the mountains to stay in a journeying-friend's big country house, only in the company of a nurse, Miss O'Bryan, where she might in solitude, which was according to the doctor's orders, sit among the fir trees, that she dearly loved, and watch the partridges care for their little chickens, or where she might enjoy the salt air and bright sunshine. During these long days of pain and silence and inactivity she read a lot but wrote very little. In November, 1904, she described to her friend, Louisa Loring, her "grind of headaches," her "prevailing fall cold" and her slow recovery, but optimistically she exclaimed, "Never mind! There ought to be time enough for everything, taking this world and the next together."

During her period of recovery, she also went to Mouse Island, Boothbay to spend time in recuperation. At

Mouse Island she was delighted that she was able to meet the poetess, Alice Maynell, the next winter after the accident.

After the accident, Miss Jewett gradually resumed her letter writing, but she confessed that she was "rather dull and confused after the accident." In a letter to Mark DeWolfe Howe she wrote, "As I am getting on so slowly that I still have to be very careful of even reading and writing notes - - I get downstairs for part of the day, and lead a really hulking life in my room for the rest of the time!" The main concern of her tragedy was not herself, however, but Annie Fields, who was sick at the same time. Miss Jewett wrote, "I know so well what a difference it would make if I were there."

After Mrs. Whitman's death in 1904, Miss Jewett graciously consented to edit the letters of her dear friend. Other activities included frequent visits by Elizabeth McCracken, a New Orleans born friend who later became an editor at *"Atlantic Monthly."* These visits over the last five years were helpful to her. Miss McCracken also introduced Julia Marlowe to Miss Jewett. Julia Marlow as a famous Shakespearean actress of the early twentieth century, but no real friendship developed between them.

In August, 1906, Miss Jewett said that she was beginning to find some pleasure again despite her occasional feeling of pain. She wrote to Sara Norton, "I have really come back to some sense of pleasure in life, though I feel like a dissected map with a few pieces gone, the rest of me seems to be put together right." She told Sarah Wheelwright that one of the pleasures of 1906 was her attendance at the Watteau Fete.

In 1907 she wrote to Violet Page that she was in a "wintry state" still, but a year later in the Spring of 1908 optimism again set in, and she wrote to Harriet Prescott Spofford that she might try writing again, "Perhaps someday now in the right place and with the right kind of quietness, I shall find myself beginning all over again; but it will be a timid young author enough!" In the summer of 1907 she wrote Willa Cather, who was then editor of "McClures" and who was her recently acquired friend, that she still had literary inclinations, "You will find that I sent a verse that I found among my papers to "McClures"—and I did it as a sort of sign and warrant of my promise to you. No story yet, but I do not despair; I begin to dare to think that if I could get a quiet week or two, I could get something done for you, and it should be for you, who gave me a 'hand up' in the spring." As a result of her resolve, her last published piece was a short story entitled, "The Gloucester Mother" that appeared in "McClures" in October, 1908, but Willa Cather recorded that Miss Jewett's writing days were then essentially over. In Cather's book, "Not Under Forty" she wrote "Some six years before she had been thrown from a carriage on a country road (sad fate for an enthusiastic horsewoman) and suffered a slight concussion. She recovered, after a long illness, but she did not write again—felt that her best working power was spent." Willa Cather made several visits to see the ailing Miss Jewett in her home in South Berwick and became well acquainted with her and her sister, Mary, whom she continued to visit after Miss Jewett's death.

In 1908 Miss Jewett made two pleasant cruises down the Maine coast in the Forbes Yacht, "The Merlin."

She continued to write letters to friends and in a letter to Mrs. Humphrey Ward and Her Daughter on June 8, 1908 she wrote of her further companionship with Mrs. Fields, where at Manchester-by-the-Sea they sat "on the piazza looking seaward over the green tree tops." She also crocheted which helped to occupy the time she had formerly devoted to writing.

On January 22, 1909, she was taken for a ride down to the frozen tide river where, as she described it in a letter to Frances Morris, "The white snow was thinly spread like nicest frosting over the fields, and the pine woods as black as they could be,--no birds, but the tracks of every sort of little beastie." She made a comment on her continuing illness when she said that "being sick is fun compared to getting well, as dear Mr. Warner used to say. Do take long enough, I have had such drear times trying to play well when I wasn't."

In March of 1909 she was stricken with apoplexy while she was staying with Mrs. Fields in Boston. Immediately, she was taken in a special railroad car to South Berwick with one side of her body paralyzed though her mind was clear. On reaching home, she kept to her wheelchair where she received her old friends. She despised any sympathy that was given, but her return home satisfied her mind, for she had wanted to live her last days in the house where she was born. As early as sixteen years of age she had said of the house that, "I was born here and I hope I shall die here and leave all the chairs in their places." Her expressed wish to die in the Jewett home was fulfilled on Thursday, June 24, 1909, when she died of a cerebral hemorrhage.

Burton W. Trafton, Jr. in the *"Boston Post"* on the centennial of her birth described the way the village reacted to her death. He wrote, "The little town where she lay was as hushed as a church steeple that day. The very air seemed reluctant to stir. The birds in her pointed firs were uncommonly still. Long, slim fingers of shade crept across the lawn from the picket fence, and the heart-shaped leaves of the dooryard lilacs wilted in the sun. The pulse of the town ceased to throb as friends, both humble and great, from far and near, gathered quietly on. Mr. Howells wrote to her nephew, 'There will be others, but what she was and what she did will never be, and never be done again.'"

Mark A. DeWolfe Howe in his book, *"Memories of a Hostess,"* told of the poem that he read at the funeral of Miss Jewett, and he recorded the tribute that Annie Fields wrote, "of my dear Sarah—I believe one of her noblest qualities was her great generosity. Others could only guess at this, but I was allowed to know it. Not that she made gifts, but a wide sympathy was hers for every disappointed or incompetent fellow creature...Sarah's quick sympathy knew a friend was in need before she knew it herself; she was the spirit of beneficence, and her quick delicate wit was such a joy in daily companionship."

Another tribute to her appeared in the July 1, 1909, issue of *"The Independent,"* which reads, "We would lay the sweetest of flowers on the grave of Sarah Orne Jewett, who died last Thursday of paralysis. She was the author of the simplest, sweetest stories and descriptions of New England life." In the tribute to her in the *"Atlantic Monthly"* in August 1909, the writer praised her heroic patience through her final years of physical disability which seemed to those who knew her an unendurable affliction.

The writer wrote that in her "there was a noble patience, a sweet endurance that could have sprung only from a heroic strain of character." The next year friends of hers set up "The Sarah Orne Jewett Scholarship Fund" at Simmons College in her honor.

After her death in 1909, a sympathetic view of Miss Jewett as an author was presented in the *"Outlook."* The critic said, "All her stories were biographic in a sense that they reflected, not the story of the happenings of her individual life, but the happenings of that wider community life into which, through sympathy and insight, she entered so simply that she came to the very heart of it almost without consciousness of the fidelity of her record. . . She opened the door to colonial homes in which breathed the refinement of an earlier New England society; she conveyed the charm of the high breeding of that older society, its love of books, its simplicity and dignity. She had the key also to the farmhouses and the little houses by the sea; and into whatsoever home she went, it was never as an intruder, but always as an affectionate and sympathetic student of the men and women she loved."

A tribute in the *"Atlantic Monthly"* in 1909, said that her stories have universal significance and should not be consigned merely to one locality. The tribute recorded, 'In the first place, this work of hers, in dealing with the New England life she knew and loved, was essentially American, as purely indigenous as the pointed firs of her own countryside. The art which she wrote her native themes was limited, on the contrary, by no local boundaries. . . It was precisely this union of what was at once so clearly American and so clearly universal that distinguished her stories, in the eyes of both the editor and reader."

In another article in the *"Outlook"* in 1912, Theodore Roosevelt expressed his delight in Miss Jewett's stories. He said, "In story after story which I would read for mere enjoyment, I would come upon things that not merely pleased me but gave me instruction." Her works have pleased presidents and peasants, young and old, Americans and Frenchmen, and have given instruction to them at the time of their pleasure.

George Baker in comparing her literary art with the painter said that her touches were delicate with the tone subdued which did not allow white lights or black shadows. He wrote, "Readers who know the work of Sarah Orne Jewett open a new book written by her with that same sense of quiet delight and gratification which possesses the connoisseur who examines a delicate bit of painting wherein the subdues, exquisitely shaded tints blend into an effect - - true not only to that in nature which all may see, but also to that something else which only an artist can divine and reveal." The short story is the form of creative writing in which she made her greatest contribution, and it is the same form that American writers in general have made a unique contribution to world literature. "Her place with the few best of these writers appears to be secure."

A poetic salute to several of her short stories was made in September, 1944, in the *"Atlantic Monthly"* by James Norman Hall. The poem is entitled *"Sarah Orne Jewett's Stories"* and is included here for the enjoyment of those readers who have read a number of her stories and have loved the characters that are mentioned again in this poem.

Sarah Orne Jewett's Stories

The news came from the husband's sister's son
The rogue who stole her farm; but I, for one,
Know that, if Mrs. Peet did pass away,
She rose not later than the following day,
Threw off her shroud, and bought a Shrewsbury
   ticket.
Dead? Mrs. Peet? No more than Cynthia Pickett
Or Mrs. Persis Flagg - - both "Orthodox" - -
Or the Free-Will-Baptist lady; she who knocks
At Mrs. Beckett's door; or Mrs. Janes,
Poor Meechin' body! With her ague pains'
Or, Mrs. Trimble, or Rebecca Wright,
Driving to Hampden in the fading light
That never fades: as golden now as when
They planned to bring the Bray girls home again.
Not one of them has "passed away" - - not one.
Miss Tempy Dent, no less than these, lives on;
As her two watchers are as safe as she
From further harm. At Byfleet; knee to knee,
Sit Betsey Lane, Peggy, and Mrs. Dow,
Old women fifty years ago, and now
Not a day older. Peggy's guarded cry:
"Ain't that Mis' Fales? There! Do let's pray her
   by!"
And Mrs. Todd's "Well, mother, here I be!"
(Heard at Green Island - - green immortally),
Ring as they did. They will be carried on
Over the hills and years when we have gone
To lie among the unremembered dead.
The hungry generations onward tread,
But the winter sun of every New Year's Day
Sees Mrs. Hand and Abby toil their way

Up to Aunt Cynthy Dallett's mountain farm
To "visit" there forever, safe from harm.
All of them safe, the folk Miss Jewett knew;
Such power has truth, when truth is added to
Clear-sighted, faithful, understanding love.
Visit her towns for ample proof thereof.
In Hampden, Woodville, every wall and roof,
And on the farms beyond, is weatherproof.
At Topham Corners, Fairfield; Dunnet Landing,
Columns of wood smoke rise from chimneys
    standing
Just as they stood those many years ago.
A century from now it will be so;
Because their life is drawn, as she drew hers,
Through healthy roots, deep as the pointed firs.

In 1911 Annie Fields closes her book, "Letters of Sarah Orne Jewett," with these words: "And so the letters went on, with the flickering lights and shadows of human life reflected on their pages, until she wrote one day in June, 1909: 'Dear, I do not know what to do with me!' Then hope died; we knew she could no longer stay with us, for like a little child, she had always planned some pretty scheme to cheer the paths of others, as well as her own, when the way was difficult. She rested on the spirit within her, which was not of herself, and dared, with a fearlessness that did not think on daring. She never put her doll away and always used her child-names, but her plans were large and sometimes startling to others. To herself her plans were joyous, every difficult time in life being met with a fine ingenuity of resource, until at the last she sent the little plaintive cry, "I do not know what to do with me!" Then she was borne away from these human trammels and her young soul was free to move in the atmosphere of Divine Love."

In 1936, Gladys Hasty Carroll of South Berwick, a fellow author, and a graduate of Berwick Academy described the feeling that the town had after Miss Jewett's death. She pointed out, however, that her death was not the end of the world. She was one of many who were and are optimistic of the future and who are helpful to their neighbors. Carroll wrote, "Very likely there were many South Berwick people who felt in 1909 that with Miss Jewett lost to them, there was little left to cling to and to row by. I am sure Miss Mary, Miss Sarah's sister, filled this high office and did this happy service for me and for all my generation in our village, and that with the closing of the Jewett house as a private residence, the heart of the town as we had known it did indeed, for a time, cease to beat." Carroll also stated that like Sarah Orne Jewett was to others, Miss Mary Jewett was to me, and some other woman of grace and dignity is now to the newer South Berwick generations. Carroll concluded with a fitting tribute to Miss Jewett. "I doubt very much that Miss Jewett ever knew she was the only artist who sat with the group around those little Boston fires. But such was the truth. She lacked only fire to be New England's fair claim to an actual literary genius. She was rich in intelligence and cultural background, but, untrammeled by the too-formal education of the time, and she lived, not in a social center, but in a little village where the natural events of every day brought her in close contact with life, with reality, and with those to whom birth and love and hate and death were bold, cruel, splendid facts."

Miss Jewett's poem, "Assurance" applies to her as well as to the others who had left a trail of memories behind with their death. In the poem she shows how it is possible for love to fill the hearts of those remaining in this life – a love that brings comfort and assurance that all is right with God's scheme of things. She wrote: "And so I think those friends whom we call dead are with us. It may be some quiet hour, or time of busy work for hand and head, their love fills all the heart that missed them so. They bring a sweet assurance of the life serene above the worry that we know, and we are braver for the comfort brought. Why should we grieve because they do not speak our words that lie so far below their thought?"

When Burton W. Trafton, Jr. was just a small boy and after Miss Jewett was only a memory in the minds of the villagers, he said that he knew an elderly man who had served Miss Jewett for many years. Trafton described how the loyalty of that servant showed itself at the graveside of Miss Jewett as the man attended the flowers there. Trafton said, "I often watched as he cultivated the old-fashioned widow's tears and bleeding hearts around her grave. It was clearly a labor of love. I knew then that she must have been a queen. Today I take her books from my shelf and know it again." Today, we too can know by picking up one of her books and by reading it, that there was a royal presence about her.

"The Sarah Orne Jewett Bibliography: 1949-1963" appeared in the June 1964 issue of "The Colby Library Quarterly" compiled by John Eldridge Frost on the centennial anniversary of Sarah Orne Jewett's birth.

Bibliography

The Harvard University Library houses the Jewett family Library and several of Miss Jewett's manuscripts. Her manuscripts are in the Colby College Library in Waterville, Maine, and the Thomas Bailey Aldrich Birthplace, Portsmouth, New Hampshire. Beside the published works of Miss Jewett, many of her stories and poems can be read in the magazines and journals in which they first appeared. Some of her work can only be read in the original publications since many of her lesser known works are still uncollected in book form. Many of her previously unpublished letters are from time to time published in the *"Colby College Library Quarterly"* which devotes its pages to the study of Maine authors and authors whose manuscripts are located in Maine colleges and libraries.

Works Consulted for this Book

Auchincloss, Louis. *Pioneers and Caretakers*. Minneapolis: University of Minnesota, 1965.

Aldrich, Lilian Woodman. *Crowding Memories*. Boston: Houghton, Mifflin, 1920.

Baker, George H. "Review of 'Country of the Pointed Firs,'" *Bookman*. 5:80. March, 1897.

Bishop, Ferman. "Sarah Orne Jewett's Ideas of Race." *New England Quarterly*. 30:249. June, 1957.

Berthoff, Warner. *The Ferment of Realism: American Literature 1884-1919.* Free Press, 1965.

Bowditch, Mrs. Ernest. "The Jewett Library," *Colby Library Quarterly,* December, 1961.

Bradley, Sculley and others eds. *The American Tradition in Literature.* New York: Norton, 1967. Vol. 2.

Brooks, Van Wyck. *New England: Indian Summer.* New York: Dutton, 1940.

Carroll, Gladys Hasty. "New England Sees it Through," *1936 Essay Annual.* Chicago: Scott, Foresman, 1936.

Cary, Richard ed. *Sarah Orne Jewett Letters,* Waterville, Maine: Colby College Press, 1967.

Cather, Willa. *Alexander's Bridge.* Boston: Houghton, Mifflin, 1912. Introduction.

Cather, Willa. *Not Under Forty.* New York: Alfred Knopf, 1936.

Clark, Lois. "Sarah Orne Jewett." *Daughters of the American Revolution Magazine,* 97;958. December, 1963.

Cleaveland, Nehemiah and Alpheus Spring Packard, *History of Bowdoin College.* Boston: James Ripley Osgood,1882.

Collyer, Robert. "James T. Fields." *The Dial.* 2:205. January, 1882.

Cunliffe, Marcus. *Literature of the United States.* New York: Penguin, 1967.

Edel, Leon, ed. *The Selected Letters of Henry James*. New York: Farrar, Straus, 1955.

"Fiction of the Early Autumn." *The Outlook*. 69:420. October, 19, 1901.

Fields, Annie. *Authors and Friends*. Boston: Houghton, Mifflin, 1893.

Fields, Annie. *Charles Dudley Warner*. New York: McClure, Phillips, 1904.

Fields, Annie. "Madame Blanc." *Century*. 66:138

Floyd, Olive Beatrice. "Sarah Orne Jewett's Advice to a Young Writer," *Yale Review*. 26:432. Winter, 1937

Garnett, Edward. *Friday Nights*. New York: Alfred Knopf, 1922.

Grattan, C. Hartley. "Sarah Orne Jewett," *The Bookman*.69:298. May, 1929.

Hall, James Norman. "Sarah Orne Jewett's Stories." *Atlantic Monthly*. 174-58-59. September, 1944.

Hicks, Granville. *The Great Tradition: An Interpretation of AmericanLiterature Since the Civil War*. New York, 1967.

Hollis, C. Carroll. "Letters of Sarah Orne Jewett to Anna Laurens Dawes," *Colby Library Quarterly*. 8:105 September, 1968.

Howe, Helen. *The Gentle Americans: 1864-1960*. New York: Harper and Row, 1965.

Howe, Mark DeWolfe, *Memories of a Hostess*. Boston: Atlantic Monthly Press, 1922.

Howe, Mark DeWolfe, ed. *New Letters of James Russell Lowell.* New York: Harpers, 1932.

Howells, John Mead. *The Architectual Heritage of the Piscataqua.* New York: Architectural Book, 1937.

Howells, Mildred, ed. *Life and Letters of William Dean Howells.* Garden City: Doubleday, Doran, 1938. Vol. 2.

Howells, William Dean. *Literary Friends and Acquaintances.* Ed. David Hiatt and Edwin H. Cady. Bloomington: Indiana University Press, 1968.

Howells, William Dean. *Literature and Life.* New York: Harpers, 1902.

Howells, William Dean. "Review of Sarah Orne Jewett, 'Deephaven,'" *Atlantic Monthly.* 39:759. June, 1877.

James, Henry. "Mr. and Mrs. James T. Fields," *Atlantic Monthly.* 106-31 (July, 1915).

Jewett, Sarah Orne. *Letters of Sarah Orne Jewett.* Ed. Annie Fields, (New York: Houghton, Mifflin, 1911.

Jewett, Sarah Orne. "Looking Back on Girlhood," *Youth's Companion*, eds. Lovel Thompson and others. Boston: Houghton, Mifflin, 1954).

Jewett, Sarah Orne. "An Autumn Holiday." *Harpers.* 61:9

Jewett, Sarah Orne. *Country By-Ways.* Boston: Houghton, Mifflin, 1881.

Jewett, Sarah Orne. *Country Doctor.* Boston: Houghton, Mifflin, 1884.

Jewett, Sarah Orne. *The Country of the Pointed Firs.* Anchor Edition, 1956.

Jewett, Sarah Orne. *The Country of the Pointed Firs.* Boston: Houghton, Mifflin, 1886.

Jewett, Sarah Orne. *Deephaven.* Boston: Houghton Mifflin, 1866 and 1877.

Jewett, Sarah Orne. "The Eagle Trees." *Harpers.* 66:608. March, 1882.

Jewett, Sarah Orne. *Mate of the Daylight.* Boston: Houghton Mifflin, 1884.

Jewett, Sarah Orne. "Missing." *Harpers*, 64:499. March, 1882.

Jewett, Sarah Orne. *The Tory Lover.* Boston: Houghton, Mifflin, 1901.

Lathrop, G. P. "Review of Sarah Orne Jewett, The Mate of the Daylight and Friends Ashore." *Atlantic Monthly,* 53:712. May, 1884.

Lewisohn, Ludwig. *The Story of American Literature.* New York: Harpers, 1932.

Longfellow, Samuel. *Life of Henry Wadsworth Longfellow.* Boston: Houghton, Mifflin, 1891. Vol. 3.

Mabie. Hamilton W. "Some Estimates of the Year's Literary Output." *Review of Reviews*, 14:743. December, 1896.

Martin, Jay. *Harvests of Change.* New York: Prentice Hall, 1969.

Matthiessen, F.O. *American Renaissance*. New York: Oxford, 1941.

Matthiessen, F. O. *Sarah Orne Jewett*. Boston: Houghton, Mifflin, 1929.

Norton, Charles Eliot. *Letters of James Russell Lowell*. New York: Harpers, 1893. Vol. 2.

"Obituary of Sarah Orne Jewett." *The Independent*. 67:52. July 1, 1909.

"Obituary of Sarah Orne Jewett," *The Nation*. 89:2 July, 1909.

Odell, Ruth. *Helen Hunt Jackson*. New York: Appleton, Century, 1939.

Parrington, Vernon. *The Beginnings of Critical Realism in America 1860-1920*. New York: Harcourt Brace, 1930.

Payne, William Morton. "Recent Fiction." *The Dial*. 5:66. July, 1884.

Payne, William Morton. "Recent Fiction." *The Dial*. 6:123, September, 1885.

"People Talked About." *Leslie's Weekly*. 85:307. November 11, 1897.

Pickard, Samuel T. *Life and Letters of John Greenleaf Whittier*. Boston: Houghton, Mifflin, 1894.

Quinn, Arthur Hobson. *American Fiction: An Historical and Critical Survey*. New York: Appleton, Century, Crofts, 1964.

"Recent Fiction," *The Critic*. 13:54. August 4, 1885.

"Recent Fiction," *The Critic.* 16;269. May 31, 1890.

"Recent Fiction," *The Dial*, 4:230. January, 1884.

"Recent Novels," *The Nation.* 39:96. July 31, 1884.

Richards, Laura E. and Maud Howe Elliott. *Julia Ward Howe, 1819-1910.* Boston: Houghton, Mifflin, 1916.

Roosevelt. Theodore. "How I Became a Progressive." Outlook, 95-195. October, 1912.

Salsbury, Edith Colgate, ed. *Susy and Mark Twain: Family Dialogues.* New York: Harpers and Row, 1965.

"Sarah Orne Jewett," *Atlantic Monthly.* 104:280. August, 1909.

"Sarah Orne Jewett," *Outlook.* 92-542-543

Sargeant, Elizabeth Shepley. *Willa Cather, A Memoir.* Lincoln: University of Nebraska, 1953.

Scudder, H. E. "Miss Jewett," *Atlantic Monthly.* 73:130. January, 1894.

Scudder, H. E. "Review of Sarah Orne Jewett, "A Country Doctor," *Atlantic Monthly*, 54:418. September, 1884.

Scudder, H. E. "Review of Sarah Orne Jewett, 'The Mate of the Daylight and Friends Ashore.'" *Atlantic Monthly,* 53:712. May, 1884.

Scudder, H.E. "Review of Sarah Orne Jewett, "Strangers and Wayfarers." *Atlantic Monthly.* 67.849. June, 1891.

Smith, Eleanor M. "The Literary Relationship of Sarah Orne Jewett and Willa Cather," *New England Quarterly.* 29:478. December, 1956.

Stern, Milton, ed., *"Nation and Region, 1860-1900."* New York: Viking Press, 1968.

Sullivan, Mark. *Colliers Weekly*, 54:11. October, 1914.

Tenison, E. M. *Louise Imogene Guiney.* New York: MacMillan, 1923.

Thaxter, Celia. *Letters of Celia Thaxter.* Boston: Houghton, Mifflin, 1897.

Trafton, Burton W. Jr. "Bookstall Gossip," *Boston Post*, October 16, 1949.

Trent, William P. and others, eds. *Cambridge History of American Literature*, New York: Macmillan, 1943, vol. 2.

"Verse on Sarah Orne Jewett," *Life,* 33:295. April 1899.

Vorse. M. H. "Review of 'The Tory Lover.'" *The Critic.* 39:470. October, 1901.

Wagenknect, Edward. *Cavalcade of the English Novel.* New York: Holt, 1952.

Ward, Mrs. Humphrey. *A Writer's Recollections.* New York: Harpers, 1918. Vol. 2.

Warner, Charles Dudley, ed. *Library of the World's Best Literature.* New York: Hill, 1896. 14:8271.

Weber, Carl J. *Hardy in America*. Waterville, Maine: Colby College Press, 1946.

Weber, Clara and Carl J. Weber. *A Bibliography of the Published Writings of Sarah Orne Jewett*. Waterville, Colby College Press, 1949.

Wickham, Gertrude Van R. "Sarah Orne Jewett's Dog." *St. Nicholas*. 16:545. May, 1889.

Wilson, Forrest. *Crusader in Crinoline: The Life of Harriet Beecher Stowe*. New York: Lippincott, 1941.

Winslow, Helen M. "Some Literary Cats." *St. Nicholas*. 28:923. August, 1900.

Workers of the Federal Writer's Project. "*American Guide Series, Maine. A Guide Down East*." Boston Houghton, Mifflin, 1937.

Made in the USA
Middletown, DE
14 October 2016